UNCERTAIN DIMENSIONS:
Western Overseas Empires
in the
Twentieth Century

Europe and the World
in the Age of Expansion

edited by Boyd C. Shafer

UNCERTAIN DIMENSIONS
Western Overseas Empires
in the
Twentieth Century

by
RAYMOND F. BETTS

UNIVERSITY OF MINNESOTA PRESS □ MINNEAPOLIS

Published by the University of Minnesota Press,
2037 University Avenue Southeast, Minneapolis, MN 55414.
Printed in the United States of America.

Library of Congress Cataloging in Publication Data
Betts, Raymond F.
Uncertain dimensions.

(Europe and the world in the Age of Expansion ; v. 10)
Bibliography: p.
Includes index.
1. Colonies—History—20th century. 2. Imperialism—
History—20th century. I. Title. II. Series.
JV151.B48   325'.3'09   84-19710
ISBN 0-8166-1308-7
ISBN 0-8166-1309-5 (pbk.)

Europe and the World in the Age of Expansion

SPONSORS

Department of History of the
University of Minnesota

James Ford Bell Library of the
University of Minnesota Library

SUPPORTING FOUNDATIONS

Northwest Area Foundation
(formerly Louis W. and Maud Hill
Family Foundation), St. Paul

James Ford Bell Foundation,
Minneapolis

For Jackie

Editor's Foreword

The expansion of Europe since the thirteenth century has had profound influences on peoples throughout the world. Encircling the globe, the expansion changed men's lives and goals and became one of the decisive movements in the history of mankind.

This series of ten volumes explores the nature and impact of the expansion. It attempts not so much to go over once more the familiar themes of "Gold, Glory, and the Gospel," as to describe, on the basis of new questions and interpretations, what appears to have happened insofar as modern historical scholarship can determine.

No work or works on so large a topic can include everything that happened or be definitive. This series, as it proceeds, emphasizes the discoveries, the explorations, and the territorial expansion of Europeans, the relationships between the colonized and the colonizers, the effects of the expansion on Asians, Africans, Americans, Indians, and the various "islanders," the emergence into nationhood and world history of many peoples that Europeans had known little or nothing about, and, to a lesser extent, the effects of the expansion on Europe.

The use of the word *discoveries*, of course, reveals European (and American) provincialism. The "new" lands were undiscovered only in the sense that they were unknown to Europeans. Peoples with developed cultures and civilizations already had long inhabited most of the huge areas to which Europeans sailed and over which they came to exercise their power and influence. Nevertheless, the political, economic, and social expansion that came with and after the discoveries affected the daily lives, the modes of producing and sharing, the ways of governing, the customs, and the values of peoples everywhere. Whatever their state of development, the expansion also brought, as is well known, tensions, conflicts, and much injustice. Perhaps most important in our own times, it led throughout the developing world to the rise of nationalism, to reform and revolt, and to demands (now largely realized) for national self-determination.

The early volumes in the series, naturally, stress the discoveries and explorations. The later emphasize the growing commercial and political involvements, the founding of new or different societies in the "new" worlds, the emergence of different varieties of nations and states in the often old and established societies of Asia, Africa, and the Americas, and the changes in the governmental structures and responsibilities of the European imperial nations.

The practices, ideas, and values the Europeans introduced continue, in differing ways and differing environments, not only to exist but to have consequences. But in the territorial sense the age of European expansion is over. Therefore the sponsors of this undertaking believe this is a propitious time to prepare and publish this multivolumed study. The era now appears in new perspective and new and more objective statements can be made about it. At the same time, its realities are still with us and we may now be able to understand intangibles that in the future could be overlooked.

The volumes in this series, even though they number ten, cover only what the authors (and editors) consider to be important aspects of the expansion. Each of the authors had to confront vast masses of material and make choices in what he should include. Inevitably, subjects and details are omitted that some readers will think should have been covered. Inevitably, too, readers will note some duplication. This arises in large part because each author has been free, within the general themes of the series, to write his own book on the geographical area and chronological period allotted to him. Each author, as might be expected, has believed it necessary to give attention to the background of his topic and has also looked a bit ahead; hence he has touched upon the time periods of the immediately preceding and following volumes. This means that each of the studies can be read independently, without constant reference to the others. The books are being published as they are completed and will not appear in their originally planned order.

The authors have generally followed a pattern for spelling, capitalization, and other details of style set by the University of Minnesota Press in the interests of consistency and clarity. In accordance with the wishes of the Press and current usage, and after prolonged discussion, we have used the word *black* instead of *Negro* (except in quotations). For the most part American usages in spelling have been observed. The last is sometimes difficult for historians who must be concerned with the different spellings, especially of place names and proper nouns, at different times and in different languages. To help readers the authors have, in consequence, at times added the original (or the present) spelling of a name when identification might otherwise be difficult.

The discussions that led to this series began in 1964 during meetings of the Advisory Committee of the James Ford Bell Library at the University of Minnesota, a library particularly interested in exploration and discovery. Members of the university's Department of History and the University of Minnesota Press, and others, including the present editor, joined in the discussions. Then, after the promise of generous subsidies from the Bell Foundation of Minneapolis and the Northwest Area Foundation (formerly the Hill Family Foundation) of St. Paul, the project began to take form under the editorship of the distinguished historian Herbert Heaton. An Advisory Council of six scholars was appointed as the work began. Professor Heaton, who had agreed to serve as editor for three years, did most of the early planning and selected three authors. Professor Boyd C. Shafer succeeded him in 1967.

Boyd C. Shafer

Preface

The following study does not attempt to embrace all the lands, peoples, and problems that are to be found in the history of twentieth-century empire. The enormity of the enterprise and the various levels at which it operated—from the suppression of Communist uprisings in Indonesia in 1926–27 to the daily sale of Darjeeling tea at Fortnum and Mason's in London—established imperialism both as a major twentieth-century force and a series of activities touching upon every continent and nearly every human concern.

To assemble these into a single historical assessment requires the exercise of selection. In the study that follows, those political units that were the older British Dominions are only slightly considered. They were part of early empire and new nations and their institutions and concerns were more in accord with the Western world than with the Third World where most of the colonial activity was now centered. Canada, Australia, and New Zealand receive very little mention, while Subsaharan African and Southeast Asia appear regularly.

Furthermore, the politics of the time, however interesting and turbulent, are treated with less intensity than are the cultural developments. The building of cities, more than the rise of nationalistic parties, has held my attention. Such an emphasis is justified by two conditions: first, the frequency with which the political history has been studied; second, the need for more general consideration of the cultural effect of imperialism—its "succession of violent shocks " to use Jawaharlal Nehru's term—on colonial populations and the structures and institutions in which they lived.

This study follows a topical, not a chronological, arrangement, which seems appropriate to the subject matter. Technology, urbanization, and ideology (one might have used the umbrella term "modernization" when it was in fashion a few years ago) are the subjects that stand out here—as they did in the minds of the major empire builders of the time, who were by and large interested in "good works." Here again, as is so frequently true in the course of human affairs, the pretensions ran far ahead of the realities: empire was in many ways a slapdash affair, not the well-articulated one that it appears to be in the books written by the apologists.

What form empire did acquire was principally determined in the early twentieth century, between the two world wars, when major conquest was over and decolonization was a neologism. The necessities of the world war— military and labor recruitment, increased production of raw materials—intensified the direct role of the state in colonial affairs. As a result, private enterprise, never very intrepid, was even more attendant upon governmental initiative after World War I.

Whatever its source of impulsion, colonial development made measurable progress. The miles of railroads and roads laid down, the number of public buildings constructed, and the sum of investments all add up to an impressive amount when placed in the context of the global activity at the time. The fixed legacy of empire—its "infrastructure"—was not only defined in the interwar years but was also largely realized then. Moreover, the questioning of the social encounter—the "colonial situation"—also intensified so that the ideologies that justified the nationalism of the years following World War II were also well-defined.

None of this activity suggested keen public interest at home. The public moods of the 1920s and 1930s were elation over the latest showing of the municipal soccer team and depression over the economy. Among King George V's last words were, reportedly, "How is the Empire?" He was one of the few who inquired.

The indigenous populations were baffled, irritated, occasionally prepared to revolt, and sometimes given to determined service. Serve they did, but usually in largest numbers in those activities that were life-threatening or menial. They served in two world wars; they served in the mines of the Rand; they constructed railroads in Indochina and West Africa. As empire crumbled, they frequently moved to London, Marseilles, or Amsterdam and there served as construction, dock, or sanitation workers. The road bed along which the new French TGV express trains move swiftly and smoothly was built primarily by North African laborers.

The colonial encounter seldom took place, a historical point that ought to be emphasized. Despite its range and the variety of its effects, imperialism juxtaposed two worlds; it did not integrate them. There was no grand synthesis of European and Asian or European and African. A very small minority of Europeans, alienated geographically from their culture, and a very small minority of Asians and Africans, alienated socially from their culture, regularly met and engaged in the business of empire. Thus, empire was the daily function of two minorities trying to reach an understanding about what had to be done. The vast majority of the Western world and the vast majority of the Third World never knew much about the purposes and the accomplishments of the various colonial acts. That is the great irony of this vast enterprise: it was, fundamentally, measured on a small scale.

The pages that follow constitute a broad introduction to the study of overseas empire in the twentieth century. I have tried to strike a balance between the human—the dedication and the disdain—and the abstract—the statistics and the trends. The great number of specialized studies, both extensive monographs and journal articles, attests to the historical importance and popularity of the subject. Much of this material has been the basis for the synthesis that appears in this study.

I am pleased to extend my appreciation to the Camargo Foundation, the American Philosophical Society, and the Kentucky Research Foundation for grants that made travel and research opportunities available. I wish to thank Dottie Leathers and Pat Willhite for typing the manuscript, which they did graciously and well.

I gladly express my appreciation to Ken, Jim, and Susan—all of whom have tolerated, with bemusement, my efforts to construct compelling topical paragraphs and, then, my demands for evaluation of them.

Raymond F. Betts

Contents

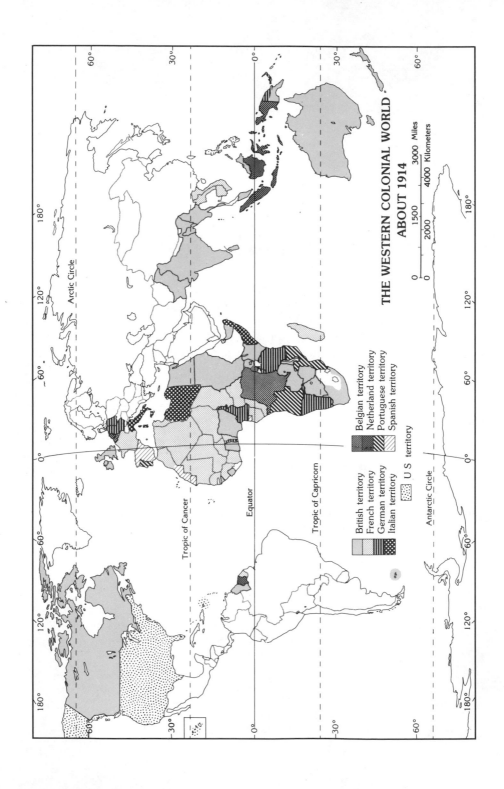

THE WESTERN COLONIAL WORLD
ABOUT 1914

British territory
French territory
German territory
Italian territory

Belgian territory
Netherland territory
Portuguese territory
Spanish territory

U S territory

0   1500   3000 Miles
0   2000   4000 Kilometers

Arctic Circle

Tropic of Cancer

Equator

Tropic of Capricorn

Antarctic Circle

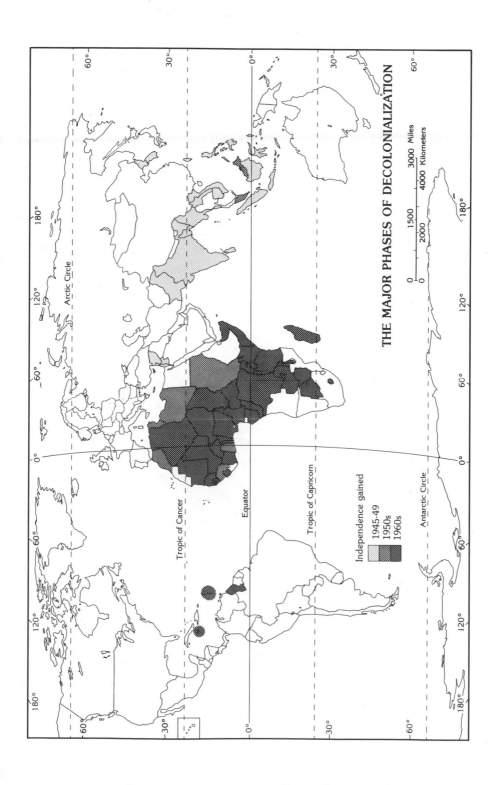

Independence gained

1945-49

1950s

1960s

Tropic of Cancer

Equator

Tropic of Capricorn

Antarctic Circle

Arctic Circle

THE MAJOR PHASES OF DECOLONIALIZATION

0   1500   3000 Miles

0   2000   4000 Kilometers

UNCERTAIN DIMENSIONS:
Western Overseas Empires
in the
Twentieth Century

The Setting

"It takes quite a lack of humor to build an empire." This summary statement, offered by the historian Carlo M. Cippola, would be difficult to match.[1] Hidden behind the stark words lie all sorts of implications about human conduct. Certainly there was a seriousness, both deadly earnest and petty, about empire-building and governance. An abundance of material is available to illustrate this point well. For instance, British imperial strategy was modernized in the interwar period by the "inverted blockade." This activity consisted of evacuating a rebellious tribe under threat of aerial bombardment, dropping a few bombs on the settlement for effect, and using airplanes to patrol the area until the tribe agreed to demands.[2] "One of the great advantages of employing aircraft in uncivilized countries is that the native is confronted with a weapon to which he can make no adequate reply," one observer blandly remarked.[3] In quite a different context there appeared a little exercise in culture contact which was entitled *The Indian Gentleman's Guide to English Etiquette, Conversation and Correspondence*. It contained the following admonitions:

Do not attempt to speak when your mouth is full . . . in laughter avoid grinning . . . do not . . . speak with your teeth closed . . . Never stand in the street and stare about you.[4]

Within the mass of regulations is found one imposed by the American administration in Guam; it prohibited individuals from whistling while passing the governor's residence.[5]

The chuckles were few indeed. Gilbert and Sullivan had earlier satirized some of the attitudes that made imperialism possible. *Punch* and *Le Canard enchainé* occasionally burst the bubble of empire with a thrust of wit. Bob Hope and Bing Crosby, masters of one-liners written in Hollywood, did likewise but in a less direct and acerbic manner, in their series of "Road" movies. In general, critics were as serious-minded as proponents, both groups thus ensuring that the words "empire" and "imperialism" were accompanied by grave connotations.

In the period between the two world wars, with which this study is primarily concerned, the serious business of empire was order and development. That the two terms might be in opposition did not trouble empire people who tried to work for both. The *pax colonia* was to ensure the internal stability that would allow economic growth and prosperity. Yet what methods and materials were needed to achieve both was not easily determined. Empire was of uncertain dimensions: it was an enterprise primarily undertaken in territories whose populations seemed to live in other ages and by other ways, yet it was an enterprise that rushed these territories and populations into modernity along the roads and railroads that Europeans proudly constructed.

The colonial literature of the interwar period is marked with terms such as "development," "betterment," and "efficiency." The "heroic" phase of empire was closed. That brief moment, when a Charles "Chinese" Gordon appeared in defeat and defiance before his adversaries in ceremonial whites and without a weapon in hand, would not be relived. The *porte-plume* had replaced the bandolier; the report in triplicate supplanted the retort of artillery. District officers in the field and colonial administrations with obligations to the League of Nations amassed statistics and undertook surveys that appeared in voluminous reports, all of which were designed to make colonization a scientific and rational undertaking, one no longer performed idiosyncratically by strong or unusual personalities who roamed worlds they did not understand.

There were exceptions, and they certainly merit to be so considered, such was the force of their personalities and the range of their impact. Hubert Lyautey and Italo Balbo made North Africa their province; they crossed their respective parts of it with a stride that drew admiration. Lyautey was resident-general of Morocco between 1912 and 1925. He was a devout Roman Catholic, strongly conservative in his political position, and brazenly theatrical in the attitudes he assumed. He was held in awe in his day but, more recently, has been remolded as a historical figure of less inspiring proportions.[6] What Morocco became as a French possession, however, was largely his doing. He respected the local culture and sought to preserve it, perhaps with too romantic an outlook. Nevertheless, he was a proconsul who ruled single-purposedly, through a loyal group of subordinates who fondly accepted the collective noun "team" as the description of their function.

Italo Balbo said that he both admired and imitated Lyautey, statements that should not necessarily be taken at face value, for Balbo was decidedly his own person. Unlike Lyautey, he has not been the subject of a first-rate biography, yet his life is the stuff from which popular television documentaries are made.[7] One of the quadrumvirate who supported Mussolini in the early days, an airplane pilot who gained world attention when he led his "aerial armada" of 24 seaplanes to the Chicago World's Fair of 1933, an individual described by all who encountered him as energetic and charming, Balbo was governor of Libya from 1933 until 1940, when he died in an air accident of a still undetermined cause. Balbo called his assignment in Libya an "exile," because he thought, as did others, that Mussolini was resentful of his popularity. Exiled or not, he played his proconsular role well, so well that the physical appearance of Libya and the spirit of the colonial officials who administered it were strongly marked by Balbo's will.

No other personalities so commanded the empire scene. Colonial administrators were more and more just that, attending to the daily business of empire and complaining more and more frequently, as do bureaucrats everywhere, of the increased paperwork and the decreased rapidity of decision-making. Most of these men were dutiful and not reflective on the meaning of the colonial enterprise.

However, there were some individuals who seriously wondered where it would all end, what it really meant. George Orwell, colonial policeman as well as novelist, had a disturbing thought on the occasion he was called on to kill a rampaging elephant in Burma:

And it was at this moment, as I stood there with the rifle in my hands, that I first grasped the hollowness, the futility of the white man's dominion in the East. Here was I, the white man with his gun, standing in front of the unarmed crowd—seemingly the leading actor of the piece; but in reality I was only an absurd puppet punched to and fro by the will of those yellow faces behind. I perceived in this moment that when the white man turns tyrant, it is his own freedom that he destroys.[8]

Such self-doubt chilled few of those who had chosen the colonial life. Better trained than their predecessors, the interwar generation of administrators

Mrs. Rudyard Boulton recording music of Tuareg tribesmen in
Timbuktu, 1934. From the National Archives.

ruled territories and peoples that frequently exceeded the traditional bounds
of government. Even if they could make the circuit, or part of it, in an automobile, there was much, perhaps too much, to know and to do with resources
and personnel available, and, more significantly, with the limited knowledge
acquired even at this time of scientific colonization. Reflecting on his own
experience, the French administrator Robert Delavignette described the colonial regime in French West Africa as the responsibility "of a few Europeans
who can only communicate through intermediaries with the masses they
govern, and from whom they are separated by ways of life, forms of thought,
methods of work."[9]

The alienation even occurred where there was a substantial colony of residential Europeans with whom the indigenous population might have had regular and mutually beneficial contact. But the Europeans consciously assumed
the position of a dominating minority, purposely withdrawn from the environment surrounding them. This was true of the situation in Algeria, according to the sociologist and political commentator Raymond Aron:

The Europeans did not understand and did not want to understand the authentic nature of the traditional culture. As the dominant minority, they feared that they would be swamped by the majority if they accorded the vanquished the civic equality which the latter had long demanded.[10]

The best of the colonial novels—E. M. Forster's *A Passage to India* comes immediately to mind—were structured around this problem, for mutual understanding was seldom achieved. The general social atmosphere was one of suspicion, if not of hostility, and of a certain correctness so that, formally, the two peoples in culture contact would get on. The revolutionary author Frantz Fanon has noted that in the last days of French empire in Algeria, when militant activity was intensifying, Algerian women in traditional veil were, for a short time, able to carry tracts and supplies for the nationalist cause because the French assumed that their behavior would be as traditional as their attire.[11] Appearances counted; correct behavior was expected because each—colonizer and colonized—had an assigned role to play.

To probe more deeply, to go beyond appearances, was difficult. Theorists soon developed a rich literature that explained the labyrinths created by both parties to the colonial act through which thought had to go before understanding was reached. Appreciating more fully the complexities of culture, colonial administrators were less sanguine about earlier policies such as the French one of assimilation by which—at least theoretically—Asians and Africans were to be made into Frenchmen, thinking as Descartes would suggest, behaving as Rousseau would prescribe. A study group of the Royal Institute of International Affairs reported in 1937 that "anthropological studies of the effects of the impact of Western civilization on more primitive ways of living have aroused serious anxiety among those interested in colonial administration."[12]

The European ways of living in the colonies were no longer primitive, as they may have been when Stanley set out to find Livingstone. The modern cities of Africa "rise dramatically from the surrounding undergrowth, with their electric lights, their phonograph music, their wide streets, their autos."[13] But modernity of equipment was not always complemented by modernity of habit. To enter the colonial world then maintained by the Europeans was to go back in time and to alter social mores. Many commentators have remarked on this interesting cultural fact, primarily with reference to India. One person has stated that interwar India was a "fragment of the Victorian world—stranded in time, like a lost world."[14] A new arrival wrote in 1921 that "in some ways life in India takes you back twenty years or more."[15] He was describing the custom of dressing formally for dinner, of using calling cards, of engaging in a sort of ritual which consumed time and thus isolated its practitioners from the pace of the alien world that awaited outside. Europeans seldom frequented indigenous society because they seldom cared to do so. For many, the colonial world was, as one critic said of Dakar, an "open air prison," in which one stayed "only by force."[16] Those novels, which focused on the colonial city, stress the petty intrigue and the gossip of a small, isolated society of Europeans given to feeding on itself.

Yet empire had grander dimensions than those of the villa in Bobo-Dioulasso in which a phonograph was playing "The Song of India" one night in 1930.[17] There were good works, even major works, to be seen and praised. Health institutes were established, educational systems developed, roads and railroads laid out nearly everywhere. The technology of empire was a very serious business and quite a disturbing one culturally. It played a special part in the maintenance of the *pax colonia*, because it shook the traditional base on which that *pax* was based. Indigenous people were uprooted to work in mines or on roadbed construction or as stevedores in the ports. Local customs and family traditions were questioned and denied by a wage economy, new work habits, and the mobility that bicycle, bus, and train provided. The technological side of empire, however, had impressive results and they filled the empire builder with pride. The British architect Herbert Baker relates the comment made by Lord Cromer, British high commissioner, when Baker was visiting Egypt:

"I suppose you will go and see the Pyramids. I think of them as the most stupendous work of human folly, while," he added with a smile, "my dam at Assouan is one of the greatest works of human wisdom."[18]

Cromer's value judgment is, of course, highly questionable, but his pride is understandable. The tangible results of modern European empire, not unlike those of ancient Rome, offered benefits that helped balance the moral account sheets. Most of the physical changes and development in the colonial territories were initiated and, in large measure, executed during the interwar period. In those years the structure of modern empire was established, what was good and bad about it was institutionally fixed. The terminal decade of imperialism—usually defined as beginning with the independence of India in 1947—was a dénouement, a rather hasty and even unanticipated unraveling of the political pattern, but not of the physical form or of the socio-economic institutions which had been created in the interwar years. The postindependence argument of neocolonialism—the assertion that old-time imperialism was being continued in more subtle and indirect ways—rested on the assumption that the structures established in the interwar years were far more durable than the politics that had governed them.

Just as there is no single event that clearly marks the end of empire, there is none that provides a sharp distinction in the developments of the early twentieth century, when imperialism was at its height. Nevertheless, the First World War is more than a convenient turning point. At first glance it may seem questionable to use an essentially European event to define change in a global activity. However, there is justification for so doing because the war was the cause of major rearrangement in the political boundaries, the generator of new sentiments and ideologies about the course of empire, and the force that created a new balance of international power.

Additionally, the war was the major European event occurring immediately after the last significant acts in the "scramble" for territory. With the Italian annexation of Libya in 1911, after a brief war against the Ottoman empire, and the French establishment of a protectorate over Morocco in 1912, after a series of border skirmishes, there was little territory around the globe that was neither claimed nor dominated by a Western power or by Japan. The so-called Great Powers had now become world powers. Six major states controlled about one-third of the globe among them—with another four states of more modest influence (Belgium, the Netherlands, Portugal, and Spain) also participants in the empire games. Outside this sphere of Western and Japanese domination, a few territories—China, Liberia, and Ethiopia the most obvious among them—could still claim nominal sovereignty. The war did not terminate colonial expansion, as the Japanese invasion of Manchuria (1931) and the Italian invasion of Ethiopia (1935) proved. However, such expansion was exceptional: the general political mood was against it and there was little space in which to maneuver without encountering a rival imperialist power.

When the major military phase of imperialism ended just before the First World War, the number of imperialist powers had reached its maximum. Along with the old colonial nations, of which Great Britain and France were the most active throughout the nineteenth century, two new imperialist powers had made an appearance: the United States of America and Japan.

America's formal imperialism was robust and short-lived. It was essentially part of that "splendid little war" which pitted an old and weary Spain against a young and ambitious United States. Before the Spanish-American War of 1898, there had been a clamor for territories. Some historians even contend that territorial expansion has been a major characteristic of American foreign policy, and that this nation's spilling over into the Pacific was only a new phase of it. Congress had finally annexed the Hawaiian Islands on August 12, 1898, nearly four months after the declaration of war against Spain. The Spanish-American War quickly increased the size of American empire, with Puerto Rico, the Philippines, and Guam all amassed, and Cuba virtually reduced to a protectorate.

William McKinley, a man doubtful and indecisive about empire building, was president during it all. Theodore Roosevelt derisively said McKinley had no more backbone than an eclair. But McKinley did make up his mind to keep the Philippines:

The truth is I didn't want the Philippines, and when they came to us, a gift from the gods, I did not know what to do with them . . . I walked the floor of the White House night after night until midnight, and I am not ashamed to tell you, gentlemen, that I went down on my knees and prayed Almighty God for light and guidance more than one night. And one night late it came to me this way.[19]

The islands were annexed.

The entrance of the American nation into the colonial world was disturbing. Not only did it change the nature of Pacific politics, but it also gave a new example in colonial rule. Despite the traditional imperialist rhetoric that they used to defend their act, the Americans were not very comfortable as overlords. As soon as peace had been established in the Philippines, there was talk of self-government for the islands and, not much later, talk of independence. The Cooper Act of 1902 was the organic act of American colonial government there: it established civil rule, provided the Filipino people with certain rights and benefits and, above all, called for a bicameral legislature with the lower house elected from the indigenous population. The democratic principles thus introduced were new in colonial affairs because they were broadly extended to non-white peoples for the first time. They were therefore potentially disturbing to concepts of European domination elsewhere.

The Japanese presence was disturbing in a somewhat different way. The successful outcome of the Sino-Japanese War (1895) and of the Russo-Japanese War (1904–05) dramatically established Japan as a major, potentially the major, power in the Pacific. French and British strategists were quick to realize this and to concern themselves with its effect on the colonial stakes in the region. The British signed the Anglo-Japanese Naval Treaty of 1902 in an effort to regulate Pacific affairs. At the same time French fear of the "Yellow Peril" intensified, even to the point that some Frenchmen thought the likelihood of holding on to Indochina in the future was somewhat doubtful and that, accordingly, French colonial efforts should be intensified in Africa, where France would be better able to protect and develop its interests.

The age of overseas expansion had virtually reached its conclusion shortly before World War I. After the war the main business of empire was of a different order. An intense effort to ensure a meaningful *pax colonia* began. Even though there were continuing problems of local militant opposition to colonial rule and new problems resulting from sophisticated forms of political protest, the major imperialist concern or preoccupation was twofold: stable government and economic development. The brief age of administrative empire was at hand. However, the policies and even many of the institutions upon which such empire was based were derived from prewar days. Their realization was a distinctively postwar activity—and this is the important point. The mark of empire on the contemporary world was made in the interwar period, when local populations were mobilized, regional resources exploited, and the general environment—both physical and cultural—altered to suit European needs.

Yet there were no neat lines of historical development. Empire in the twentieth century was as confused as it had been previously, a varying combination of good intentions and hesitant governmental support, of cultural condescension and experiments in education, of improvement of health facilities and exploitation of indigenous labor, and of grand official residences and squalid slum housing.

It was an unsettled time in which individuals coped with empire of uncertain dimensions. Unknowingly, an American tourist, traveling by train through South Africa in 1921, witnessed what might now serve well as a symbolic scene depicting it all:

Little black boys . . . began to beguile our stops with offerings of grotesquely carved giraffes—made in Japan![20]

CHAPTER 1

Empires at War

In the early afternoon of February 1, 1921, the Prince of Wales unveiled the Chattri that had recently been constructed in Brighton, England. The correspondent of *The Times* covering the event commented: "The Chattri is impressive because of its architectural originality—or, at the least, the unfamiliarity of the whole design—and all the more so because of its situation on the Sussex Downs."[1]

The unfamiliarity was an outcome of World War I, and of the contribution made by the soldiers of empire to that essentially European conflict. The Chattri was a war memorial, in the design of the Indian funeral temple after which it was named. Erected near Brighton hospital, to which Indians wounded on the western front had been brought, the marble structure marked the location of the pyres on which the bodies of those who had died were cremated. "It is befitting that we should remember and that future generations should not forget, that our Indian comrades came when our need was highest," the Prince of Wales remarked.

Yet just before the outbreak of the war no one contemplated either such a need, or a response that brought 1,440,337 Indians into army ranks. Of these, 62,057 were killed in battle, battle for which they had not been trained, to support a cause that certainly was not theirs. Indeed, the Royal Navy and the army, which had plans drawn up for the defense of the far reaches of empire, had given little thought to the manner in which that empire might participate in a European war. The convoying of hundreds of thousands of colonial troops to Europe was not imagined to be a naval task at all, although the first

12

sea lord, Admiral Sir John Fisher, once remarked that the "Army was a projectile to be fired by the Navy."[2]

The war as an imperial experience was not uniquely British. All of the colonial powers who assembled their forces along the crude lines of trenches found their relationship with their overseas possessions and peoples altered. By the time the guns had ceased to fire on the western front, Europe looked out on a different world scene in which empire had been reshaped and intruded upon by new technologies, problems, and cultural conditions. Few individuals questioned, as did the grim prophet H. G. Wells, whether empire would long endure. But almost all who favored imperialism recognized that the war had been, as General Charles de Gaulle would later say of war in general, an agent of revolutionary change.

The political geography was the most obviously rearranged. The German colonial empire had disappeared, absorbed chiefly by victorious Great Britain and France, and by Japan. Japan, hitherto deferential to Great Britain, now emerged as the dominant power in the Pacific, with British and French statesmen resigned to the fact that their continuing imperial role there would depend on the sufferance of the Japanese. The Turkish empire had collapsed, and as a result, several of its parts were subsumed under British and French authority, thus making these two European nations factors in the Middle East on a scale not contemplated earlier. Such imperial expansion—Lord Asquith mentioned a "scramble for Turkey"[3]—soon required new justifications because of the moral authority assumed by the United States, or more particularly, by its president, Woodrow Wilson, who had denounced the concept of "spoils." There followed an internationalization of colonial activities, a theory of judicial accounting that pronounced that colonies were a "sacred trust," held for the well-being of the indigenous populations. As with all matters human, the gap between theory and practice was great, but the ideology of imperialism had been altered as a result—and so would be altered the ideology of the discontented, those individuals under colonial rule who asked for colonial reform.

Across the diverse colonial landscapes new images roamed. Rolls-Royce armored cars negotiated the sands of Libya and the Arabian peninsula. A German zeppelin, the LZ-59, laden with 11 tons of small arms ammunition and three tons of medical supplies, undertook a mission to embattled German forces in East Africa. The airship had flown from Jamboli, Bulgaria, to the vicinity of Khartoum, Sudan, before it was successfully recalled by wireless on the morning of November 23, 1917. During the Gallipoli campaign of

1915, British submarines succeeded in slipping silently beneath the waters of the Strait of the Dardanelles to torpedo ships in the harbor of Constantinople. In the summer of 1917, a Handley-Page biplane flew 2,000 miles to Constantinople, with refueling stops en route, to bomb the German warship *Goeben* and the Turkish war office. The raid was successful. In the same year a proposal was made by a British official to establish a "chain of aerodromes under our control or on British territory in East Africa and in the Middle East." The suggestion was first "greeted with derisive laughter," but was later approved.[4]

No dimension of empire was more readily and dramatically altered than the demographic one. Migration to the colonies had been slow and insignificant before the war, except for migration of the English to the "settlement colonies" of Canada, New Zealand, and Australia. Indeed, the lack of a large European population in the newly acquired imperial estates had been a major concern of theorists and practitioners alike. Now, in sudden and reverse order, colonial populations converged on Europe, for the single purpose of supporting the European war effort. If, as has been argued, the world war was a "war of usury," it forced upon Europe an incredible debt to empire. The general statistics demonstrate that accounting:[5]

Territory	Soldiers Mustered
Canada	828,964
New Zealand	128, 525
Australia	412,953
India	1,440,337
Algeria	172,800
Tunisia	60,000
Morocco	37,150
French-Equatorial Africa	17,910
French West Africa	163,602
Indochina	48,922
Madagascar	41,355

Elated European statesmen and proponents of empire saw this military experience as a sign of imperial solidarity. It was what the British prime minister Lloyd George called "a spontaneous rally to the flag," and what a Frenchman described as a "living empire." Illusions regarding the new meaning of empire rose dreamily out of these harsh statistics. General Jan Smuts of South Africa, a major figure in imperial politics throughout the interwar period, stated in a speech at a parliamentary banquet on May 15, 1917:

Here you have from all parts of the British Empire young men gathering on the battlefields of Europe, and whilst your statesmen keep planning a great scheme of union for the future of the Empire, my feeling is that very largely the work is already done.[6]

It was not, of course, nor would it ever be. Empire was only effectively joined in the theories of its exponents. But if the concentration of colonial manpower in Europe allowed the assertion of grand thoughts about unity and solidarity, it more clearly demonstrated the relevance of the widely held belief that the fate of the colonies would be settled in Europe. Decades before the war, the German chancellor, Otto von Bismarck, had said as much, and now there were more such assertions. "The future of Morocco will be determined in Lorraine," commented Frenchmen. "I knew the fate of the colonies . . . would be decided only on the battlefields of Europe," wrote the German military commander in East Africa. The British War Committee made policy of such statements when it announced in December 1915 that "from the point of view of the British Empire, France and Flanders will remain the main theatre of operations."[7]

Military activities elsewhere were often contemptuously dismissed as "sideshows," but this sentiment was little more than a wartime equivalent of the "sideshow" that empire had been for Europeans all along. Aside from grand moments, such as Queen Victoria's two jubilees, little attention had ever been paid to overseas matters. French colonial propagandists, a small but hardy lot, wondered at French public indifference, and one writer mistakenly inferred, after commenting on Parisian insouciance, that in London "everything reminds the Londoner that he is the citizen of a World Empire."[8] Yet the seat of the British empire in London, Westminster, only resounded with debate over the condition of that global institution three days a year, with India alone occupying two days of this annual debate. In its founding issue, the procolonial publication, *The Round Table*, stated: "No one can travel through the Empire without being profoundly impressed by the ignorance which prevails in every part, not only about the affairs of the other parts, but about the fortunes of the whole."[9]

Nevertheless, the fortunes of the whole were given consideration of sorts during the war, and not by the British alone. Each of the belligerent powers found the war an unexpected opportunity to anticipate possible new territorial

Indian troops, supported by British grenade thrower, charge German trenches
at Neuve la Chappelle. The Indians were praised for gallantry.
From *Illustrated London News*, March 27, 1915.

arrangements in the colonial world, but notably in the most recent center of
high activity, Subsaharan Africa. Then, when the Ottoman empire stumbled
into the war in the autumn of 1915, its loosely held lands, curving around
the eastern basin of the Mediterranean and long inviting European diplomatic
attention, became another field for the play of imperialist interests. In the severe metaphor provided by General Smuts, there was now British need for
"tearing off from the Turkish Empire all parts that may offer Germany the
opportunity of expansion."[10]

Even though imperialist thoughts and actions never cluttered the agenda
of the governments directing the day-to-day operations of the war, the political conditions of the moment were attractive to those personalities who still
thought in terms of prewar imperialism. The Russian foreign minister, Serge
Sazonov, put it directly, in a line that brings to mind the plight of the Walrus

Sikhs and Hindus in the British trenches. From *Illustrated London News*,
January 16, 1915.

and the Carpenter: " . . . though the criminal thought of starting a European war in order to gain them [the Strait of the Dardanelles] never occurred to us, Russian diplomacy could not fail to concentrate its attention upon [the matter] once the war had been begun by someone else."[11]

Statements of this sort were variously voiced in imperialist circles throughout Europe. Those who had championed imperial expansion and consolidation before the war now were interested in "straightening out ragged edges," to use the homely phrase of a British committee set up in 1915 to consider Middle Eastern problems.[12] The most plaintive expression of this idea of realignment came from the Italian colonial minister, Gaspare Colosimo, who in his program of 1916 hoped that Italy might get out of the war the "re-establishment . . . of that which should have been under our exclusive influence [in Ethiopia] if sad events, human errors, and, let us even say, ill-will on the part of our present allies had not caused the collapse of twenty-five years of italian diplomatic and colonial activity."[13]

Yet for all this talk, colonial planning in wartime was sporadic, sketchy, and most frequently undertaken by very small coteries of dedicated imperialists, not by governments at large. In both Germany and France the strong proponents were the colonial ministers and certain private colonial associations. In both countries these associations cooperated with the minister in drawing up plans for postwar empire. In France, the *parti colonial*, a loose combination of politicians and propagandists, used the occasion of the war to foster objectives that never would have been given serious consideration on any other occasion. It was less imperialism and more the broader and amorphous idea of "national prestige" that aligned politicians like President Raymond Poincaré and, later, Premier Georges Clemenceau with the imperialists.[14] These politicians were determined not to let Great Britain dominate the region formerly held by the Ottoman empire. They wished France to have its place in the sun, too.

French concerns were then, as before, largely an expression of suspicion over British intentions. The seemingly effective alliance on the western front was not complemented by a similiar approach to colonial matters. One French military officer, regarding British activity in the Persian Gulf, provided as good a summary statement of this suspicion as any: "Arms in hand, England is now profiting from the War to establish her politics in the north of the Gulf on an unshakable base."[15] The sentiment was reciprocated. The British had long considered France a nuisance to their imperial system, and they continued to so regard it. A month after the war ended, Lord Curzon insisted that "the great power from whom we have most to fear in the future is France, and I almost shudder at the possibility of putting France in such a position. She is powerful in almost all parts of the world, even around India."[16]

Curzon's opinion was that of one of the "New Imperialists," an ardent little band whose members had insisted before the war that British foreign policy and diplomacy be figured in imperial terms. With the advent of David Lloyd George to power in late 1916, members of this band quickly moved into positions of authority. Lord Curzon, former viceroy of India, and Lord Milner, former high commissioner in South Africa, became cabinet members and, consequently, strong voices in the new War Cabinet that Lloyd George put together. The War Cabinet was itself complemented by the Imperial War Cabinet, another creation of the moment, which included the dominion prime ministers and General Smuts of South Africa.

Outside of these two cabinets, and literally outside of the prime minister's residence at 10 Downing Street, was found the "Garden Suburb," a brain trust of able and ambitious advisers to the cabinet who were temporarily housed in small buildings in the garden of the residence—hence the name. Among these advisers none was more persistent or more dedicated to the imperialist cause than Leo Amery. Amery wished to solidify the British empire and ensure it a common executive and parliamentary body so that it could become a true federation. He saw the Imperial War Cabinet as one such method of achieving his objective. More significantly, he wished to extend wartime considerations and postwar aims away from the western front. He imagined a "Southern British World which runs from Cape Town through Cairo, Bagdad and Calcutta to Sydney and Wellington," a world which can "go about its peaceful business without constant fear of German aggression."[17]

Such thought as this was given its best summary statement by Lord Milner, who seemed to speak for imperialists of all nations when he said that his desire was that Great Britain "should get out of the War a really consolidated Empire."[18]

In most similar pronouncements the tone was less that of bravado than of resignation. The British feared the war would end in a stalemate. The lack of any major British military success on the western front, and the continuing thrusts by the Germans, who on several occasions threatened the lines of the Allies and thus the very security of France, led individuals like Milner and Amery to assume that British colonial gains would be compensations for possible losses in Europe.

The Germans had quite a different perspective. Sure of the efficacy of their arms, they drew up their postwar maps on the basis of total victory, in which they would dispose of territory as they saw fit. Thus, even as the German colonial empire was being dismantled by the British, German planners saw this as a temporary inconvenience that would be reversed grandly at the peace table.

Both in the early fall of 1914 and in the late spring of 1918, two occasions when victory seemed imminent, the Germans reworked the maps. Despite the kaiser's claim at the outset of the war that "no lust for conquest" had inspired his government, anticipated military victory inspired great territorial expectations. Accordingly, the Germans, the only nation to go into such detail, drew up elaborate war aims. The chief concern was with a vast *Mitteleuropa*, which would ensure German domination of the Eurasian land mass, but there was also consideration of a grandly proportioned *Mittelafrika*, which would consist of most of the southern half of that continent. In the fall of 1914, the foreign minister, Theobald von Bethmann Hollweg, spoke of the need for a "continuous Central African Empire," and the colonial minister, Wilhelm Solf, assumed that soon-to-be defeated France would yield most of its black African colonies to Germany. In addition, the Belgian Congo and portions of Angola and Mozambique—to be acquired even though Portugal was a neutral country at the time—would handsomely augment German imperial holdings. Should Great Britain be eventually defeated, Solf assumed that Germany would acquire Nigeria in order to round out the new *Mittelafrika*.[19]

Great Britain's concern with Africa at the outset of the war was more modest and more immediately naval. In other words, the concern was more imperial than colonial—a matter of defense. On August 5, one day after Great Britain's entry into the war, a special cabinet committee, awkwardly named the "Offensive Sub-Committee," recommended the immediate seizure of the German colonies. The reason was best summarized by General Smuts in his résumé of war aims a few years later. The first aim, he declared, was the "destruction of the German colonial system with a view to the future security of all communications to the British Empire."[20] The British feared that the German colonies would serve as naval stations and that the powerful wireless transmitters located in several of them would provide the necessary communications to coordinate effective naval operations. Of particular concern was the Pacific squadron, under Admiral von Spee, and based at the leased Chinese port of Kiaochow. This squadron, nearly as powerful as the British forces in the region, might roam the Pacific, raid British shipping, and find a haven in the various German island possessions.

Great Britain moved with dispatch. As several writers have stated, the first British soldiers to have military contact with the enemy were those in West Africa, not those on the western front. Anglo-French troops overran Togo

Anglo-French military expedition in German Cameroon, December 1914.
From *Illustrated London News*, February 13, 1915.

with ease in August, and another joint force moved against the Cameroons, but with more difficulty so that victory was delayed until January 1, 1916. A South African army, requested by the British to engage the enemy, invaded German Southwest Africa, which surrendered on July 9, 1915. More complicated and drawn-out was the action taken against German East Africa. At first Indian troops, dispatched by the government of India, invaded in order to protect the "red line of empire." The lack of military progress, however, brought the home government to request reinforcements through the reassignment of the South African troops, now victorious in the southwest. The South Africans joined the Indians in 1916, and, assisted by troops from the Belgian Congo and the colony of Rhodesia, moved relentlessly against the Germans. However, the German commander, Colonel von Lettow-Vorbeck, adroitly resorted to guerrilla tactics, which enabled him to remain in the field until a few days after the armistice was declared on the western front.

If the British government was responsible for initiating and directing most of the military activity against the Germans in Africa, it did so with the support of the French in West Africa and, to a much more modest degree, the Belgians in East Africa. All three nations, therefore, anticipated an enlargement of their possessions in Africa as a result of their military activities. Furthermore, they were joined in such anticipation by the Italians who, through the Treaty of London signed on April 26, 1915, agreed to enter the war on the Allied side in return for territorial compensations, notably in Africa.

At first British official opinion varied on what might be the ultimate disposition of the conquered German colonies. Even late in the war there were individuals and groups who urged the return of some, if not all, of these colonies. However, two planning committees, the Committee on Territorial Change (1916) and the Committee on Territorial Desiderata (1917), favored the retention of what had been conquered. But if British arms were not crowned with victory, the 1917 committee urged that German East Africa be retained, with the territory in West Africa returned as compensation. In British eyes, East Africa, which fronted on the water routes to India, was a matter of primary concern. The persuasive arguing of General Smuts precluded any return of Southwest Africa.

For France, the African continent was of different political proportions. West Africa remained of primary concern.

French interest in Africa had intensified in the early years of the twentieth century. Morocco, which the French had acquired as a protectorate in 1912, was now imagined to be the doorway to France's African empire, and that empire was seen as the most promising portion of *France d'Outre-mer*. Since 1906, when Onésime Reclus had published his *Lâchons l'Asie, Prenons l'Afrique* (Let Asia Go and Take Africa), attention to the future potential of Africa had grown, both because of the region's ability to be defended and because of its seeming susceptibility to successful economic development. A French commission, appointed by the minister of colonies in 1917, principally to amass documentation for intelligent determination of possible postwar policies, was converted into a committee of advice-and-recommendation by one of its members. As head of the African department of the ministry, Albert Duchêne had obvious priorities, and it was therefore West Africa that he wished to be secured and strengthened by territorial enlargement. France was necessarily excluded from East Africa, because its small possession of Somaliland was of no consequence in the determination of politics there. Duchêne argued for the retention of those portions of the German colonies in Togo and the Cameroons that France had acquired in military cooperation with Great Britain. Also, he hoped that by diplomatic negotiations and trade, France might acquire much of the British, Spanish, and Portuguese territory in West Africa, with a protectorate established over Liberia for good measure.[21]

The two other nations that had an interest in the military outcome of the campaigns against German Africa were Belgium and Italy. The Belgians played an active, if very limited, role in East Africa and occupied the rich territory of Ruanda-Urundi. In discussions with the British, the Belgian government indicated a disinterest in any territorial expansion in that sector, but a strong desire to gain control over the mouth of the Congo River and to acquire Portuguese territory in Angola in order to strengthen their position around the river. Such negotiation would no doubt have meant compensation for the Portuguese in those territories seized by the British from the Germans in East Africa. Although the British government strongly disfavored such an arrangement and the foreign secretary, Lord Grey, so told the Belgian government, the planned Belgian expansion, at a time when Belgium was occupied by Germany, adds an ironic note to the history of empire.[22]

The Belgians could make such claims because of the old rights of war and conquest, but the Italians could not. Italy was the one European nation that made promises of territorial acquisition a condition of its entry into the war. The Treaty of London stated that Italy would receive additional territory in Libya, Eritrea, and Somaliland—the elements of its African empire—in the event that Great Britain and France decided to retain any of the territory that they had acquired when they conquered Germany. The Italian minister of colonies, Gaspare Colosimo, went further, however, and drew up a maximum and a minimum plan for territorial expansion, by which Italy might belatedly gain what had long been desired and denied. "Rarely has any colonial ministry drafted such ambitious colonial projects for a nation whose claim to 'compensation' was so tenuous,'' one scholar has stated.[23] What the minister wished was a sphere of influence over Ethiopia—(hence the elimination of British and French interests there); the acquisition of British Somaliland; the doubling of the size of Libya, through a southward extension into territory claimed by the French; and a sphere of influence over Angola. In seeming proportion to their size and significance, each of the colonial powers was generating plans for territorial expansion in Africa that were quite grandiose. The prewar ''scramble'' was to be rectified by postwar realignment. This anticipated third stage of the partition of Africa—following upon the ''paper partition'' of the 1880s, and the ''pacification'' by military means in the 1890s—was complemented by activities occurring in the Pacific.

Just as Great Britain had initiated the military action in Africa and had tolerated French and Belgian cooperation there, so did that nation do much the same in the Pacific. There is one important and obvious difference, however. The actual role played by the British armed forces was minimal. More significant, even the traditional authority of the British navy was diminished in the region.

In naval planning, as in all else, the war was essentially a European war. British naval strategy, as urged by Winston Churchill, first lord of the admiralty in the years just before the outbreak of hostilities, had called for concentration of the fleet in the North Seas where it would either battle or bottle up the German High Seas Fleet. The ships of the ''outer stations,'' the naval bases serving the empire, were, according to this plan, to be reduced to the tolerable minimum. Although the British Chinese squadron was considered somewhat stronger than the German one, and it was obvious that the new Australian battle cruiser, *Australia*, was more powerful than any ship the Germans had at their disposition, the combined British-Dominion naval force would be insufficient to guard all imperial interests in the Pacific in the event of war. British strategy, again as chiefly defined by Churchill, called for increased dependency on the Japanese for support.[24] However, British relations with Japan at the time could be described as being more testy than friendly.

The Naval Treaty of 1902 had formalized these relations, but not to everyone's satisfaction. Admiral Sir John Fisher said that the treaty was ''the very worst thing that England ever did for herself.''[25] Yet the treaty certainly seemed to have much merit at the time. Negotiations leading to the alliance had been initiated out of British fear of a possible strategic disadvantage in the Pacific because of the Franco-Russian Alliance of 1894–95. However, that fear soon paled before a greater one aroused by Germany's naval expansion policy, the creation of a German Pacific Squadron, the leasing of Kiaochow from China as a Far Eastern base, and the rumbling diplomatic noise of *weltpolitik*. In short, Kaiser Wilhelm II spoke as if he wished to stride continents—and step on British toes in the process.

The naval treaty was due to be renewed in 1915, but had become the subject of much discussion well before then. Although the Committee of Imperial Defense had mixed opinions about the treaty's ultimate value, most of its members were worried about possible developments in the Pacific if the treaty were allowed to lapse. A key question was the exposed position of Hong Kong, which some strategists said could not be defended from a Japanese assault, should one be mounted.

The treaty was thus renewed because of two elements of distrust, one concerning Japan, the other Germany. Allied to Japan, Great Britain would not fear its possessions subject to possible Japanese imperialism. Allied to Japan, the British would not need to maintain a large fleet in the Pacific, thus allowing concentration of forces in the North Sea. This was the condition of naval affairs in the Pacific when Great Britain, in the person of the foreign secretary, Edward Grey, appealed to the Japanese on August 6 to enter the war. The appeal ran against Grey's previous intention to neutralize Japan; on August 2 he had refused a Japanese proposal to provide assistance in the event of war. Now, however, the fear of a possible German naval assault on British shipping caused Grey to change his mind in haste.

The story of the flurry of negotiations that occurred between August 6 and August 23, the date on which Japanese hostilities began, is an unusual example of diplomatic confusion and hesitancy on the part of the British. Grey had hoped to restrict the extent of Japanese involvement to forays against any German raiders, but the Japanese government announced that it alone would define the range of its wartime activities. The diplomatic matter was further complicated by the fears generated in the United States and the Netherlands, both neutral countries, that Japan might move aggressively against their possessions at this time of British distress and distraction. The Dutch were particularly worried about the obvious vulnerability of their East Indies to Japanese attack and absorption.

After some successful political maneuvering to accommodate these concerns, which even included the temporary withdrawal of the request for assistance, Grey assented to what was now a condition beyond his assent. The Japanese had dispatched an ultimatum to Germany on August 10, requiring that nation to withdraw its naval forces from Pacific waters and to turn over its base at Kiaochow to Japan. The Germans made no reply; accordingly, the Japanese attacked and seized those German possessions within reach. Faced with what was a naval *fait accompli*, Great Britain recognized a line of demarcation in the Pacific, along which Japanese and Australian expansion had actually run: the Japanese were given control of the German colonies north of the equator; the Australians and New Zealanders control of those they had invaded south of the equator. Under further Japanese pressure, the British signed a secret treaty with Japan in 1917, in which the Japanese claim to retention of these colonies after the war was endorsed.

Of equal value to this approval of Japanese imperialism was British endorsement of the subimperialism of the Dominions. Neither New Zealand nor Australia wished to give up the German possessions they had seized. Nor was the Union of South Africa of a different opinion about German Southwest Africa. It was more at the urgence of the Dominions than of the home government that Prime Minister David Lloyd George appointed the Committee on Territorial Desiderata in 1917 to regulate such colonial matters. The Dominion prime ministers and General Smuts got their way at that time, as they would get it again during the peace conference.

It may be asserted that Great Britain was overwhelmed by events in the Pacific and perplexed by events in the Middle East. Certainly the naval simplicity and rapid success of the former were contrasted with the military complexity and long trials of the latter.

An area of European military activities throughout the modern era, and most pronouncedly during Napoleon's Egyptian campaign of 1797, the rambling and crumbling Ottoman empire was converted once again into a theater of war. This development ran against British and French wishes: both nations wanted to keep Turkey out of the war because they had neither manpower nor equipment to divert without severe sacrifice to another front. However, Germany sought such Turkish involvement and made the government a number of attractive postwar promises. Of immediate influence was the German provision of two magnificent warships to the Turkish navy soon after the British had seized two warships commissioned and constructed in Great Britain for Turkey and paid for by Turkish public subscription.

This little British blunder of war turned into a bigger blunder for the Turks. They commenced hostilities. A sudden attack on Russian Black Sea ports by the two German warships and other units of the Turkish navy was to be the *casus belli*. After avoiding a political collapse for two centuries, the

Turkish government found itself in a war that would prove to be beyond its capacity to endure. Nevertheless, German financial and military assistance, accidentally complemented by British military incompetence, allowed the Ottoman empire to carry on for a few more years.

From a European imperialist perspective the military activities now begun in the Middle East were but another aspect of age-old Anglo-French rivalry. The French—or more accurately, the imperialists—had long feared British intrusion into this area, an area that Frenchmen, out of a romantic reading of history, thought was theirs to dominate culturally. Shades of the Crusades blended with more recent images of France's role as protector of Christian religious interests in the holy land. On a more mundane level, French commercial interests—ranging from efforts of Lyonnaise entrepreneurs to begin a silk industry to the construction of tramways and the publication of French-language newspapers—allowed the French to consider the Middle East as a region of clear and vested interest.

As might be expected, the British understood, if they did not respect, French claims. T. E. Lawrence, who was a notorious francophobe, stated in 1915, shortly before his enigmatic personality was given a diamondlike luster by rubbing against the course of events, that he would like "to biff the French out of all hope of Syria."[26] Syria, a large and ill-defined province, which in French eyes ran northward from Egypt to the Taurus Mountains, would be the key to Anglo-French negotiation and irritation. These conditions developed quickly upon British military intervention.

Great Britain initiated action in the Middle East for a number of reasons, which were a mix of older imperialism and newer wartime considerations. As was feared, a belligerent Turkey upset all nineteenth-century considerations and strategies. During that century of British expansion eastward, the Ottoman empire had served as a buffer between India and potential enemies from the West, primarily Russia. Now, however, threats were multiple. The Suez Canal seemed vulnerable to a German-Turkish attack. Egypt and India, both with large Moslem populations, might question and resist a war waged between Christians and Moslems. India could be easily threatened by German-Turkish military action through Persia. The newly worked Persian petroleum fields, which were sending vitally needed petroleum through the Persian Gulf, might be jeopardized and, so, consequently, would fuel for the British navy.

If the reasons for military action were several, the action itself was complicated by tangled chains-of-command. The British diplomat, Mark Sykes, said that it took 18 agencies of the British government to respond before a decision on the Middle East could be reached.[27] The viceroy in India, the high commissioner in Egypt, the sirdar—or military commander—in the Sudan, the army, the navy, and the foreign office all had their say. It was a situation suited to the combined wit of Gilbert and Sullivan and one that engendered controversial debate.

Two geopolitical visions of the war were fixed in Great Britain. The "Westerners" wanted the war fought and won in Europe; they perceived no other route to victory and considered any deployment of troops away from that region an egregious waste of manpower. The "Easterners" thought action in the Middle East was imperative and might be decisive. The badly pressed Russians were seeking relief, and "the soft underbelly of Europe," to use Winston Churchill's phrase, might be easily penetrated. The "Easterners" were first supported by Churchill in his capacity of first lord of the admiralty, and by the imperial secretary of state for war, Lord Kitchener. Lloyd George joined this group as prime minister, bringing a romantic view of biblical history and a critical appraisal of current military activities. The "Easterners" did extend the war to the Middle East, but they did not cover the region with bursts of British military glory.

Writing about the first campaign, that of Mesopotamia, which was also the most strikingly colonial in character, Lloyd George employed the sarcastic mode:

It was an ideal professional soldiers' campaign, lacking even a minimum of supervision from the muddlesome politician. Tradition places the Garden of Eden in the land between the Euphrates and the Tigris. In this blissful enclosure there appeared in 1916 the Paradise of the Brass Hat. He reigned alone in unfettered and unrestricted sway over this garden for nearly two years. . . . Let us see what kind of Paradise he produced. It is a gruesome story of tragedy and suffering resulting from incompetence and slovenly carelessness on the part of responsible military officers.[28]

Lloyd George exaggerated the environmental qualities of this "Paradise," perhaps to make better felt his bitterness at the miserable military performance, but he certainly was not off the mark in his appraisal of incompetence and carelessness. The campaign had been ill-prepared, and it was foolishly conducted. Yet its beginning foretold little of these two conditions because early encounters suggested to the British the beginning of just another colonial campaign in the old style, in which luck substituted for planning.

The first objective was to secure the safety of the oil supplies. This involved the seizure of the refinery at Abadan and the city of Basra, the Ottoman port through which oil from the Persian fields flowed. A military force from India approached the area in order "to show the flag," just before the outbreak of hostilities, and then moved quickly to the completion of its newly assigned task once war with Turkey had begun. Securing the two objectives was a rather easy task, aided by the failure of the Turks to create an effective blockade of sunken ships at the estuary of the Euphrates River.[29]

The following spring, the new commander, Sir John Nixon, received permission—or rather was told to use his judgment—to extend the military operation northward, up the Euphrates and the Tigris. Nixon soon looked far forward, some 300 miles to Baghdad and the magic that city suggested—and to the military renown its capture might provide. The actions of his force began as a cavalier performance in the tradition of colonial romance. As the Anglo-Indian force moved quickly up the waterways, the Turks fell back in chaotic retreat. The field commander, Major General Charles Townsend, raced after them on the deck of one of his two steamers with a handful of men (actually 100 men and another officer). Their most Kiplingesque success was the capture of the city of Amara with its garrison of 2,000 Turks.

Such careless action was ventured again in the early fall as Townsend plunged on, this time with a division of soldiers. Soon thereafter, the tide of battle changed dramatically just as did the meanders of the River Tigris on which it was to be fought. Once Townsend had reached and taken the town of Kut, he considered his advance to be at its maximum, and he therefore did not desire to proceed farther. But Baghdad beckoned to Nixon, and the campaign continued. The reasons for Townsend's hesitancy were soon starkly justified, for a superior, well-trained Turkish force now descended on the Anglo-Indians, forced them to retreat to Kut, and besieged them there. On April 29, 1916, after several futile attempts at relief by Nixon, Townsend's decrepit force surrendered, a sad conclusion in imperial history, a useless outcome in the history of the war.

Top command was again shuffled, and the battle resumed. Now with caution, the British moved into Mesopotamia and took the city of Baghdad in March, 1917. It was a victory that did not ease the memory of what had occurred earlier, as Lloyd George's *Memoirs* remind us.

The historical conclusion to be drawn from the second Middle Eastern campaign waged on water and over land is no brighter. The only successful action at Gallipoli was the withdrawal of the troops, once it had been determined that further involvement would be futile.

Gallipoli is a peninsula, shaped like a hind leg, that forms the western shore of the Strait of the Dardanelles. It was to Gallipoli that the strategists in London turned, once plans for a naval "forcing" of the Straits went awry. Finally and geopolitically, Gallipoli was to be used to provide relief for the embattled Russians by opening another front.

The British navy, supported by the magnificent new battleship *Queen Elizabeth* and a small collection of older vessels, including a few supplied by the French, began its bombardment of the Turkish forts guarding the famous waterway on February 19, 1915. As in Mesopotamia, there was initial success, and the flotilla moved inward until it encountered minefields. Three ships were sunk (including one of the French), and a new battle cruiser was damaged. The British naval and military commanders considered the score bad enough to withdraw and to convert the naval action into the largest amphibious action undertaken prior to World War II.

The new campaign was about to begin brightly, at least in the minds of many young men, whose romantic anticipation was expressed by the poet Rupert Brooks. "Will Hero's Tower crumble under the 15-inch guns?" he questioned, with historical allusion. "Will the sea be polyphloisibic and wine-colored and unvintageable? . . . Should we be a Turning Point in History?"[30] None of these questions would be answered in the affirmative, and none of these questions would be answered at all for the young poet. Just as the campaign was getting under way, he died of heatstroke contracted while he was at the staging area in Egypt.

From April 26, 1914, when the first troops disembarked in the confusing darkness of early morning, until December 19, 1915, and January 8, 1916, when mass evacuations were undertaken in the same obscurity, the British forces maintained a tenuous hold on the high land that rose sharply from the narrow beaches of Gallipoli. It was the western front exported: a hastily contrived form of trench warfare. Four hundred thousand men—English, Australian, and Indian—fought against 300,000 Turks. That was the simple sum of it all, a costly diversion that brought the war no closer to an end and succeeded only in provoking political and historical controversy over its meaning.

The third campaign was the only one crowned with triumph, but even this came belatedly. What was called the Syrian campaign, undertaken by the Egyptian Expeditionary Force, began early as an effort to protect the Suez Canal. It paralleled the coast in its eastward thrust, until the force was checked, not once but twice, at Gaza in 1916. A change of military leadership

Australian troops at Gallipoli, 1915. From *Illustrated London News*,
July 31, 1915.

was therefore made. General Sir Edmund Allenby, nicknamed "Bull" and characteristically British in his idiosyncratic interest in insects and classical literature, firmly assumed command. With a force that ultimately numbered 300,000, many of whom bore the depressing experience of Gallipoli in their memories, he took the offensive in late 1917 and moved onward in October of 1918 to the conquest of Damascus. Less than two weeks before the Germans surrendered on the western front, on October 30, 1918, the Turks capitulated.

Allenby's most spectacular moment, and indeed that of the entire war, occurred when he and his forces entered Jerusalem, thus providing the British with the Christmas present that the biblically minded Lloyd George had earlier requested. On December 11, 1917, Allenby entered the holy city as the first conquering Christian since the days of the Crusaders. Whether this claim was one to trumpet or to temper, Allenby had a proper sense of history as he approached the city. He staged a modest entrance. He walked through the gates, his boots dusty and his uniform dishevelled from campaigning.[31]

Somewhere behind Allenby, as part of the retinue, came T. E. Lawrence. Lawrence had helped make the Arabian aspects of this campaign "the last of the picturesque wars," according to the novelist E. M. Forster. The picturesque quality derived from the desert skirmishes undertaken by camel-mounted, rifle-swinging Arabs. Among them was the colorful, sardonic, and self-advertising Lawrence.

Weighing less than 100 pounds and standing only five feet, five inches tall, Lawrence was nevertheless a commanding personality who magnificently wove fiction out of fact and thus provided a number of biographers with the difficult task of between-the-lines psychoanalysis.[32] Before he was so treated, he followed his sympathies for the Arabs through desert encampments to the headquarters of Allenby in an effort to assist Arab independence and, more personally, the authority of the Emir Faisal, son of Sharif Hussein, ruler of Mecca, and the man Lawrence considered the most likely candidate for ruler of the region.

The immediate British objective, to which Lawrence willingly lent himself, was the enlistment of Arab support in the war against the Turks. "The job is to foment an Arab rebellion against Turkey," Lawrence wrote, "and for that I have to try and hide my frankish exterior, and be as little out of the Arab picture as I can. So it's a kind of foreign stage, on which one plays day and night, in fancy dress, in a strange language, with the price of failure on one's head if the part is not well filled."[33] Lawrence was exhilarated by it all and able to convert political and military activity into a series of sensuous experiences that suited the needs of his haunted personality.

British problems were more pragmatic, but every bit as complicated as Lawrence's personal ones. The overall objective was, as described later by the government of India, a "Monroe Doctrine,"[34] in which nominally independent states would be under British suzerainty. However, the British knew the French were determined to maintain their imagined prestige in the region by the simple effort of ensuring their presence there.

What would finally emerge as the Sykes-Picot agreement, later to be denounced as the most blatant wartime example of imperialistic conquer-and-divide, began somewhat obliquely in the direction of the Dardanelles. In an atmosphere of "old diplomacy," by which the "new imperialism" had been characterized, the Russian government asked for Constantinople and the Straits, should the Gallipoli campaign be successful. Great Britain and France reluctantly agreed, the latter continuing its reluctance until April 9, 1915. The French felt themselves victims of circumstance, for, although the Russians supported France's claims to Syria, the hard-pressed French army could spare no troops for the Syrian campaign the British were now mounting. French politicians considered such action without strong French participation tantamount to a "catastrophe."[35] The rhetoric was not matched by troops, however; French participation remained minimal throughout the war. To compensate for this weakness, the French imperialists did their best diplomatically—and did quite well at that.

The efforts of this diplomacy were rewarded on October 21, 1915, when Grey first suggested joint negotiations over the territorial definitions of a French-controlled Syria.[36] Grey decided to take this initiative because of the intensifying negotiation with the sharif Hussein, which would certainly require some French cooperation and support. The Arabs had been initially approached on September 24, 1914, by Lord Kitchener, who was then high commissioner for Egypt. He discretely inquired, by way of an intermediary, and through one of the sons of the sharif, whether the sharif might support or oppose the British in the event of war. Discussion and correspondence continued after the war did involve Turkey, and all of this led to the sharif's demand that his support would require British endorsement of Arab independence and of the creation of a large state over which he might rule as caliph or king. Kitchener's replacement in Egypt, Sir Henry MacMahon, spoken of by historians as being both consciously ambiguous and unconsciously vague, approached the sharif's demand indirectly. When the sharif then showed impatience with such British muddling-through, negotiations were quickened, with the British providing a communication, dated October 24, 1915, that acceded in general to the sharif's demands. But a conditional clause did stress the need to respect "French interests" in the region.

Grey had already begun to ascertain these interests by his suggestion that joint Anglo-French negotiations begin. The representatives selected were two able men. Mark Sykes was a Francophile, energetic, and well-acquainted with the Middle East. François Georges-Picot, who had formerly been the French consul-general in Beirut, was an ardent member of the *parti syrien*, a pressure group in France determined to protect French interests in the Middle East. By February 1916, the two had arrived at an agreement that divided the area of contention in a colorful way. The French were to have a "Blue Zone," which included the Mediterranean coast and Cilicia, as well as Mosul. The British were to have a "Red Zone" in southern Mesopotamia. In these color-coded areas, each nation was to be free to establish its own form of control and administration. There were, moreover, two areas of protectorate—"A" (French) and "B" (British)—over the region to be designated as an Arab state or confederation of states. Here the two countries were to have exclusive commercial rights and the right to provide advisers to the Arab government.

These proposals were approved by both the British and French governments and then submitted to the Russians for consideration. The Russians made some amendments that gave them territory in the eastern portion of the "Blue Zone," and the French were compensated with other Turkish territory. Final modifications were made after Italy declared war on Germany in August 1916 and then intensified its territorial demands. In April 1917 a "green zone" was added, along with a "C" protectorate to provide Italy with territory between Mersina and Smyrna. Thus, quite simply, in primary colors and by use of the first three letters of the alphabet, the Allies neatly labeled the planned partition of the Ottoman empire.

The inconsistencies between the promises made to the sharif in the British letter of October 24, 1915, and the conditions of the Sykes-Picot agreement were to plague future Anglo-Arab relationships and to call forth the old accusation of "Perfidious Albion." By the end of the war, however, the British were already a long distance from the agreement, even though the French stayed close to it and insisted that it be the basis for postwar policy in the region.

The measurement of this distance can be found in the convention of September 30, 1918. It was this statement that attempted to regulate the ambiguous and unsettled relationship between British military occupation and French political representation in the areas assigned to the French. The fact is that General Allenby disregarded the stipulations of the Sykes-Picot agreement on several occasions. Beyond an effort to address this problem, the convention called for the issuance of a joint declaration of intention about the future disposition of the former Ottoman territories. That declaration appeared on November 8, 1918, and stated that both the British and the French would help establish indigenous governments in Syria and Mesopotamia and would have "no other care" but to support the freely chosen governments of the region. The French interpreted the declaration as a refinement of the Sykes-Picot agreement; the British interpreted it as a rejection of that agreement.[37]

The British and the French found themselves far apart on one other matter in the Middle East, and this was Palestine. The Sykes-Picot agreement had called for the "internationalization" of Palestine. Yet by 1917, British involvement with the Zionist cause had deepened so that "postage stamp" piece of land—to use Balfour's description of Palestine—had grown to major proportions. The war in the Middle East had rather obviously aroused Zionist hopes, and these hopes were strongly expressed in Great Britain. Led by Chaim Weizmann, a renowned scientist who would later be the first president of Israel, the Zionists campaigned in the press and along the corridors of political power.

Their interests and British imperialist interests were seen to dovetail nicely. The Zionists therefore came to support the idea of a British protectorate over Palestine; and, in turn, the British promised the establishment of a "Jewish Homeland" within this protectorate. The substance of this arrangement appeared in the famous Balfour Declaration of November 2, 1917, in which the foreign secretary affirmed the government's support for the idea. The French government did not support the Balfour Declaration, although its interest in Zionism was originally not dissimilar to that of Great Britain. On June 4, 1917, Jules Cambon, secretary-general of the foreign office, had issued a letter to the chairman of the Zionist International Committee, in which he endorsed "Jewish colonization in Palestine."[38] However, the progress of the war and a glance toward peacetime conditions convinced many in the French government that political rapport with the Moslem Arabs would be badly impaired by further overt support of the Zionist cause. Moreover, French Jews, who had little desire to migrate because of their generally assimilated condition in French society, were not strong supporters of Zionism. Finally, the French were disturbed that the British had already occupied Palestine militarily and refused French participation. On the other side, Weizmann had already written the French off, declaring that "the less we involve ourselves with the French the better."[39]

The Palestinian issue and the mutual suspicion with which the French and British regarded each other's presence in that part of the world added to the complexities of Middle Eastern affairs. In large measure the history of modern imperialism has been the history of Anglo-French rivalry, of which the Middle East was one irritating example. Yet even if distrust was the attitude most pronounced in the wartime diplomacy of imperialism, the distrust was clearly over the "spoils" that victory would eventually present. Because of the sum of territory involved in anticipated territorial changes in the Middle East, Africa, and the scattered islands of the Pacific, it is easy to reach the conclusion that the war had not diminished the enthusiasm for empire building. True, some individuals did question whether additional territory would strengthen or weaken existing imperial structures. Winston Churchill even went so far as to announce tersely just before the outbreak of the war, "We have got all we want in territory."[40] Yet the acquisition soon went on, as did the planning for redesigned political maps that would suit the imagined conditions of a postwar world. The British Committee on Territorial Desiderata, in its meetings of April 1917, allowed its collective imagination to roam around the world and, en route, to contemplate the possibilities of territorial shifts and acquisitions in nearly every sea and on all continents. Lord Curzon, commenting on this geopolitical exercise, stated that someone might get the impression "that we are meditating the carving up of the world to suit our own interests."[41] Whether said in dead earnestness or lively jest, the statement showed how far removed from impending realities the "New Imperialists" of old empires were.

Away from the chancelleries and other high-ceilinged offices of state, the perspective on empire was often neither so bright nor so clear. The outbreak of the war raised the fear of local disturbances and the concern that the shift of military power might mean a tip in the scales of local political power. In Haiphong, Indochina, the English wife of a French medical doctor noted the split in sentiment between the French soldiers who desired to leave immediately for the western front and the French civilians who feared local uprisings and plundering if such military support were withdrawn.[42] The situation in Morocco presented a grim appearance as well. There, the resident-general, Hubert Lyautey, was requested to send some 35 batallions home immediately and, in the process, to withdraw his remaining troops to the more easily defended coastal regions.[43] This would have meant the abandonment of much of Morocco, which was not yet under adequate French control. Lyautey offered an alternative plan which allowed the dispatch of the requisite number of troops but also allowed the maintenance of the outposts, although with reduced numbers of troops. The plan worked, but the situation remained somewhat unsettled. German-inspired agitation, initiated in Spanish Morocco, did cause trouble and fear: an attack in 1914 cost the lives of 33 officers and 650 men. Yet throughout the difficult months of 1914 and 1915 Lyautey responded with determination and a touch of showmanship. He started construction on his official residence in Rabat to give visible proof of the French intention to stay for a long while.[44]

The Italians were far more disturbed by the problems that they quickly encountered when they entered the war. As one of the newest colonial powers, and one whose control was far from secure when it declared war in 1915, Italy was confronted with major difficulties in Somalia and in Libya.[45] In Somalia, the Turks encouraged the opposition of the chief Islamic leader by supplying him with arms and recognizing him as king. He took the offensive and defeated an Italian unit in March 1916. The Italians were therefore forced to dispatch additional troops but were unable to gain control in Somalia until 1921. In Libya the situation was graver still. There a general revolt in 1915 forced the Italians to retreat to the littoral region, a retreat further accelerated by an uprising among the Sanusi. The Italians held securely only to a few coastal towns until the war's end.

Along the shores of the British empire there were problems as well. A military insurgency in Singapore containing "the classic ingredients of every Indian mutiny—ineffective officers, disruptive influence from without, and military grievance,"[46] occurred in 1915 at a time when a new troop movement was planned. English officers hopefully anticipated assignment to Mesopotamia, but were soon destined for Hong Kong. Under the illusion that they would be shipped to the Middle East, the Indian soldiers, already uncertain of the outcome of the war, were deeply disturbed by the thought of fighting Turks, fellow Moslems. Thus, a combination of religious resistance and political confusion sparked mutiny among four of the eight companies. Of greater proportions and of enduring significance was a rebellion among Afrikaners at the time of the invasion of German Southwest Africa. For a while the British authorities were frightened enough to consider the diversion of Australian troops, destined for the Gallipoli campaign. But General Botha, both military leader and premier, was able to contain the rebellion. One leader was executed, another 281 were tried for treason. "The pathos of the rebellion," commented one historical observer, "lies mainly in its character as a civil war between Afrikaners."[47] But its importance lies in its effect on later Afrikaner nationalism.

Perhaps the most widely observed and remembered British colonial upheaval occurred very close to home. This was the Easter Rebellion of 1916 in Ireland. The immediate cause was the impending threat of Irish conscription, but long-range causes were deep in Irish history, reaching back to Oliver Cromwell and the conquest of Ireland, and to the absentee land ownership that still characterized the agrarian sector of the economy. Impatient with British promises, and now irritated by the thought of conscription, which appeared to be nothing less than impressment, the Irish Revolutionary Brotherhood and the Irish Volunteers, a paramilitary organization, prepared an attempt to overthrow British rule. Some support was secretly obtained from the German government in the form of a planned small arms shipment, but the general organization was badly timed and managed. Orders and counterorders created further confusion. First planned for Easter Sunday, the rebellion actually took place on Easter Monday, yet without the nationwide support that had originally been anticipated. The center of militant activity was Dublin, where the rebels established and valiantly held their headquarters in the general post office. From there they issued their manifesto proclaiming the Irish Republic: "We declare the right of the people of Ireland to the ownership of Ireland, and to the unfettered control of Irish destinies, to be sovereign and undefeasible."[48]

The declaration was greeted with swift reprisals from the British, and so the Easter Rebellion passed into history, yet as a memory not to be forgotten.

The declaration would be reworked in different languages and different idioms within a few decades when colonial empires everywhere were in advanced states of collapse. But generally the wartime experience was perceived as tending to modify imperial structures, rather than to destroy them. The worst of the war swept wide of the colonies. The editorial writer of the *Gold Coast Leader*, who published the following statement in 1915, knew this: "We shall play the role of passive spectators with loyalty, determination and devotion in order to qualify for greater trust."[49]

In general the colonies did not encounter war; they stood aside as their youth embarked on an imperial task that caused consternation and anxiety as well as pride. "If the Empire fails, we fail with it," dramatically intoned Prime Minister Hughes of Australia in 1916. "The Empire is fighting for its life. Britain has asked us to do our share. The question is—are you going to do it?"[50] When Hughes so spoke, he was in the middle of a campaign to persuade the voters to approve a referendum for conscription. This was a new issue, a military and imperial one that had not disturbed colonies previously.

It was not just an Australian or a British empire problem but one raised as well by the French in their African colonies.

Certainly the issue was a major one. "The history of conscription in Canada is practically the history of Canadian politics for 1917 and part of 1918," an official history stated.[51] By extension, it was a major part of the political history of both empires in those years. The dire loss of soldiers and the disturbing success of the great German spring offensive of 1918 frightened Allied leaders into a search for larger sources of manpower. Great Britain itself had broken with its own military tradition by introducing conscription in early 1916, and now the dominions followed. While there was little dispute in New Zealand, the other two dominions were the setting of keen and acrimonious debate. As Canada prepared to confront the issue politically, French Canadians rioted in Quebec City in March 1917, and several persons were killed by troops brought in to quell the disturbance. The conscription law was finally passed on August 29, 1917, but the French Canadians ardently fought it and assiduously avoided the draft, in protest against an empire they felt abused them.

The situation in Australia was equally complex and subject to intense debate. Both referendums on conscription, one in 1916 and one in 1918, each championed by Hughes, were defeated. Australians seemed to want to keep whatever conscripts they needed home in Australia, a policy they pursued in both wars. What proved to be the main factor determining the outcome of each vote on the two referendums was a general perception of Australia's place in the world; that is, whether the territory was "part of an Empire fighting for its life" or "a new nation whose business was both to defend and insulate itself from European squabbles."[52] The outcome of the conscription issue was thus an expression of Australia's growing national awareness and diverse reactions to it.

In contrast, there were few diverse reactions to conscription in Ireland. No policy was more clumsily executed, so little likely of any success. "We might almost as well recruit Germans," remarked H. E. Duke, chief secretary for Ireland, when the bill for Irish conscription was passed.[53] The fault lay directly with Lloyd George, who, appalled by the German spring offensive of 1918, desperately turned to Ireland to provide 150,000 of the 550,000 conscripts believed necessary. In so doing, he reversed his original opposition to such a plan. Moreover, he quickly departed from the dual policy he had previously thought necessary: the promise of home rule to make conscription acceptable to the Irish. Perhaps it was too late for a home rule bill to satisfy the Irish; certainly it was too late for the Sinn Fein party, which ardently wanted nothing less than national independence. But the introduction of the conscription bill without any immediate consideration of home rule doomed all hope for any Irish support. The results were disastrous. A general strike broke out in April; the hierarchy of the Catholic church denounced conscription as a "scourge," and riots occurred across the land. In the end the British dropped the idea of Irish conscription, but their political retreat was to no avail. Rather than gaining men needed for the war effort, they lost the last opportunity for a parliamentary solution to the age-old Irish question. In the elections of 1918 the Sinn Fein party won, its success largely an outcome of public indignation over the conscription issue—and its success an indication that the days of British colonial rule in "John Bull's Other Island" were about over.

France's results with conscription in its black African colonies were not greeted with such dramatic and unfavorable conclusions. Yet the political consequences were of importance. France considered its colonies a manpower "reservoir" because of a declining birthrate at home. In stark terms, there would be far fewer French youths to combat the many more German youths in any future war. The idea of using African troops gained in popularity in the early years of the twentieth century, principally with the publication of *La Force noir* (*The Black Army*) by Lieutenant Colonel Charles Mangin. Mangin assumed that approximately 30,000 troops could be recruited each year in black Africa, and their deployment in North Africa would release French troops for service on the frontiers of the homeland. Furthermore, he praised the virtues of African fighting men in terms that carried the racist overtones of the day. The Africans "have all the qualities required for the long struggles of modern warfare: ruggedness, endurance, tenacity, instinct for combat, absence of nervousness, and an incomparable shock value. Their arrival on the battlefield will be demoralizing to the enemy."[54]

Such recruitment began in 1912, and was intensified with two major levies during the war, in 1915 and 1918.[55] As a result of the first levy, which met with riots and, in addition, depleted the manpower needed to raise foodstuffs also required by the French, the local authorities in Africa were hesitant about a second draft. The governor-general of French West Africa was particularly bothered by the thought that if the British did not undertake a similar draft in their colonies, "we would turn over to them our commerce and our populations, which is to say forty years of efforts."[56] These objections did not enter the official thinking in Paris; the second draft was endorsed. More-

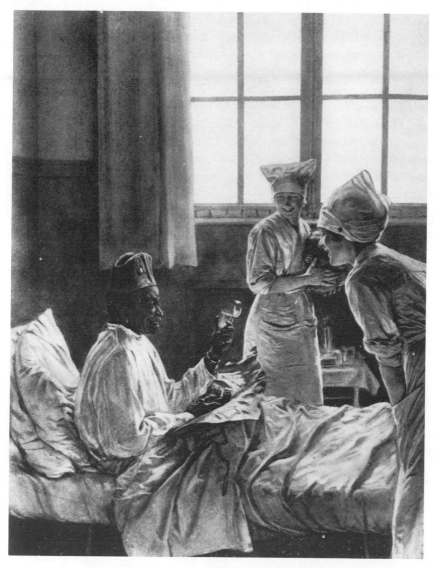

Drawing of a wounded Senegalese soldier receiving a gift from nurses in a
French hospital. From *Illustrated London News*, January 16, 1915.

over, its chances of success were considered high, because the individual entrusted with the task of recruiting was an able politician from Africa.

Blaise Diagne, recently elected representative to the French parliament, the first black African to achieve this authority, was made high commissioner of the republic for recruitment.[57] His position was equal in authority to that of a governor-general, a status that caused some irritation among French colonial officials. Diagne did his job well, exceeding any quotas the French could have imagined. His contribution was not, however, the result of unalloyed or misplaced patriotism. Diagne looked to his own political interests and to those of the people he served. In speaking before the French parliament, he said that he had undertaken the task for two reasons: the first, respect for France and recognition of its service in Africa; the second, the assurance for African soldiers of "the ransom for their political liberty in the future."[58] The war, in this way, served as part of the modern political awakening of Africa.

North of the equator, the contribution of manpower to the war effort gave rise to the thought and hope that the British imperial structure would change. "But is it possible," asked the Canadian press magnate, Lord Beaverbrook, "that they [the dominion soldiers] should return without having stamped upon the loose constitution of the Empire articles at once more formal and mutual than those with which until this war we have on the whole been content?"[59] The peculiar nature of the British empire, the core of which consisted in the several white settlement colonies, recently termed "dominions," made Beaverbrook's question irrelevant to all other empires.

During the war certain imperialists had hoped that a federal system would emerge, bringing the empire together in a meaningful, political way. The Imperial War Conference, for instance, was anticipated by some as the first step toward an imperial parliament which would sit in deliberation of the affairs of this world empire. In a speech before the House of Commons on May 17, 1918, Lloyd George furthered such ideas when he stated: "We hope that the holding of an annual Imperial Cabinet to discuss foreign affairs and other aspects of Imperial policy will become an accepted convention of the British Constitution."[60] The prime minister of Canada, Robert Borden, went furthest in his proposal to the Imperial War Conference of 1917, which would become the famous "Resolution IX." Stating that constitutional considerations should be postponed until after the war, the resolution said in part:

The Imperial War Conference . . . deem it their duty . . . to place on record their view that any such readjustment, while thoroughly preserving all existing powers of self-government and complete control of domestic affairs, should be based upon a full recognition of the Dominions as autonomous nations of an Imperial Commonwealth, and of India as an important portion of the same.[61]

The anticipated postwar constitutional convention to effect these changes never occurred, but the resolution was a clear notice that the fundamental assumption of European imperialism from the fifteenth century on—that the colonies existed for the benefit of the mother country—was out of date. The principle of nationhood, existing within an amorphous commonwealth, was a new, twentieth-century idea that found its resonance in the political vocabulary of one of the century's most influential statesmen, a figure who was patently anti-imperialist.

Woodrow Wilson, as he and all of his biographers have stressed, was a moralist. Self-righteous, confident in his knowledge, liberal in his political outlook, neatly academic in his efforts to reorder world affairs, Wilson converted his personal ideology into a meteorological condition that he was certain would shake the world. "There is a great wind of moral force moving through the world," he stated, "and every man who opposes . . . that wind will go down in disgrace."[62]

It was a wind that would blow unfavorably across empires. Wilson abhorred war and imperialism, both of which he saw as being generated out of petty and selfish interests, and to the detriment of the people at large. As a Progressive, Wilson regarded the business community with suspicion; as a student of constitutional history, he assumed that the benefits of democracy might be conferred upon the world. Ignorant of foreign policy, he nonetheless applied his principles abroad. The most frequently cited example of his activity was the 1914 treaty with Colombia, in which the United States indicated its "sincere regret" for the political maneuvers by which Panama was established during the Theodore Roosevelt administration—and for the purpose of getting the "Big Ditch" underway. The "regret" was also given a value, for the treaty called for a $25,000,000 indemnity to be paid to Colombia. Roosevelt, still alive and feisty as ever, got his friends in the Senate to prevent passage of the treaty. The incident clearly indicates the difference in attitude between the president who was a pious liberal and the president who was a rude expansionist.

The war in Europe also aroused the conscience of Wilson. He sought to play the role of mediator and sent Colonel Edward House as his emissary to bring sweet reason to the embittered chiefs of the European states. House failed, but he was not ignored. The goodwill of the United States as a neutral power was of major importance and had a "powerful restraint," according to Lloyd George, "on the proclamation of extravagant or rapacious war aims."[63] By the time the United States did enter the war—brought to this decision by the resumption of German submarine warfare—the major principle later identified with Wilson, "national self-determination," had been much discussed. The principle was accepted for Europe, but its application to the colonial world was quite another matter. In a speech of January 5, 1918, Lloyd George tried to place Great Britain in a favorable light by announcing that self-determination was as applicable to the former German colonies as it was to the occupied European territories. But the applicability went no further; there was no affirmation of self-determination for the colonies of the British empire, or for the French for that matter. The French, like the British, observed Wilson's words and actions with great caution. The foreign minister, Stephen Pichon, told the French Chamber of Deputies on January 13, that the French government was in accord with Wilson on war aims, but he made no specific reference to the colonies.[64]

Wilson himself gave the matter its lasting rhetoric in the fifth of his famous Fourteen Points, presented in his speech of January 8, 1918. He requested:

A free, open-minded, and absolutely impartial adjustment of all colonial claims, based upon a strict observance of the principle that in determining such questions of sovereignty the interests of the populations concerned must have equal weight with the equitable claims of the government whose title is to be determined.

The question Wilson addressed was complicated and made embarrassing by the new Soviet regime, which in late 1917 disclosed the contents of the secret treaties to which the Tsarist government had been a part. This was followed by denunciations of imperialism made by Lenin, as well as by the Soviet government's urging of independence for all colonies. Empires were not yet to tremble because of such verbal onslaughts, but the language represented new attitudes that would have to be considered.

The war generated more than a new rhetoric that was soon directed to the colonies. The arrangement of institutions and social relationships was also altered, but in ways that have not yet been closely examined by historians.[65] Beyond the obvious effects of German's disappearance as a colonial power, beyond the significance of the service provided by millions of Africans and Asians in the war, a number of local and regional developments stand to be recognized. The departure of Europeans for the war front, from West Africa as well as India and Indochina, meant that indigenous personnel were able— because now required—to occupy positions hitherto denied them. The wartime demand for more agricultural and mineral products increased production and thereby involved more people in the European-based economy. Conversely, the shortage of shipping meant for India the increase of homespun cotton piecegoods, with the result that the import of these British goods virtually stopped after the war.[66] In West Africa, however, a similar British shipping shortage provided European merchants with a commercial edge, because they could command scarce space with an authority that the Africans could not.[67]

More widespread in occurrence and effect was labor mobilization. Not only were individuals enlisted and even forced into the armed services but the need for regimented labor to meet new production demands intensified. The local reaction was one of discontent occasionally extended to resistance. Between November 1915 and July 1916, for instance, Upper Volta was in a state of turmoil because of French recruitment efforts, aggravating already widespread discontent over taxes, labor practices, and general colonial policy.[68] In Kenya Africans were forced to serve as porters to British troops, to the extent that 75 percent of the male population was taken from the colony.[69]

The extraordinary mobilization and the production that the war generated demonstrated, however crudely and inhumanely, the ability of the local economies to serve European needs.[70] As the imperialist state intruded more boldly into colonial affairs, the first suggestions for economic planning were adumbrated. It has been suggested that the genesis of the Sarraut plan for economic development, of major importance in the interwar period,[71] occurred during the war. As early as 1916, a group of Englishmen were considering how the colonial economy might be strategically organized to relieve the nation of its increasing war debt.[72]

In ways such as these the European war was brought to overseas possessions. The effect was a disturbance that suggested the need or possibility of more intense development to the Europeans—and that aroused some hope and indignation among the local populations.

The Prince of Wales would understand some of this change when he arrived in India in 1921 and found his visit shunned by the Indian population. "Wherever he was taken," later wrote Jawaharlal Nehru, "he was met with *hartals* [strikes] and deserted streets."[73] Edward, Prince of Wales, was a popular figure who probably did not expect any such reception when he had planned his first empire tour to India, one of four goodwill tours that took him some 35,000 miles around the British empire after World War I.

The Reuters correspondent covering the initial departure from England did so in ponderous language, in what might be called the "imperial vernacular."

The governor of Bombay and his wife, with the governor's bodyguard, 1933.
From the National Archives.

The Prince, in the uniform of a post captain, with aiguilettes, emerged into a little patch of sunshine, that last approving smile of the drooping orb.[74]

As the sun set on that autumn day, not many people perceived that it would soon be setting on empire as well. The war had intensified and diversified imperialist activities, even disguised them in new language, but had not undermined the institutions or destroyed the beliefs upon which imperialism was structured. The soldiers who had come to fight in the European war did so to support that abstract concept of "empire." The concept, and the parts of the world it denoted, still remained after the soldiers had returned home.

CHAPTER 2

Colonial Rule and Administration

Few of the world war's effects on imperialism were so swift and complete as that which occurred in the European compound of Tientsin, China, when news of the armistice arrived at 7:05 P.M. on November 11. A German statue, erected in commemoration of the Boxer Rebellion and deriseively known as "Tin Willie," was pulled from its pedestal with one heave by British, French, and other celebrants. The mutilated form was dragged through the streets until it finally reached the grounds of the French Club where the remains were hacked into pieces for souvenirs.[1] The immediate disappearance of German influence in the colonial world was in no way matched by comparably dramatic alterations in the situation of other colonial powers.

The war weakened many European beliefs and destroyed many European institutions, but the underlying assumptions about empire and the structures based upon those assumptions withstood it well. The "strong citadel of self-seeking imperialism" remained, even if buffeted by new winds of adversity.[2] This is the point: critical appraisal of empire intensified and imperialist theory was modified to reflect the concerns of the age, yet the general enterprise went on in the interwar years much as it had done before. Change was modest and gradual, not radical and immediate: Certainly the signs of protest within the colonial territories were being manifested more glaringly, but by and large they were considered containable. According to the former director of the French Ecole coloniale, writing in 1937, European authority was being contested and opposed, "but everything allows the conclusion that, except for

47

catastrophe, it is far from exhausting all its resources for lasting a long time to come."[3] Moreover, any such opposition was considered not to be in the best interests of the subject peoples who, it was granted, may have had the right to self-government but were not yet at the stage of development where they could effectively exercise it. The transfer of authority to the protestors, it was frequently declared, would only lead to renewed anarchy or absolutism of a precolonial sort.[4]

The sentiment of the age was still that which was found in the rhetorical question asked by President William McKinley about the Filipinos at the time of the American annexation of the islands: "Did we need their consent to perform a great act of humanity?"[5]

An "act of humanity" remained the basic justification for empire, but with significant modification. To "civilizing mission," which had been hailed in the nineteenth century, was added "sacred trust," which was to be the watchword between the wars. The latter concept both enlarged and shifted the responsibility of colonial rule, so that in principle such rule became the concern of the international community, not solely that of a particular nation, while the well-being of the subject populations, rather than the ambitions of the colonizing power, was to have priority. Article 22 of the Covenant of the League of Nations, which addressed the status of the territories and colonial possessions of the defeated powers, stated that "there should be applied the principle that the well-being and development of such peoples form a sacred trust of civilization and that securities for the performance of this trust should be embodied in the Covenant."

This assertion of international responsibility was what gave "sacred trust" its unusual quality. Theorists dedicated to colonial questions, notably writers in Great Britain, had progressed in their thought during the war from concern with the need for international regulation to acceptance of international supervision as a desirable condition.[6] Although new in modern colonial policy, the idea of accountability was not at all new in principle. It had made an early appearance in Edmund Burke's famous statement voiced during the parliamentary debate on Fox's East India Bill of 1788. Burke then argued that "all political power which is set over men . . . ought to be some way or other exercised ultimately for their benefit." He continued: "If this is true . . . then such rights are all in the strictest sense a *trust*: and it is of the very essence of every *trust* to be rendered *accountable*." As liberal, and then democratic, principles suffused European politics of the nineteenth century, variations on the Burkean idea appeared in a number of documents, even finding vague expression in the debates and the conclusions of the Berlin West African Conference of 1884–85 and the Brussels Convention of 1890, in which the participating nations jointly agreed to uphold their responsiblity for the betterment of subject peoples.

The concept was, however, essentially English in development, not international. The postwar acceptance of trusteeship by all of the colonial powers and its enshrinement in League of Nations documents has been considered a victory of sorts for British colonial principles.[7] However, trusteeship ought to be seen as a refinement of imperialistic ideology to meet the needs of the times: to respond to the moral issues raised by the war, to assess new research and theories from anthropology in terms of colonial administration, and to provide a set of general principles by which to justify and guide current colonial rule.

By the 1920s the age of imperialism had been replaced by the age of empire. Administration generally meant maintenance of the public peace and economic development, and these indeed were the principal objectives promoted after the war. The era of "scrambles" was over, although rapacious acts of imperialism still marked the times. Japan's invasion of Manchuria in 1931 and Italy's invasion of Abyssinia in 1935 were the notable examples. But these acts were condemned, not condoned, by the other imperialistic states, which were now more interested in development than in further expansion. Their immediate problem was how to govern territories that had only recently been invaded and then occupied by the military.

Every imperialistic power had soon recognized that its newly acquired territories posed a new set of problems in administration. These regions were described as "dominations" or "tropical dependencies" and were deemed unsuitable for extensive white settlement. They were, therefore, not colonies at all but territories populated by "backward races" over whom Europeans would serve as managers or instructors. The nineteenth-century metaphor had been anatomical: Europeans supplied the brains, "natives" the muscle. As a lesson in anatomy, this assessment of colonial rule was crude and was seldom repeated after the war. However, the general asymmetrical relationship it clearly described between the two peoples remained.

This relationship was one that colonialists regarded as primarily necessary in black Africa but the condescending attitude of administrators, when combined with the European economic imperative—the development of colonies at least to the point of fiscal self-sufficiency—was certainly not restricted to a single geographical or ecological region. The one notable exception to this generalization, and the most striking development in the mobilization of labor in a colonial situation, was introduced by the Italians during the Fascist regime.

"Demographic colonization" was new in the twentieth century, but, in general appearance, seemed a reversion to the older concept of "plantation"—or transplantation—which was widespread in seventeenth- and eighteenth-century Europe. Of all the colonial powers, Italy could least afford overseas expansion. Its economy was weak, its international indebtedness high. For the Fascists, however, colonialism was justified by its prestige and as a means of ensuring the immigration of part of a population too large to be supported by the home peninsula.[8]

Initially anticolonialist in mood, Mussolini soon embraced the idea of a "new Roman empire" and lent his person to the enterprise by undertaking a state visit to Libya in 1926. Two years later he ardently endorsed—some say he initiated—the new policy of "demographic colonization." This state-directed effort to relocate thousands of Italian peasant families on the arable soil along the coastline of Libya was designed to create labor-intensive economic development by a country that was weak in capital resources. Actually, however, the policy did not have much impact until Marshal Italo Balbo became governor of Libya in 1933 and seized the project as his own.

With that special panache for doing things with a touch of the theatrical, which led one observer to call him "a bearded buccaneer, a product of the modern aviation school,"[9] Balbo contrived the relocation of 20,000 Italians on the anniversary of the Fascist March on Rome. The *Ventmilia*, described by one historian as "part country carnival and part military parade,"[10] was an exodus that brought 1,800 families to Genoa and Naples for embarkation. They sailed in a small armada of nine ships, escorted by eight destroyers, across the Mediterranean, arriving at Tripoli on November 2, 1938. The "pioneers" settled in specially constructed farms, clusters of which encircled small villages. All was new, neat, and white, the entire arrangement graphically different from the somber situation many of the émigrés had left behind.

This effort in agricultural colonization did lead to a notable increase in olive and wheat production, but it also resulted in the harsh relocation of the original Arab population. Although the Italians created Arab villages as well, the land on which they were relocated was unsuitable for agriculture. Thus, the Arabs in Tripolitania, like the Bantus in South Africa, and the Indians in the United States, were relegated to the status of a "reservation" population on lands not needed or wanted by the white colonial population.

Italo Balbo with some of the twenty thousand Italian peasants setting off for
Libya, 1938. From the National Archives.

Widely acclaimed at the time, "demographic colonization" was an aspect
of twentieth-century imperialism peculiar to Libya and to the Fascist state that
briefly controlled it. The ideology of that state, initially unmarked by racism,
did, with the progress of time, the bluster of Mussolini, and the influence of
Nazi Germany, take on a racist quality.[11] Officially, Mussolini and the Fascist state stood as protectors of the Moslem population, and citizenship for
that group within the Italian state—Libya was integrally incorporated into the
kingdom—was possible. However, the Sahara area of Libya was excluded
from such consideration because parts of its population were considered to
be negroid.[12]

Even so, few persons in Italy and fewer still elsewhere, except the racist
theorists in Nazi Germany, publicly entertained the crude Social Darwinian
notions that had made late nineteenth-century imperialist thought so noxious.
Anthropological studies, refined and enhanced by the introduction of serious
field work in the early twentieth century, had put behind these earlier, simple
historical arguments, which had grounded Africans in some primeval past
and arrested the Chinese in centuries long gone by.

If there was a time line, it was the "base line" that marked the local cultural configuration just before it was entered, and hence disturbed, by cultural carriers from the West, notably the colonialists.[13] Distinctions among cultural systems were now perceived as being more of kind than of time. The "advanced" peoples of the West organized their social patterns of behavior differently, and they thought about the world differently than other peoples. It was not so much the new in conflict with the old as it was the modern in opposition to the traditional that Europeans saw as the nature of this culture contact.

The strategic term employed in the 1920s and 1930s was "primitive." It was frequently used interchangeably with "backward," but it gained dominance as the antonymn for all that modern Europe supposedly represented. The contrast between "primitivism" and "progressivism" was first made in the late nineteenth century, but the addition of complicated cultural connotations to "primitivism" only occurred in the early twentieth century when noun and adjective became popular anthropological terms. The French anthropologist Lucien Lévy-Bruhl remarked that these terms had not yet been adopted by the French in 1910 when he wrote his first book, *Les Fonctions mentales dans les sociétés inférieures*, or he would have employed "primitive" in place of "inferior."[14] Yet by 1919 Robert Briffault, author of the popular book *The Making of Humanity*, used the term in its modern sense with familiarity. He wrote: "Primitive man does not think at all unless driven by direct need."[15]

The extremes of civilized development were characterized by entirely different thought systems, "mentalities," to employ the French term. Psychological, far more than historical, distinctions separated the Westerner from the Australian aborigine, for instance. The refined expression of these distinctions was the lifetime work of Lévy-Bruhl, who first was alerted to the enormity of the subject when he read some translated Chinese philosophy that he found incomprehensible. To appreciate the obstacles standing in the way of cross-cultural understanding, Lévy-Bruhl turned to analysis of one extreme, the "primitive."[16]

His general conclusion was that primitives were "pre-logical." It was not that primitives were incapable of logical thought, but that they were indifferent or opposed to it; it was not required to explain phenomena or events in their world. "Mysticism" prevailed. For the primitives there was no process of causality, for theirs was a natural world guided by outside forces that spirited things as they would. Instead of events with explicable causes, there were "occasions" in which these unseen forces intervened. The result of these conditions was that among primitive peoples "there is a decided aversion to rational thought."[17]

The analysis that Lévy-Bruhl provided in his several books was sophisticated and sensitive, unmarked by either rigid or simple distinctions. He appreciated the significance of change through time, just as he observed certain continuities, the "residues" of "mysticism," which existed even among those peoples whose principal mode of observation was rational. But he added an authority to the word "primitive" that helped ensure its wide acceptance at a time when serious scientific study of differing cultures and civilizations was being made.[18]

Lévy-Bruhl's professional interest in cultural antithesis, the extremes marked by the primitive and the modern, the backward and the advanced, reinforced research interest in those people who were most unlike Westerners, those whose cultures were apparently simple and small-scaled. American Indians, Polynesians, and black Africans were the major subjects of the new field research.

As a cipher, "primitive" served the advocates of empire well. It complemented the concept of "sacred trust" because it suggested a scientific basis for the need of colonial rule. The "primitive" peoples were deemed to be without the intellectual apparatus and the institutions that would allow them to cope with modernity, with "more complicated and efficient ways of doing things."[19] No doubt "primitivism" was an improvement over "inferiority" as a term of distinction because it substituted manageable cultural differences for fixed racial ones. However, it is questionable whether it did much to alter the colonial administrator's perception of the subordinate position of the indigenous populations in the colonial situation. Lord Lugard's brief catalog of the major characteristics of the "typical African" included most of the adjectives that were currently used, but in varying combinations, for all the colonial peoples. According to him, the African was "a happy, thriftless, excitable person, lacking in self-control, discipline, and foresight."[20]

The immediate concern of colonial rule was to cope with these characteristics; the long-range concern was to move the "primitive" world into the "modern," to integrate the resident populations into a different cultural order, one that was technologically advanced and centered around a market economy. Although most of the colonial administrators on the spot were captivated or overwhelmed by the rusticity of the environment in which they worked and therefore cast themselves more in the role of feudal lords than captains of industry or members of a managerial elite, the general premise of modern colonial theory was consistent with the Western spirit of progress: to lead the subject peoples forward to a "better," more westernized, way of life. What would appear in twentieth-century European thought and practice as "social democracy," the responsibility of the state for the general well-being of its citizenry, had a colonial variant. The latter, however, was imposed, not negotiated; it was alien, an outgrowth of European concerns, not needs felt and defined by the indigenous populations. Jomo Kenyatta, the future president of Kenya and a student of anthropology in the 1930s, wrote that European education for Africans was "a policy that has been carried out without due regard for the ideals and aspirations of the people concerned."[21]

Kenyatta's accusation, in general accurate, is one proof that the imperialist mentality had neither been shattered nor reformed by the war experience. The principal alteration was one of scope or perspective, not of attitude. Imperialism was now seen as a global concern exercised primarily for the benefit of subject peoples. Thus, the need for European domination was not to be lessened but slightly redirected. The most telling statement was that found in the British White Paper issued on Kenya in 1923:

His Majesty's Government regard themselves as exercising a trust in behalf of the African population . . . the object of which may be defined as the protection and advancement of the native races.[22]

There was more to it than a particular moral tone. The liberal political philosophy that provided the principal bias of twentieth-century imperialistic ideology was paralleled by economic concerns, which, like that philosophy, had been well established in the nineteenth century. These concerns, generated by the industrial revolution and the dominance it ensured Europe in the world, were three: the need of raw materials, the extension of markets, and the search for new places of investment. Both advocates and adversaries of imperialism had made the economic argument the primary one. Frederick Lugard, as forceful a proponent of empire as would be found in the twentieth century, insisted that the British "should understand . . . how vital to our industrial life are the products of the tropics and its markets for our manufactures."[23] Nikolai Lenin, chief theorist and most influential figure in the Communist camp, agreed on this point, although his argument suggested a more intense degree of urgency:

The more capitalism is developed, the more the need for raw materials is felt, the more bitter the competition becomes and the more feverishly the hunt for raw materials proceeds throughout the whole world, the more desperate becomes the struggle for colonies.[24]

No proponent of empire in the interwar period would have described the situation as a "desperate struggle." The rhetoric then employed was not as strident nor as dramatic as it had been at the end of the nineteenth century— and as it remained in Lenin's assessment. The terms which were now used stressed nobility of purpose, the benevolence of colonial activity, even the generosity of spirit animating the European nations.

Throughout the colonial world, development was the current key term, *mise en valeur* in French. But it was to be development of idealistic proportions: first, for the betterment of the "backward races," and second, for the benefit of mankind in general through the release and utilization of resources previously ignored or untapped. The two aspects formed the "dual mandate."

The term and the most persuasive definition of it were the work of Frederick Lugard, former British high commissioner of Northern Nigeria, chief sponsor of the concept of "indirect rule," and an author of some note. Lugard's book, *The Dual Mandate in British Tropical Africa*, attracted sufficient attention to go through four editions between its first publication date, 1922, and the outbreak of World War II. More than 600 pages in length, this compendium of British Africa contained recommendations for the layout of private residences, discussed tax and land use systems, reviewed methods of colonial administration, and *inter alia*, praised the British "genius" for colonial rule and the "dual mandate" that had been so responsibly followed. In one grand historical sweep Lugard summed it up in a manner that must surely have pleased the ghosts of Joseph Chamberlain, the earl of Cromer, and Cecil Rhodes.

As Roman imperialism laid the foundations of modern civilization, and led the wild barbarians of these islands along the path of progress, so in Africa today we are repaying the debt, and bringing to the dark places of the earth, the abode of barbarism and cruelty, the torch of culture and progress, while ministering to the material needs of our own civilizations.[25]

The dependent clause tells all. Earlier in his argument Lugard admitted that no undiluted philanthropy caused the British to sally forth into Africa; economic concerns were the chief reason, and so they remained. In Lugard's opinion, the wealth of the world could not—should not—lie untapped because of the inability or the incompetence of the people to exploit those resources that were all about them. The new responsibility of the trustee was therefore the second element of the dual mandate: " . . . the development of [the colonial territory's] material resources for the benefit of mankind."[26]

Monument "À la gloire du génie colonisateur de la France," just before its
dedication in Algeria, 1933. From the National Archives.

The latter idea has its roots in nineteenth-century imperialistic policy. It
was a reworking on another plane and in another idiom of the old "open
door" policy, which was to reduce international friction by assuring free
trade in certain areas of colonial rivalry, of which the Congo Basin, Morocco, and China were the most famous examples.

In brief, there was nothing particularly new in the overarching principles
of imperial responsibility that were defined and praised at the peace table. It
was the intensity with which they were stated that makes them distinctive
from previous statements. However, that intensity resulted more from an accident of history than from a calculated change of heart. German military
defeat in Europe required new consideration of colonial questions.

Even as the war raged, theorists and politicians debated what would become of the German colonial empire, which had already been militarily occupied. From this debate, particularly keen in British liberal and socialist circles, one idea gained in authority and was most cogently expressed in 1916
in an article appearing in the *New Statesman*:

If the Allies determine at the end of the war to retain control of the German colonies, they might and ought give a solemn undertaking to hold these territories in trust for civilization, to treat the interests of the natives therein as paramount, and to preserve in perpetuity the Open Door in the fullest sense of the term.[27]

Moreover, it was obvious that a war, in which victory was finally victory galvanized by a nation whose president professed his intention to "make the world safe for democracy," was one in which the old rule of "spoils to the victor" could hardly be announced as public policy. Finally, the exclusion of Germany from the small band of self-styled civilized nations presented ideological problems for which quick solutions were necessary.

The Germans, who had begun their colonial enterprise in the same spirit as the other European states and who had employed much the same rhetoric and tactics, were suddenly outcasts, victims of their own pride and of their enemies' propaganda. Germans had gone abroad some 30 years before triumphantly bringing *Kultur*; they returned defeated, bearing the label of "Hun." Along with general war guilt, the Germans were accused of "colonial guilt." This was officially registered in the Allied Note of June 16, 1919, to the German Peace Delegation, in which the membership was told that Germany would have "to renounce all her rights and claims to her overseas possessions" because of her "dereliction in the sphere of colonial civilization."

German behavior overseas, as is now well-known, had been no worse and, on occasion, was much better than that of the other colonial powers.[28] But Germany's colonial fate was sealed with the invasion of neutral Belgium.[29] The horror stories that were fabricated out of the twisted ruins of that small country were easily transported overseas. The resulting propaganda was, as Heinrich Schnee, a former governor of German East Africa, wrote, "organized, and in large measure invented, without the slightest regard for logic or consistency," and for the purpose of "sheer cupidity."[30] At least one British colonial official later, but discreetly, concurred in this judgment when he commented on a British Foreign Office note in 1936:

One would almost believe that Mr. Perowne [author of the note] still thinks that the seizure of the German Colonies after the war was justifiable on the highest moral grounds, and was not a carefully disguised act of conquest.[31]

The disguised act had its particular advantages. It enabled advocates of colonial rule to reinforce their arguments about the need for good government as a major justification for the European presence. Germany could be made the exception that proved the rule. Because that nation had "outraged" the populations under its jurisdiction, it had forfeited its moral right to colonies.[32] In this simple argument the colonial system was in no way questioned, but an egregious violation of it was the subject of condemnation. Postwar French and British critics were, in effect, doing little more than saying in their own way what President McKinley had said when he defended the substitution of American for Spanish rule in the Philippines: " . . . we could not leave them to themselves—they were unfit for self-government and would soon have anarchy and misrule over there worse than Spain's was."[33]

The dilemma that proponents of empire had willingly imagined was the one that the earl of Cromer had defined in 1910, when he wrote that the imperialist

is in truth always striving to attain two ideals, which are apt to be mutually destructive—the ideal of good government, which connotes the continuance of his own supremacy, and the ideal of self-government, which connotes the whole or partial abdication of his supreme position.[34]

The dilemma was not a dilemma at all but rather a very effective rationalization for the continuation of European domination. It avoided the appearance of a major inconsistency: democratizing states acting as imperialistic powers.

Twentieth-century imperialism might be succinctly defined as conservative rule directed toward distant liberal objectives. The two were compatibly aligned ideologically in the tropical environment that Europe controlled. The mediating element between the two was history, improvement through time, that meliorist doctrine that bore the name of progress. In political terms the doctrine received its most concise statement in the title of a book written by the Italian philosopher Benedetto Croce. *History as the Story of Liberty*, which appeared in 1941, upheld the thesis that the course of Western civilization was the movement toward greater personal freedom.

Transported to the colonial world, the concept of political progress became a vague ideal. The unidirectional course of history was, in European opinion, henceforth to be followed by Africans and Asians. Even though there was talk of the fusion of East and West into some grand future synthesis, and even though there was intensifying interest in the structure of other political and legal systems, Europeans still expected the colonial peoples to march forward to a European drummer.[35] In principle, therefore, the colonial world was also to be made safe for democracy, or at least for responsible government, but at some future date. This result would be ensured through the guidance provided by colonial rule. Sir Charles Lucas, a popular British author on the subject, extended historical generalization to its hyperbolic limits when he wrote of the British Empire that "it has infected the whole world with liberty and democracy."[36]

Few imperialists would have gone nearly so far. In their perception of things, Lucas was not describing a present condition at all. The way had yet to be paved to the future of self-government. "Western leadership must remain until the foundations [of the nation] have been constructed," asserted—in italics—a well-known Dutch author of colonial affairs, A. D. A. Kat de Angelino.[37] William Howard Taft, the first American civilian governor of the Philippines, and a judge of great eminence at the time of his appointment, had also made historical necessity out of political contingency:

it is absolutely necessary, in order that the people be taught self-government, that a firm, stable government under American guidance and control, in which the Filipino people shall have a voice, should be established. Nothing but such a government can educate the people into a knowledge of what self-government is.[38]

The inner logic of such arguments was unhistorical. The course of European and American political development had not been measured by outsiders determining when liberty and self-rule were appropriate. "Give me liberty or give me death" would have been rejected as an imperative with falsely limited alternatives, had it been stated in Swahili or Urdu between the world wars. In asserting the right to continued colonial rule, Europeans and now Americans were twisting their own history to new uses. Their defense was that the rigors of modern life—what Article 22 described as "the strenuous conditions of the modern world"—required the exercise of managerial skills and instruction in good government. Tutelage, "indispensable tutelage"—to use a phrase of Georges Hardy[39]—that was what modern empire was all about, its main justification, its principal activity.

Even a cursory reading of the major works that appeared and the governmental debates that occurred in the interwar period would quickly lead anyone to the conclusion that Europeans of nearly every political persuasion saw empire as a required activity that would continue until the day, still projected into a distant future, when the colonial possessions would change form through absorption, autonomy, or independence.

Among the political factions within the colonial nations, only the Communists demanded immediate withdrawal. Where there were party cells composed of Europeans in the colonies, such as in Algeria, the participating Communists responded as whites as frequently as reds, and therefore hesitated to support such withdrawal unreservedly. Politicians of every other

Blaise Diagne inaugurating French West Africa pavilion at the International
Colonial Exhibition in Paris, May 1931. From the National Archives.

political persuasion usually indicated in public debate that the time was not
ripe for the end of colonial rule, however desirable that end might be. Thus,
the French Socialist Léon Blum replied to the French Communists in 1927
that he was in agreement on the issue of independence but could neither advo-
cate insurrections by the colonial peoples nor support "immediate withdrawal
because of the perils this would entail both for the colonists and for the
natives themselves."[40] The colonial policy of the British Labour party was
of the same order. In 1918 a program was defined that began with expressed
opposition to "the Imperialism that seeks to dominate other races" but which
then accepted "the moral claims upon us by the non-adult races."[41]

What the non-Communist Left generally advocated was a policy of reform, not a sudden retreat from empire. They, too, accepted the idea of a
"sacred trust." Even though their rhetoric stressed the evils of social inequity
and economic exploitation, they were as concerned with the need for governmental stability and the fulfillment of necessary social conditions as were
their opponents wholeheartedly serving in the colonial administration. As late

as 1949, the Labour Party Advisory Committee on Imperial Questions could affirm that:

His Majesty's government in the United Kingdom would be well advised to lay the foundations of a sound economy in the colonies and nurture it to strength, lift the masses from poverty and raise their level of literacy before handing them over to new rulers.[42]

The remark did not lack sincerity, however archaic and even condescending it may have sounded. The good-intentioned were as perplexed by the developments in colonial rule and administration as they had been earlier. Certainly in such a vast and varied enterprise as European empire there was great difficulty in establishing consistent and long-range political plans or patterns. But nothing stood still. In some instances spectacular change did occur. The Irish Free State came into existence in 1921, thus dividing Britain's oldest colony. Egypt was granted nominal independence in 1922, with Great Britain still controlling foreign and financial affairs. India moved closer to dominion status and internal self-rule through reforms culminating in the India Act of 1933. The Philippines were made a commonwealth in 1934 and promised their independence in 1944. Whether these changes may be considered indicative of a retreat from empire is, at best, questionable.[43] Elsewhere the colonial situation seemed quite settled, promising continuing European control. Margery Perham, active in colonial affairs at the time and later a biographer of Lord Lugard, recalls hearing a senior Colonial Office official tell a delegation to a conference on West Africa: "Well, at any rate in Africa we can be sure that we have unlimited time in which to work."[44] The year was 1939.

The British may properly be credited with a more dedicated and sincere interest in the realization of future self-government for their colonies, but they did not hurry along in that direction either. In retrospect it is quite clear that few colonial officials were genuinely interested in substantially modifying their patterns of activities, except when forced to do so. Throughout most of Asia and Africa, empire remained, nearly to the end, based on a paternalistic attitude; colonial change was more rhetorical than factual. William Howard Taft spoke gently of "our little brown brothers" before World War I; Albert Sarraut spoke of "our little nephews" shortly after the war.[45] Such usage was not popular anymore, but even the newer terms suggested little more than a continuing condescending attitude that directed all policies gathered under the rubric of "tutelage." Léopold Sédar Senghor, poet and future president of the Republic of Senegal, saw the problem best from the colonized's point of view when he said after World War II that the African's need was "to assimilate and not to be assimilated." The cultural process had to be one of choice and selection, not one of imposition. Nevertheless, imposition was the general colonial mode of doing things in 1945 as it had been in 1885.

The persistence of old ways was revealed in the debates and decisions made about the one important change in colonial status that occurred immediately after World War I: the disposition of the German colonies and the detached territories of the former Ottoman empire. The mandates system was the solution to the problem.

The delegation by international authority to a particular nation of the responsibility for the governance of other peoples had no historical antecedents, even though theorists scurried through the past, as far back as Rome, to provide some precedent for this idea that was doubtfully received and that was actually proposed as an expedient. The language of the mandatory's charge was certainly lofty. The mandate over the Cameroons, established in 1923, made Great Britain "responsible for the peace, order, and good government of the territory, and for the promotion to the utmost of the material and moral well-being and social progress of its inhabitants."[46] Yet this variation on the theme of "sacred trust" did not persuade everyone of a changed colonial order. At the peace conference itself, Robert Lansing, then an American delegate, saw the mandates system as "a subterfuge which deceived no one." He found that "it worked in favor of the selfish and national interests of the Powers who accepted the mandates."[47] As if in agreement, the French colonial minister, Henry Simon, said to George Beers, chief American colonial delegate, "There is no real difference between a colony and a mandated area."[48]

The mandates, as many historians have pointed out, were the means by which to effect a satisfactory compromise between opposition to outright annexation and opposition to international control. Woodrow Wilson was the most ardent anti-annexationist; his position is summarized in his Fourteen Points in which he called for a peace without annexation. Lord Balfour, a member of the British delegation to the peace conference, was one of those individuals determined to restrict internationalization. He expressed himself unmistakedly at a League of Nations meeting in 1923, where he said: " . . . the Mandatory Power should be under the supervision—and not the control—of the League."[49]

The idea of international supervision and control of the colonial areas had been bruited about during the war in the British press and within American liberal circles. However, the principal designer of the mandates system was an empire man himself, Jan Smuts. He devised the system as an arrangement to be resorted to only if the possibility of direct annexations failed.[50] While Smuts and some of the British politicians openly endorsed the idea, only Woodrow Wilson was enthusiastic, indeed adamant, about it. The prime ministers of the British dominions which had conquered German territories were strongly opposed to it; the Japanese had already announced their intention to hold on to the territories they had seized; and the French colonial minister went so far as to make a forceful speech during negotiations in which he stated that annexation, direct and simple, was the only feasible solution. He did justify his position with the usual rhetorical flourish: "All the Great Powers worthy of the name considered their colonies as wards entrusted to them by the world."[51]

Wilson was unmoved and unbudgeable. His position was a strong compound of general opposition to imperialism and great enthusiasm for the League of Nations. "The League of Nations would be a laughing-stock if it were not invested with this quality of trusteeship," Wilson said.[52] During the debate on the mandates, the dominion prime ministers made common cause against Wilson. They offered a number of arguments, each tailored to their particular situation but all similar to those used by the expanding European powers some 50 years before. Wilson's chief adversary was Prime Minister William Hughes of Australia, who, in blustery prose, defended his ground. Wilson was soon irritated and directly asked the prime minister if he would "defy the appeal of the whole world" were Australia asked to approve the principle of a mandate over the islands adjacent to it and currently occupied by it. Hughes answered with no hesitation and little respect, "That's about the size of it, President Wilson."[53]

In the end the matter was compromised in a way that gave the dominions control of these territories in all but name. A special "C" class of mandates was created over which the mandatory power ruled as if it were sovereign, the justification officially being that these territories were "remote from civilization" and therefore needed such control. The fact was that the obduracy of the prime ministers had paid off. The outcome was well described by Lloyd George, who wrote: "Three out of the four [dominions] thereby established little empires of their own within the greater Empire of which they are an integral part."[54]

The rest of the confiscated territory was divided into "Class A" and "Class B" mandates. The "A" mandates were established over the former Turkish territories where France and Great Britain, as the mandatories, were confined in principle to offering administrative advice only, as these territories were seen as nearly ready for self-government. The "Class B" mandates were delegated to the same powers—with Belgium belatedly added after protest—over the German colonies in Africa. The United States had been invited, indeed encouraged, by the British to assume a mandate, preferably over Armenia. In this way it was hoped that the United States would be more closely allied to the British cause and, according to Lloyd George, American involvement "would remove any prejudice against us on the ground of 'land-grabbing.' "[55]

One world war later, one international institution later, and after the total collapse of colonial empires, the "C" Mandate that the Union of South Africa had received in 1919 was still retained when it became the Republic of South Africa in 1960. Nor was this the only example of such political absorption. By an order of council, dated June 21, 1923, the British made permanent the temporary arrangement whereby they had administered the Cameroons as a part of Nigeria.[56] In the following year Britain imposed the Nigerian legal system on the mandate. The actions made sense, even though they were inconsistent with mandatory responsibilities. The debate over the establishment of mandates had found the South Africans arguing that two territories, both contiguous and culturally similar, would be hard to administer differently by a single power. Out of such administrative convenience, as well as out of simple desire, the mandates became, as their critics had anticipated, colonies in all but name. The "A" mandates in the Near East fared little better than the others. Only Mesopotamia changed its status and became independent as the Kingdom of Iraq.

The reason for this tendency to treat mandates as colonies was the nature of the system of League supervision. A Permanent Mandates Commission had been established to watch over the behavior of the mandatory powers and to advise the League council on matters relating to the mandates. However, the commission was rather an academic institution. It sifted carefully through annual reports submitted from territories its members never visited. The League budget provided no money for such visitation, and members of the commission, colonial figures like Lord Lugard and Martial-Henri Merlin, former governor-general of French Equatorial Africa, were opposed to it. "Such a course would be a signal for local trouble," Lord Lugard declared.[57]

The disinterest of the commission in being more assertive was partly due to its membership, which included many former colonial officials. Lugard served for 13 years but was no doubt continuously comfortable in deliberations with French, Belgian, Japanese, Italian, and Portuguese colleagues, all representing nations with vital colonial interests, if not mandates.

The chief function of the commission was advisory. Indeed, its principal activity was to receive the annual reports required of each mandatory. Its institutional value was therefore educative: it forced the mandatories to consider and evaluate what they were doing; and it accumulated and published materials on indigenous affairs that might not otherwise have been available.[58]

The membership focused its attention more on the "B" mandates in black Africa than on the others, primarily because of their familiarity with the region. But it was also in black Africa that the issue of "native policy" seemed most pressing. There, the colonial challenge was perceived as being the most difficult and the most promising.

There also, colonial rule was the most recent and the most tenuous. Vast territories, sparsely populated, were flimsily controlled by ill-trained administrators who did not have adequate financial or military means at their disposal. This was the state of affairs at the beginning of the twentieth century. In romantic lore, the era was that of the "bush officer" who ruled by wit, not by the book, and whose communication with the people under his jurisdiction was through an interpreter—or with an unholstered pistol.

The disparity between available European resources and the scale of responsibility forced the conclusion that any form of direct administration would be both difficult and inadvisable. As a result, an ad hoc form of collaborative administration took place, in which the local colonial administrator acted as representative of the colonial power, but through the agency of the local chief. The French administrator Robert Delavignette explained the articulation of the system well, and in a way meaningful for more than the French West African situation, when he wrote: "There is no colonization without native policy; no native policy without a territorial command; and no territorial command without native chiefs who serve as links between the colonial authority and the population."[59]

Although no observer or critic has doubted that activities of the chiefs were integral to the colonial system throughout the continent, there has been a considerable academic debate about the uses to which the various European powers put these chiefs. The major question has centered on the difference

French military personnel at the Fort of Inslah in the Sahara, 1925.
From the National Archives.

between direct and indirect rule, between delegation of European authority to the African rulers and European mediation of traditional authority enjoyed by these rulers. While most scholarly interest has been directed to the distinction between the British and French modes of control in Subsaharan Africa, where procedures, if not ultimate effects, were distinctive, the issue is perhaps best placed in historical perspective by a general review of continental policy, but with special attention still given to the activities of the British and French.

The most famous explanation of the importance of the "Native Authority" to the colonial order was that of Lord Lugard, who encased in theory the most discussed and imitated method of domination: indirect rule. As did so many administrators in the colonial realm, he made a virtue of a widespread necessity, but few wrote so persuasively of that virtue.

Confronted with the large territory of Northern Nigeria to administer after the transfer of the Royal Niger Company's authority to the state and faced with a shortage of men and funds, Lugard realized that any suggestion of direct control was out of the question. But such a conclusion was also supported by his belief, formed during his prior service in Uganda, that the use of existing indigenous institutions was the best method of colonial administration. Therefore, in his service as high commissioner for Northern Nigeria between 1900 and 1907, Lugard developed his general practice and offered a detailed explanation of it in his many *Political Memoranda*.

The best résumé of his policy is found in a set of instructions he issued to his officers in 1906, in which he argued for "a single Government in which the Native Chiefs have clearly defined duties and an acknowledged status, equally with the British officials."[60] The basis of what was to become the system of indirect rule was therefore one of collaboration, not subordination, with the British resident acting primarily in an advisory, not an executive, capacity, and with the African "chief"—in this instance, the Fulani emir—continuing in a traditional role which was now loosely guided by the imposed colonial administration. In this attempt to integrate the emirs into the colonial system, Lugard wished to have them retain most of their old responsibilities, functions, and perquisites of office so that they would continue to appear as the legitimate rulers in the eyes of the local populations.

The essence of Lugard's rule was to use existing authorities in existing capacities, but something more was intended. Modifications along European lines were expected in matters such as justice and taxation. "The great task of indirect rule," wrote Lugard's biographer in an article defending his policy, "is to hold the ring, to preserve a fair field within which Africans can strike their own balance between conservatism and adaptation."[61] That task depended in large measure on the knowledge that residents had of local customs and institutions—and, of course, upon the willingness of the Native Authorities to make such adjustments toward modernization within the context of their own institutions.

Although Lugard's example and his written explanation of it gave indirect rule a special British cachet, the practice had been tried by other colonial administrations. The Dutch had a long history of dominating the East Indies through control of the area's precolonial bureaucracy. One observer of that system stated that "the old political order had not so much been totally destroyed as it had been decapitated."[62] The Dutch worked through an indigenous aristocratic class, the *priyayis*, who ably represented colonial interests, but in the process were divorced from the society they still served.[63]

Close by, in Indochina, the French were experimenting with a similar arrangement. Some French people highly praised the Dutch effort at indirect rule, while others lavished praise on the British in India. Among the latter was a conservative colonial theorist, Jules Harmand, who offered one of the best explanations of the new *politique d'association*, the French equivalent of indirect rule, in a long segment of his influential work *Domination et colonisation*, published in 1910. Association, he stated therein, is "indirect administration, with the preservation but improved governance of the institutions of the conquered peoples, and with respect for their past."[64] With the postwar publication of Sarraut's *La Mise en valeur des colonies francaises*, the policy was given the aura of official sanctity.

Originally suggested for Indochina and later extended as policy to Africa, "association" was nonetheless geographically limited as a colonial practice. Only in Morocco did the French seriously consider it, and there primarily because of the attention given to indigenous affairs by Resident-General Louis-Hubert Lyautey, who, in the initial years of the protectorate, ruled with few restrictions from the metropolitan government. Throughout Morocco the forms of the Cherifian state were preserved, while at the local level administrative activities were strikingly similar to those proposed by Lugard. The French *contrôleur civil* was to perform in an advisory, not a supervisory, capacity, with respect to the *cadi*, a Moslem official fulfilling magisterial functions in accordance with the *Shari'a*, the Islamic book of law. A comparable arrangement existed in the Spanish-dominated portion of Morocco where the *cadi* was guided in his role by the *Inventore*, the Spanish counterpart of the *contrôleur civil*. The *cadi* was also administratively retained as before in Italian Somalia, but there he was joined in the responsibilities of local government by assigned warrant chiefs.

In theory such indirect administration also applied to French colonial activities south of the Sahara, but in fact practice was at severe variance with it. In a 1917 statement frequently referred to as most descriptive of the methods of the French actually pursued in this region between the wars, the governor-general of French West Africa, Joost Van Vollenhoven, said: The chiefs "have no power of their own, for there are not two authorities in the *cercle* . . . there is only one! Only the *commandant du cercle* commands; only he is responsible. The native chief is but an instrument, an auxiliary."[65] Despite official pronouncements, therefore, the French used indigenous authorities not indirectly, but directly and subordinately in their colonial administration. And so did the Portuguese.

Lugard's form of indirect rule was initially successful in Northern Nigeria and was then extended after the war throughout much of British Africa, including the newly acquired German possessions of Tanganyika and the Cameroons. Moreover, it was even adapted to their uses by the Belgians in the Congo. Although conditions were nowhere else so optimal or the results so successful as in the Hausa-Fulani region of Nigeria, the British did try to follow local custom so that even newly devised institutions, like local councils, were consonant with indigenous forms of organization. The egregious exception, however, was South Africa where the concept of "Native Authority" was the means by which the white minority ensured local administration of Africans now displaced by the policy of segregation to territorial reserves.

Throughout Subsaharan Africa of the interwar period the chief became an administrative agent, not a "Native Authority." This shift in position, even in regions submitted to indirect rule, is easily explained. Most obviously, traditional functions were distended by new demands, such as the collection of taxes, the taking of censuses, or the recruitment of labor and military conscripts. Where there appeared to European eyes no satisfactory individuals in positions of traditional authority, other personnel, such as veterans, non-commissioned officers or clerks, were installed as chiefs. Then, chiefs were sometimes endowed with political significance that had not previously inhered in their office, or on other occasions they were installed in chiefless societies where they previously had no administrative purpose. Examples of these two developments are found among the Ibo of Nigeria, the Kikuyu of Kenya, and the Langi of northern Uganda.[66]

With the rationalization of European administration, chiefs were manipulated as if they were administrative personnel who might be reposted or removed to satisfy colonial needs. Chieftancies were abolished where considered superfluous, created where considered colonially useful. Perhaps the most striking example of this process occurred in the Belgian Congo where, after 1918, the reforms proposed by the colonial minister, Louis Franck, led to a drastic revision in the colonial order of things. The number of chieftances was reduced from 6,095 in 1917 to 1,212 in 1938. Furthermore, an entirely new administrative unit, called the *section*, was introduced for purposes of consolidation. Along similar lines, the French in West Africa also created a new unit, a grouping of villages into a *canton*, which, in the words of one governor, "is placed under the authority of an *indigenous administrative agent* who assumes the name of canton chief."[67] In Libya the populations were subjected to new administrative organization by a royal decree of

August 31, 1929, which notably allowed for the division of the nomadic peoples of the colony into tribes and subtribes at the discretion of the governor and upon the advice of the regional commissioner. And even the British made such alterations in the eastern district of Nigeria when indirect rule was introduced there shortly after 1900. Faced with an elaborate number of local rulers, whose range of authority they were then unable to discern, the British introduced the principle of the warrant chief whose authority extended over districts of many thousands of people but derived directly from the warrant issued by the colonial government.

Operating as a disruptive agent in connection with these factors was the local administrator. Whatever his intentions, he invariably became a surrogate chief. As Delavignette described the situation with satisfaction, the colonial administrator was not an administrator at all, but a commander, and recognized as such by the African population under his control. His primary function, asserted Delavignette unequivocally, "is to act as a chief."[68] Later, a British anthropologist would say of the district officer that he was "a new kind of territorial chief."[69] The reserved and unobtrusive role that the colonial administrator was supposed to enjoy in the system of indirect rule was never enacted in French and Portuguese territories, where the European was prominent in the exercise of local authority. Although the Italian administrators in Somalia came closest to the British in their relationship to the local chiefs, even among these groups Lugard's principles were modified because of the exigencies of the local situation and the individuals involved in it. Truly, the master of indirect rule was an exceptional person and, however appealing the policy may have been to individuals raised in the public school and university tradition of Great Britain, it was hard to maintain.

The perplexing difficulty of how to reconcile stable government, which meant the retention of local customs and laws, with growing economic needs, which meant change, was one that lasted throughout the colonial era.

The "native question" was never solved, because "native policy" required the paramountcy of indigenous interests, and such an arrangement would have changed the purpose and the power relationships in empires. Nowhere was this better understood and more strongly denied than in South Africa.

"Native policy" there meant domination and manipulation. Even before it was officially construed in the policy of *apartheid*, racial segregation as a means of African subjugation had been widely practiced. Africans had been restricted in land use and in forms of employment early in the twentieth century. In the interwar period, the South African government moved to further restriction and thereby denied the realization of liberal principles the British had hoped would occur. The Nationalist party campaigned in the election of 1924 for social and conomic segregation and for the removal of Africans from the common roll of Cape Colony, an electoral privilege that had been enjoyed since the imposition of British rule. If the Nationalists under J. B. M. Herzog were more racist than the South African party headed by Jan Smuts, there seemed to be little general disagreement between the two about urban policy. The cities were, quite severely, to remain a white preserve. The infamous pass laws assured the condition. The Native Urban Act of 1923, passed while Smuts was still prime minister, controlled black African movement to the cities by requiring passes of all who would enter and leave. An amendment of 1937 further tightened the system, making the African tolerated, not welcomed, as part of the urban life. The Transvaal Local Government Commission put the matter in severe terms when it declared in 1922 that the African in the city "should depart therefrom when he ceases to minister to the needs of the white man."[70]

Certainly South Africa was not the norm for social relations between colonizer and colonized, but the practices in that land did brutally and starkly emphasize a fundamental, some would say, the fundamental problem, of all modern colonial empire. The conversion of an economic system to alien purposes was culturally and socially disruptive. European observation of Asian and African economic behavior led to the conclusion that the people were "backward," not yet prepared or capable to assume those major responsibilities that a modern economy required. In 1934, Pierre Ryckmans, then governor of the Belgian Congo, remarked that "what we must overcome in order to lead the Black to work is not so much his laziness as it is his distaste for *our* work, his indifference to *our* wage system."[71] Lugard had even been bleaker in his assessment. He wrote that the African "lacks the power of organization and is conspicuously deficient in the management and control alike of men or of business."[72] Even though such statements had been intelligently refuted in the remarkable study of Ida G. Greaves, *Modern Production Among Backward People*, published in 1935, the general assessment was of the need for rigorous European supervision of the economic development of the colonial territories.[73]

Such supervision in the past had depended much more on force than on incentive. Those basic conditions, subsumed under the term "infrastructure,'' had to be realized before a modern economy could function. Expenditure of labor in the colonial world preceded accumulation of capital. This was the logic used. Various forms of impressment were therefore tried initially. The French used the *corvée* or labor tax in their colonies, with able-bodied males required to serve a certain number of days in ''public works'' projects. It was not until after the Blum Socialist government came to power in France that legislation was passed—in 1937—that allowed the *corvée* to be transmuted into a money tax and that both reduced and standardized days of service required.

The French were not alone. Variations of forced labor existed in every colonial region from the Dutch East Indies to the Belgian Congo. The Dutch system of *heerendienstein* was not dissimilar to the French *corvée* and was also applied to public works. It had virtually disappeared in the interwar years, as had the worst effects of portage in the Belgian Congo. Yet the *prestation*, or labor tax, in the French African territories continued until 1946; and the *Luwalo*, a precolonial work tax of one month's labor, was continued by the British in Uganda until 1938.

Increasingly conscious of the deleterious effects of forced labor practices, and acting in light of changing attitudes in Europe toward the work force, the colonial powers began to regulate labor conditions. The earlier concern with the provision of labor was slowly replaced by a concern with the protection of labor.[74] From 1935 to 1936, for instance, the International Labor Organization, now monitoring such behavior, reported enactments that limited night work by women and children, established minimum wages, provided workmen's compensation, and limited work hours in a number of African territories under French, British, and Belgian control.[75] Even trade unionism made a hesitant appearance in a number of colonies.

The appearance of left-of-center governments in the two major colonial powers, Great Britain and France, aided this development. A Colonial Office Labor Committee was established by the second Labour government in 1930. The secretary of state for colonies, Lord Passfield (Sidney Webb), requested that all colonial governors initiate legislation to assure the legal rights of trade unions. In France, the Blum government sent a commission to the colonies to investigate and consolidate labor practices. Under the aegis of the able colonial minister, Marius Moutet, work hours were reduced, factory inspection legislation passed, and paid vacations for indigenous labor provided.

The results were mixed at best, as Robert Delavignette has noted. Moutet ''had to mobilize the European settlers and administrators as well as the masses, whose uniqueness and social structures were not understood by the mother country.''[76] In other words, the practice did not match his intentions. Moreover, informal impressment continued throughout the colonial empires, as local chiefs often forcibly gathered together a work supply that had been requested so that they might pay taxes or even obtain a personal profit. In this manner the requirements of the new colonial economy occasionally exacerbated previously established indigenous codes of behavior. The French extension of the Indochinese equivalent of the *corvée* is a well-remarked example.[77]

The gap between the colonial office at home and the colonial administration in the field was nowhere greater than in labor policy and practice. As the Royal Institute of International Relations study group wrote about the colonial problem in 1937, ''the danger lies in the possession of practically despotic powers [by the colonial administration] which may perhaps unconsciously be employed to promote the advantage of the employers.''[78]

In acknowledging the unrestrained nature of colonial authority on the local level, the study group unintentionally gave evidence in behalf of those critics who argued that imperialism had changed only its appearance, not its form, during the interwar period. The administrator in the field could do almost as he wished. That personal authority was defined with rhetorical flourish by Lloyd George in his often quoted ''steel frame'' speech of 1922 that described the Indian Civil Service as the steel frame of the British Raj. ''Their every word is a command, every sentence a decree,'' he said of the administrators.

The excess of Lloyd George's prose did not, however, exaggerate actual conditions. Memoirs and reminiscences of individuals who were in service at the time clearly describe the unusual relationship between freedom and authority then enjoyed by colonial officers. A French colonial governor, for instance, offered this retrospective comment in 1965: ''In my thirty years in the colonial administration, I never received an instruction from the ministry of colonies. We were the real rulers of the empire; no one told us what to do.''[79] What another officer in southern Burma described as ''this somewhat heady draught of independence and responsibility''[80] derived from three conditions: geographic isolation from European centers of power; political insulation from any local indigenous control; and the psychological compulsion to retain power. (''It is not easy to give up power,'' commented one member of the Indian Civil Service at the end of the colonial era.)[81]

Often in charge of a district that was the size of an English county, and frequently without the support of an administrative staff, the colonial officer found his "faculties were kept at full stretch."[82] The responsibility for colonial rule was the responsibility of a small number of individuals—about 1,200 in the interwar Indian Civil Service to serve a population of 300,000,000, for instance. That they succeeded in their responsibilities, that they "held the ring," was in part a testament to their ability but also an indication of the non-technical functions they were required to perform. If analogies are useful, the average colonial administrator might be compared to the eighteenth-century squire or constable, the figure who mediated conflict and maintained the public peace.[83] "Those days," wrote an Indian member of the Indian Civil Service about the 1930s, "governmental activity was limited; administration did not touch the life of the ordinary citizen at many points."[84]

However limited the number of assigned responsibilities might be, the colonial official was a vital center, his idiosyncrasies marking the administration of his district, and his isolation and independence often generating a spirit of paternalism about "his people." Service was unidirectional: it was given to the local population, not required or defined by them.

The rhetoric surrounding "sacred trust" did not change the nature of imperial rule in any dramatic way. Such rule continued to be dependent on cooperation of certain indigenous elements—chiefs, notables, headmen—and the acquiescence of the rest of the population. Indirect rule, whatever its regional form, tended to be conservative and supported the status quo. In Indonesia, for instance, the *priyayis* retained their social position and did not change their cultural outlook, as they were neither disturbed nor disrupted by the colonial presence.[85] In Tanganyika, a decision made in 1926 to establish a Native Authority, an obvious aspect of indirect rule, included the provision that the traditional rulers be retained.[86] Even where rulers were removed or reassigned, the colonial intention was not to radicalize government. The hesitant steps taken in India as an advance toward local self-government frequently confused or bothered the district officer. "It is hard to serve where you have ruled," commented one of them about this shift in function.[87]

The reconstitution of the social and political order from within, in preparation for self-government, was inhibited, even where it was seriously entertained, by the support the colonial system gave to the existing order of things—and vice versa, of course. Margery Perham, reflecting on the conditions in that region of the colonial world considered least ready for self-rule, indicated that she thought "the African parts must be helped to grow slowly and naturally, outwards from within, into the larger whole."[88] Nothing of the sort occurred. The colonial whole, those units given names like Nigeria and Ivory Coast, were forced together from without by Europeans seeking administrative convenience and economic advantage. A general problem confronting most post-colonial nations was the conversion of such units into nations, which was the business of creating a social order out of a bureaucratic structure.[89]

There was a certain sameness about rural colonial administration, whatever the year, wherever the place. Removed from the main concourse of world affairs, generally out of earshot of the complaints registered against imperialism, the local administrator and the people he was officially assigned to supervise, continued their limited relationship in an outwardly unchanging way. As late as 1951, a young British colonial officer, newly arrived in Nigeria, had these thoughts:

The simplicity, peace, and sense of continuity of prosperous Hausa village life was something to admire. It seemed so unnecessary to disrupt it for the sake of progress, yet the Hausa peasant could not avoid contact with the century in which he lived and whose aircraft droned overhead. Introducing change without destroying stability, bringing new values but retaining the old, was to be the essence of my job.[90]

It was also the essence of the jobs held by most of the colonial administrators who had preceded him by a generation or two. As they, too, questioned the necessity of disrupting the old order for the sake of progress, modernity intruded. Commercial aircraft flew regularly over Nigeria, beginning on February 13, 1936.

CHAPTER 3

Imperial Designs:
Technology and Economic Development

Benito Mussolini, dictator of Italy, paid a visit to the movie set of "Scipio Africanus" in January 1937, where he watched Libyans playing the role of Hannibal's soldiers.[1] It was an obvious example of political propaganda and a historical evocation that twentieth-century technology made both possible and monumental. There were no Hollywood musicals about empire, but the drama of large-scaled expansion, the heroic role it invited sturdy men to play—these were part of the film director's imagination and the appeal to avid moviegoers, of whom Mussolini was one.

If empire had a heroic phase, which is doubtful, it was gone by the twentieth century. The "Lives of a Bengal Lancer" and "Beau Geste" were now filmed, not lived. But the technology that produced the cinema also produced the new networks that gave the illusion of imperial unity.

The development of air transport will shrink our world Empire to the size of a single continent. . . . The immense reduction of Empire distances . . . will make it possible for the Empire to become a single economic and political entity.[2]

As this statement suggests, the new British "red line of empire" was to be drawn through the clouds as it had earlier been extended across the surface of the water, but now with less effective results. To speak of the airplane as the means to "buckle" or to provide "links" in the "imperial chain," as indeed some of the English did, was to confuse metaphor with reality.[3]

Yet the airplane revealed a new truth because it assured a new perspective.

76

The land trod by explorers, turned over by plantation owners, and dug by miners, was still unknown in parts. The South African author Laurens Van der Post describes, in *Venture to the Interior*, his 1949 mission to Nyasaland to further reconnoiter two regions about which the British were still poorly informed. Earlier ground observations were now seen as inaccurate: "The knowledge that was being gained from flying over them by aeroplane suggested more and more that the maps were misleading, if not spurious, and in any case woefully inadequate."[4]

The contrast implied in Van der Post's statement was perhaps the most telling of all the contrasts that highlighted modern empire. Twentieth-century technology was expected to serve nineteenth-century empire, which, in turn, remained an alien force among cultures that were generally small and rural.

The literature of the interwar period is rich in explanations of the effects of this contrast. African and Asian, as well as European, authors expressed their personal opinions, in addition to constructing theories upon which to strengthen their observations. The most popular and influential concept was defined by the British anthropologist Bronislaw Malinowski. His analysis of contemporary Africa led him to conclude that there was "only one correct conception of culture change in such areas: the fact that it is the result of an impact of a higher, active culture upon a simple, more passive one."[5] The Danish novelist Isak Dinesen, then living in Kenya, cast the problem in a more poetic mode:

We can make motor-cars and aeroplanes, and teach the Natives to use them. But the true love of motor-cars cannot be made, in human hearts, in the turn of a hand. It takes centuries to produce it, and it is likely that Socrates, the Crusades, and the French Revolution, have been needed in the making.[6]

Such perceived contrasts between the old and the new, between the traditional and the modern, were grossly exaggerated, even when beautifully phrased. What colonial administrators and, occasionally, cultural anthropologists fixed in separate categories, more recent critics have graded in terms of evolutionist or structural distinctions. The contrast should not have been made between an undifferentiated local past and a rapidly changing European present. Modern research has, for instance, led to the conclusion that a form of merchant capitalism, not dissimilar to the European, appeared in sixteenth-century India and grew thereafter,[7] and that some of the elements contributing to the rise of industrialism in Western Europe had their counterparts in pre-partitioned West Africa.[8] Conversely, many of the rural regions of Europe in the late nineteenth century were more aligned in method of production with Southeast Asia than with the industrial complexes found a short distance away.

All is change and continuity, as philosophers have said for ages, and so it was in the countryside of Africa and Asia as it was in Provence or Sussex. Yet the contrasts made between a modern technological grid and the quiltlike pattern of local African or Asian life on which it was imposed became major arguments in the ideology of modern imperialism and provided some of the reasons for subsequent resentment and protest. To supporter and opponent of imperialism alike, the Europeans seemed to have brought their colonies to the periphery of the capitalist-industrial order, but no further.

This influx of technology was not announced by the engines of the trimotor airplane Cirene, which took off on its initial flight of the Tripoli-Benghazi route in December 1931, or by the first crackle of the short-wave receiver that indicated the inauguration of the British Broadcasting Service's Empire Service in December 1932. Western forms of technology and punctuality had long since been taken overseas. Printing presses, telegraph lines, and tinned foods marked the procession of European industrialism around the globe.

The twentieth century witnessed the acceleration of this procession, a change of tempo that sharpened cultural contrasts and stimulated further commentary on them. But, in plain terms, it still was the old game, only now played with new equipment. There was little different about what had been said before in a statement like this: "nothing in the story of Africa, from the time of Van Riebeck to Rhodes and Stanley is more deeply moving than the efforts to complete her conquest from the air."[9] Nor had much changed in the nature of the complaint registered over the narrow width of the new Carter bridge, opened in Lagos, Nigeria, in 1930. The planner, it seems, "did not make any allowance for the difference between the black man driving a car and the white man, which is very considerable."[10]

The appearance in Asia and Africa of Europe's industrial products, which allowed such expressions of cultural condescension to become commonplace, had occurred decades before the first trucks bounced along the laterite roads of the Sudan in 1899. The primary vehicle of colonial expansion was the steam engine. The impact made by this, the most significant technological improvement of the nineteenth century, can be measured historically by a comparison of two statements made about British India, one at the opening of the steam era, the other at its close. In 1846, Sir William P. Andrew looked to the future of the subcontinent and intoned: "A magnificent system of railway communications would present a series of public monuments, vastly superior, surpassing in grandeur the aqueducts of Rome.''[11] In 1959, John Strachey, a severe critic of imperialism, looked to the past of the subcontinent and solemnly wrote: "The trunk railways, with their huge steel or masonry bridges, over the great rivers, will surely remain the memorial of our empire in India, as do the Roman roads in Europe to the Romans''[12]

Within the period separated by these two dates, the railroad had appeared on the surface of every major colonial territory. Most of the African construction, however, occurred in the early twentieth century, with the major lines completed after the world war. Wherever the railroad was undertaken, its building was not accompanied by any spirit of romance. Poor labor conditions, bad management, insufficient surveying of the land for the roadbed, and major physical obstacles combined to make the process generally costly and difficult. These conditions were particularly noticeable in Africa, where, often, the lack of suitable ballast for the roadbed required importation of the material or hauling it for long distances from other regions. In the Gold Coast, to cite one major instance, the initial use of local wood for the railroad ties had to be discontinued because of destruction by ants; steel ties were then imported from England.[13] Faced with such obstacles, the Europeans found the completion of the railroad a slow business. The Yunnan Railroad in Indochina, a line only 863 kilometers long, was started in 1901 and not completed until 1910. In striking contrast was the construction of the Bechuanaland line, begun in 1893 and finished only 17 months later, a real and unusual triumph, given the fact that the rails extended 106 miles.

The railroad was perceived as the means of joining the hinterland to the coast, moving heavy raw materials, such as minerals and wood timber, more easily than any other form of transportation, and enhancing military security. The railroad was made a colonial device, and as such it occupied much of the colonial budget and administration because it was a major factor in local economies.

As late as the 1920s, when the gasoline engine had effectively challenged the steam engine, the Belgian colonial minister Louis Franck undertook a major development program in the Congo in which approximately 75 percent of the funds went to railroad and port construction. In the same period the Executive Council of the Indian Railway Board planned to lay 1,000 miles of new track every year, beginning in 1924. In 1928–29, that anticipated figure was exceeded by the 1,282 actual miles constructed. However, this latter mileage was exceptional; a total of only 5,360 miles was built between

Opening of the Benguela railroad at Luao on the Anglo-Belgian Congo frontier, 1929. From the National Archives.

1925 and 1932.[14] Yet the figures remain impressive and stand as proof of the importance assigned the railroad.

The range of transportation provided by the railroad, exceeded by no other form of land transportation at the time, was what stimulated the imagination and inspired the dreams of continental-visionary imperialists. The turn of the century was the era of the "trans" railroads, the lines that were to bind continents and fix new definitions of empire. The most famous of these was far removed from any European tropical estate; it was the Transsiberian, which was completed in 1903. But there was also the Transaustralian, 5,160 kilometers long, completed in 1913; the Transsudan, uniting Port Said and Khartoum, completed in 1924; the Transethiopian, begun in 1896 and completed in 1918; and, the most remarkably delayed and expensive of all, the Transindochinese, which eventually extended 1,735 kilometers along the coast, and took from 1898 to 1936 to complete.

There was also a line of romantic imagination, a Jules Verne inspiration. It was the Transsaharan, never put down on land but constructed many times over on paper. Between the 1870s and the 1930s, French technicians played with this idea of uniting North and West Africa, of creating an imperial geometry that would allow a straight line of rail to run southward. By the postwar era, they envisioned the line as electrified, with trains swiftly moving the French across the desert wastes. As late as 1931 the project was revived again, now with an added function: the line would serve as an emergency landing area for disabled aircraft.[15]

The Transsaharan was not built, but the assertion of its potential significance to aircraft was far from ridiculous. In 1923, the French airline, Latécoère, relayed its aircraft between Toulouse and Dakar in six stops and five days in winter and in three stops and three days in summer. Early pilots carrying the mail were given some assurance of personal well-being by a backup plane, which flew within sight of the principal aircraft and was prepared to assist in an emergency. An Arabic-speaking interpreter was often brought along to assist in social emergencies as well.[16]

British aerial problems were similar in those early days. Flights over the Arabian peninsula were guided by car tracks and, in some instances, by specially plowed markings. Circles were inscribed on the ground at 20-mile intervals to serve as emergency landing fields, for airplanes were often troubled by malfunctioning carburetors or leaking fuel lines.[17]

The 1920s and 1930s constituted the era of heroic flight. The spirit of adventure was taken aloft principally by biplanes and trimotors, but only after the anticipated victory of the huge airships turned into fiery defeat. Empire builders initially assumed that variations of the zeppelin would be the long-distance craft of the near future. Even before the war, Rudyard Kipling, in one of his two pieces of science fiction, ''With the Night Mail,'' imagined hydrogen-filled airships soaring gracefully over the oceanic expanse between London and Montreal. After the war the French tried to realize some measure of that fiction by experimenting with long-distance travel in the *Dixmude*, a confiscated and renamed German wartime zeppelin, now in use as a naval vessel. On December 21, 1923, on a return flight from southern Algeria, the airship fell into the Mediterranean, the fate of its crew a watery mystery.

British dreams were similarly dashed when the huge R-101 was destroyed on its inaugural flight from London to Karachi, with a planned intermediary stop at Cairo. The airship was charged with an atmosphere of urgency as it departed on the evening of October 4, 1930, because Lord Thomson, the air minister, wished to fly to India, pick up representatives, and return in time to attend the Imperial Conference in London. Thompson thought the success

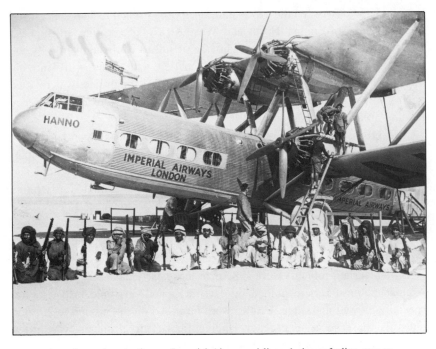

Armed guard protecting an Imperial Airways airliner during refueling stop at
Fort Sharjah, 1934. From the National Archives.

of the venture would confirm the role that airships would play in imperial
communications. In the early morning of October 5, the airship crashed.
Underpowered because of a hasty extension of its size, weighted down by bad
weather, and lost because of poor navigation, the R-101 lumbered along, nar-
rowly missed the spire of Beauvais Cathedral in France, and hit the ground
shortly thereafter leaving 38 of the 44 aboard dead.[18]

Meanwhile, airplanes flew on, gaining more altitude, traversing greater
distances, increasing in size and comfort. In the 1920s the planes were essentially the means of fast mail service, and the *pilotes de ligne* were a hearty
group, begoggled in open cockpits, flying long hours behind loud motors,
never quite sure if their aircraft would land where destined. The poet among
them was the Frenchman Antoine de Saint-Exupéry, who has left behind a
few works that are now considered minor classics and have earned their
author a place in world literature as well as one in the annals of aviation. In
Wind, Sand and Stars, Saint-Exupéry describes the quality of wonderful

R-101 on test flight over London, October, 1929, before an extension
increased its size. From the National Archives.

aloneness that every early pilot must have known. Flying low over Tripolitania as the sun was setting, he took off his sunglasses to better view the scene
that opened before him.

The sands were golden under the slanting rays of the sun. How empty of life is this planet of ours . . . What an amount of the earth's surface is given over to rock and sand!

But all of this was not my affair. My world was the world of flight. Already I could feel the oncoming night within which I should be enclosed as in the precincts of a temple—enclosed in the temple of night for the accomplishment of secret rites and the absorption of inviolable contemplation.[19]

Few wrote—or flew—as did Saint-Exupéry. Many turned out books, however. A new element in that well-read literary genre, travel tales, took off with the airplane. The flights over colonies and across the wide expanses of empire were duly recorded, often in painful detail. R. J. Minney wrote *Across India by Air* in 1921. R. J. Paru and J. C. MacIntosh wrote *The Record Flight from London to Calcutta* in 1921. B. Bennett wrote *Down Africa's Skyways* in 1932. J. and J. Tharaud wrote *Paris-Saigon dans l'Azur* in the same year. A. Viruly wrote *We Vlogen Naar India* in 1934. M. E. Johnston wrote *Over African Jungles: 60,000 Miles by Aeroplane* in 1935. And there were many others.

For more general travelers on empire business, who numbered in the hundreds daily in the 1930s, the airplane inspired no literary effort but proved to be an arduous means of voyage. By contemporary jet aircraft standards, it was a form of primitive travel. Sand-swept airfields; improvised lunches in corrugated-iron hangers; train rides from Paris to Toulouse to catch the flight to Dakar, or from Paris to Milan and then on to Brindisi to catch the flying boat to Cairo; defective engines necessitating emergency landings— these were the common characteristics of such flights.

Yet it all worked well at times, or, better, it improved with time. The initial KLM flight between Amsterdam and Jakarta was made in 1924, and it took some 55 days to cover the 9,600-mile distance. Beginning in 1929, KLM offered fortnightly service to Jakarta with only 12 days required. In 1936 the first passenger service was inaugurated between Toulouse and Dakar. The French publication *Illustration* boasted of the relative ease of such modern travel, and used as its proof the presence-as-passenger of the 82-year-old former governor-general of French West Africa, Ernest Roume.[20] The homeward trip on which this notable embarked took 20 hours, with intermediate stops.

Such slow progress aloft seemed to be the hallmark of British Imperial Airways. Although its flying boats, manufactured by Short Brothers beginning in 1928, rose lugubriously out of the water, their passengers were treated to a particular elegance once the craft were airborne. The cuisine was elaborate, the seats were very comfortable, the neatly uniformed personnel were most courteous. In sum, the service was shipshape, in keeping with the nineteenth-century maritime tradition.[21] Van der Post, winging his way to Africa in 1949 aboard a fast and noisy American aircraft, grew nostalgic for the "Imperial" way of doing things. "I longed for the slower, more comfortable, British flying boats, with their obstinate, old-fashioned respect for privacy and individual needs."[22]

The world the Short flying boats soared over was being transformed more markedly by another form of transportation, the motor vehicle. The great French automobile manufacturer André Citröen stated in 1923, just as one of his several motor expeditions was getting under way, "I have already wondered why motor cars could not be used as explorers. In fact they are the best explorers one can dream of in the world."[23] Automobiles gained in significance in the interwar period. Not as explorers, but as economic factors. The motorized expeditions that Citröen and others sponsored had their own romance, granted, and they provided good reading to subscribers of the *National Geographic Magazine*, but they were only the more spectacular or exotic aspects of motor trends.[24] More significant, if less noticed, was the fact that 55 motor vehicles were operating in the French Sudan in 1901, at a time when France led the world in motor vehicles, with 5,608 on the streets and roads. At the same time, there were 392 in Belgium, 304 in Great Britain, and 268 in Germany. It was through the enterprise and ambition of one Felix Dubois, who foresaw the potential of such transportation in the economy of colonial Africa, that the trucks, vans, and cars were imported to the Sudan.[25]

Other Frenchmen also anticipated an important role for the motor car in a tropical setting. General Joseph Gallieni—later famous for mobilizing the taxis of Paris during the First Battle of the Marne in 1914—had arranged to have three 12-horsepower Panhard-Lavassor cars shipped ahead of him to Madagascar when he returned from France to his governorship of that island in 1900. With these vehicles and an improved road he had earlier had constructed, Gallieni was able to travel the 80 kilometers between Mahatsara and Beneforona in three hours, whereas the trip had previously required three days by primitive conveyance.[26] Across the globe, in Indochina, a similar transportation improvement had been achieved. There, the world's first motorized postal and bus service had been established. By 1904, when the Americans and the French were introducing comparable services, the Cochinchinese (Vietnam) automobile industry was assuring a regular run over a distance of 450 kilometers.[27]

As might be imagined, the French were not alone in motorizing colonies at an early date. Motor transport began in the Belgian Congo in 1906. In the following year the Dutch government in the East Indies introduced a similar service, while the Niger railway company began a motor service to connect surrounding areas to its railroad. All of these efforts were tenuous, only secured and extended after the world war, when the motor age appeared almost everywhere in the non-Western world, but nowhere with more noticeable results than in the Near East. Of this particular development a German journalist concluded in 1930:

Today the automobile is the most common form of transportation throughout the Orient. The camel has been quite outmoded and is waging the same vain struggle against the motor car that the horse of Europe has already fought and lost.[28]

The hyperbole was not excessive, certainly not when measured against the intrepid entrepreneurship of the Nairn brothers. These two New Zealanders, who had served under General Allenby during the war, had stayed on in the Near East to begin what was a most successful and lauded motor service. The historian Arnold Toynbee, crossing the Arabian desert as part of an adventuresome trip to a conference in Japan, succinctly described what the Nairns had achieved. "As the Nairns saw it," he wrote, "the obvious thing to do was to push out into the desert in a car and go on pushing until they reached Bagdad; and, sure enough, by 1923, Bagdad had been found and the transdesert route established."[29] Four years after Toynbee had made his trip, in 1934, the Nairns purchased an impressively outfitted American diesel cab and passenger coach—69 feet long—that allowed the 470-mile trip between Damascus and Baghdad to be made in 24 hours, the comfort of the 35 passengers assured by an onboard refrigerator and stove, both maintained by a steward.[30]

Although the Nairn Transportation Company offered bus service quite unrivaled in any part of the world, the company's contribution to the colonial transportation revolution was not unusual. The automobile was widely and quickly accepted during the interwar era, as statistics verify. In 1928 there were 10,000 cars in Morocco; in 1930, there were more than 100,000 gasoline-propelled vehicles, motorcycles included, in the Dutch East Indies. In 1929 alone India imported 19,569 automobiles. Even the Tonga Islands in the Pacific had 125 automobiles by that time.

Serviceable roads also increased in number and length, although the all-weather highway was exceptional. Surfacing roads with material such as asphalt or even crushed stone was very expensive, and, moreover, costs were intensified by the need to ship in equipment and, often, basic materials. Most colonial roads were therefore of dirt surfaces, rather easily constructed by local labor. Nonetheless, interwar road building amassed impressive results. In India, approximately 22,000 miles of metal-surfaced roads were constructed between 1920 and 1929. In Indochina, thanks to Governor Albert Sarraut's "prophetic vision of the importance of motor travel,"[31] an extensive program began in 1913 and resulted, by 1931, in 25,000 kilometers of roads, half of these stone-paved. The most impressive statistics were compiled by the Dutch in the East Indies and the Belgians in the Congo. By 1930 there were 60,000 kilometers of roads, half of them with asphalt surfaces, in the East Indies. The Congo network, which began with 2,550 kilometers in 1920, reached 74,000 by 1939. For sheer innovation in technique, however, engineers in Malaya deserve the credit: they experimented with the use of surplus rubber as a surfacing material on a few lengths of road in the 1930s. An American, driving over one of these stretches, wrote that "the surface is soft like tar but more resilient."[32]

Yet, of all the road-building efforts, none was more spectacular—or opened with greater ceremony—than the Litoranea Libica, constructed during the governorship of Libya by the colorful and energetic Italo Balbo. The road that Balbo pushed along—with the labor of 11,400 workers, of whom 800 were Italian—extended 1,822 kilometers from the Egyptian to the Tunisian border, thus uniting Tripolitania and Cyrenica by a modern communications system. The road was opened in May 1937 by a motorcade of 120 automobiles, one containing Mussolini and Balbo. A monumental arch straddled the road in the desert where Tripolitania and Cyrenica met, an arch described by a French commentator as "proud and boastful at having taken possession of the empty space."[33] Equally monumental was the lavish seven-course meal, complete with three wines, that had been flown in from Rome to greet the motorcade—and its 120 correspondents—as it stopped at Arae Philenorum in the desert.[34]

Not only for the flamboyant Balbo but also for less notable colonial administrators, the construction of a road was the opportunity to make a mark, to impress their moment on colonial history. Rudbeck, the young administrative hero of Joyce Carey's novel *Mister Johnson*, learned this fact from an old hand, who commented, "When you make a road you know you've done something—you can see it."[35]

Benito Mussolini and Italo Balbo in the motorcade inaugurating the Litoranea
Libica, 1937. From the National Archives.

The importance of a modern road network had not been visible to most
colonial administrators until late in the interwar period. The railroad was generally regarded as the best line of economic development, and for easily appreciated reasons. Modern imperialistic expansion, notably the late nineteenth-century "scramble for Africa," occurred when European railroad
building had already been achieved and the economic importance of the railroad established. In the colonial vision, therefore, the railroad was the best
and quickest means of economic penetration. It was well-suited to the regular
movement of bulk goods, the primary materials that the imperialists wished
to extract from the hinterland. In 1925 an English student of African economics referring to Nigeria, wrote: "The export trade in tin and coal and cotton
and ground-nuts is the creation of the railways."[36] Assuming, as most important administrators did, that the railroads were the main arteries, planners
considered the road a "feeder" into that system by connecting it with out-
lying communities. Lord Lugard offered the following dictum:
"Roads . . . being ancillary to the railways should be constructed as
feeders and not parallel to them, so as to compete for freight."[37]

The triumphal arch on the Litoranea Libica, 1937.
From the National Archives.

Yet the competition for freight explains, in part, the growth of motor transport. After the war the light truck replaced the heavier vehicles which required well-bedded roads. The Ford truck, introduced at this time, became the new colonial beast-of-burden, capable of moving over lightly surfaced roads without destroying them.[38] With such a vehicle, small quantities of goods could be carried profitably from areas still unserved by the railroad to rather distant markets. As such activity intensified, colonial officials registered grave concern because the economic viability of the railroad was threatened. Generally constructed at great expense with state funds, often completed only shortly before the motor vehicle was introduced, served and regulated by colonial officials, the railroad was usually the most significant and costly economic investment made.[39] It also was the chief land element in the imperial economic network by which the movement of raw materials was regulated by Europeans, chiefly for European benefits.

The dramatic departure from the railroad imperative, and it was so described at the time, occurred in 1938 when the "Transdesert Road," designed by the British to link Haifa with Baghdad, was started after a railroad survey for a similar route had been completed and approved. This planned railroad was peremptorily discarded for the road, a 600-mile asphalt-surfaced undertaking.[40]

Only the Italians during the Fascist era gave precedence to the road in colonial geography. Italy's own road-building program had been highly praised in the 1920s. An element in Fascist ideology with its emphasis on modernism, road building was of economic, strategic, and even propaganda value, as the length of the Litoranea Libica measured.[41] Yet the most frenetic and extensive road building by the Italians was also the most disastrous in effect: the roads built for and during the invasion of Ethiopia.[42] Plans for that military venture, already advanced in 1932, called for an efficient, modern transportation system by which to speed along men and supplies. Work began in the neighboring colony of Eritrea, from which the military thrust would be made. After the original effort to use local labor was discarded, Italian workers appeared in ever-increasing numbers during 1935; 50,000 of them were at work when the war began.[43] The criticism of the roads they hastily constructed was widespread. Poorly engineered, badly affected by rainy weather, and overcrowded with military equipment, the roads were frightening to use. A writer for *Collier's* somberly summed up the results: "It is certain that in the first three months of the war, more Italians died under wheels, and in plunges off cliffs, than in front of the rifles and spears of the Abyssinian warriors."[44]

The only other road-building effort of the time that matched the Italian in military haste and engineering difficulty was located on the periphery of imperial affairs. The Burma road, which attained fame in World War II, was a heroic undertaking. Although sections had been started as early as 1925, the 650-mile section linking Kumming to the Burmese border was only started when the Sino-Japanese War began in 1937. Approximately 120,000 laborers built that section almost entirely by manual labor. After the port city of Canton fell to the Japanese in October 1938, the Burma road became China's major economic artery, along which supplies were pumped by 1,000 American trucks delivered in early 1939.[45]

The statistics tell much, but not all, about the transportation revolution that took place in the colonial world in the early twentieth century. The social maps of Africa and Asia were being transformed much as the maps of Europe and America had been somewhat earlier. Temporary migration from countryside to city intensified. Manual labor in the transportation field grew, and, although it often took on the form of impressment, it did bring many individuals into the European money economy as wage laborers who spent their earnings on European goods and acquired, in some limited measure, the taste for a different, materialistic life.[46] Local economies were replaced by regional economies, with cultural effects that have been debated.[47] Certainly the new transportation system further divided the dual economy—European-export, local-consumer—far more than it amalgamated it. [48]

Yet in an unexpected way the motor vehicle conveyed some new economic opportunities to Africans and Asians. A number of individuals and groups established their own transportation companies, engaged in trade that Europeans ignored or considered to be too small to be of consequence. In Nigeria and the Gold Coast the cocoa farmers maintained their own motor transportation system by which their product was moved quickly to market.[49] Motor transport was one means by which a small percentage of the colonial population could enter the technological sector of the European-imposed capitalist economy in other than a menial position.

However, here was the exception that proved the rule. The transfer of technology from Europe to the colonies was rather like the roads on which motorized transport moved, a surface affair. "Technology transfer"—the contemporary term describing the cultural process by which the rational, industrialized organization of production, and the managerial skills which direct it, are moved from one civilization to another—did not occur, or occurred so imperceptibly that it had little effect on the colonial population of the interwar era.

Were the reason for this condition the conventional one that the colonial

Aerial view of switchbacks on the Burma Road, 1942.
From the National Archives.

economies were primarily pastoral and primitive and, therefore, not in need
of any innovation or "rationalization," the issue might be dismissed or ignored. However, the concept of development had already entered the impe-

rialist lexicon, decades before the word and the idea it represented became fashionable in American academic circles.

"Development" as a colonial consideration seems to have originated with the British colonial minister, Joseph Chamberlain, who first used the term in a speech of 1895. On that occasion he described the British empire as an "underdeveloped estate." He added: "If the people of this country are not willing to invest some of their superfluous wealth in the development of their great estates, then I see no future for these countries."[50] Little of that "superfluous wealth" was so invested, and when such investment did seem compelling, it took place in an era of financial stringency, at a time when the major colonial powers were wracked first by the Great Depression and later by the ill effects of World War II.

There was nonetheless a widespread willingness to reconsider the nature and purpose of colonial economics in the interwar period. It was Leo Amery, Chamberlain's lineal descendant in the colonial office, who offered the most timely definition of development. Borrowing the theme from Lord Milner, Amery states that "the twin keys to development were improved communications and research."[51] Because so much of the road and railroad building of the time was undertaken with this thought in mind, one may conclude that the total length of these transportation arteries is as good a measure of the acceptance of Amery's definition as any that will be found.

Regardless of particular national issues, all colonial technicians agreed that extended infrastructure would make the territories more profitable. The major consideration was determined to be the increase of the flow of raw materials outward to Europe. The plans that the French minister of colonies, Albert Sarraut, called for in his major study, *La Mise en valeur des colonies françaises* (1922), concentrated on infrastructure: port extensions, road and railroad building. This activity, he anticipated, would result in the tripling of the economic output of the colonial empire.[52] More modest variations of the Sarraut grand scheme were devised by the Belgian minister of colonies, Louis Franck, and the governor of the Gold Coast, Frederick Guggisberg. Franck's plan, put before the Belgian parliament in 1920, called for a variety of public works, with railroads in the forefront. Moreover, by way of a new departure, the state was to provide a special annual allocation of 15,000,000 francs to pay the interest on loans during the construction time. Franck himself offered the cautionary comment that a project of this magnitude required overall planning and coordination of the stages of the work.[53]

Guggisberg went further. He was the first colonial officer to develop a plan, indeed a ten-year plan, that seemed to forecast what would be the standard governmental procedure after World War II. As a military engineer and an individual who could cope with detail, Guggisberg first prepared in 1919 what he called a "Programme," which was, in fact, a long-range plan that would, in his words, "give as clear an idea as possible of the material development necessary for this country."[54] Chief emphasis was first placed on railroads, next on port facilities, and third, on roads. Yet Guggisberg realized the meaningfulness of the progress in road building. Discussing the subject, he expressed his pleasure at being the first administrator able to travel by automobile to areas hitherto inaccessible and then evaluated the economic impact of the new transportation system. "The new motor roads are steadily opening up trade in the Northern Territories."[55]

The technological imprint that motor roads were making on the geography of empires was a highly visible, but not an exclusive, element in the European effort to arrange and order the colonies according to the principles of an industrialized West. Prior to the interwar years little had been known about the potential of these "tropical estates" because little was known about their contents. "Scientific colonization," as the Germans called it with justifiable pride, had begun on a small scale at the turn of the century. This certainly was the next logical step now that the claims to land had been "staked out." That American miner's metaphor, consciously employed by Lord Salisbury in his appraisal of late nineteenth-century colonial expansion, implied that territory had been acquired with the hope of future returns, not with an appreciation of actual contents. What was therefore required was a careful survey to determine what resources were to be found where.

The coincidence of colonial expansion overseas and scientific positivism in Europe is a noteworthy one. The intensification of industrialism in the Western world and the late nineteenth-century creation of a rigorous scientific method—what Alfred North Whitehead once described as the "invention of the method of invention"—suggested to some colonial officials and technicians the need and value of carefully prepared inventories of natural resources, the importance of experimentation with possible cash crops, the need for investigation and control of debilitating environmental factors, like the tse-tse fly.

In some measure each colonial power accepted the idea of "scientific colonization," as was evidenced by the proliferation of agricultural and medical clinics and research centers. Among those established before the World War, none was more highly regarded or more serious about its responsibilities than the *Biologisch Landwirtschaftliche Institut* at Amani in German East Africa, which concentrated on agricultural studies. The French would speak with pride in the interwar era of their several *Instituts Pasteur*, all of which did valuable work in the investigation and treatment of tropical diseases. The British founded a major College of Tropical Agriculture in Trinidad in 1927; and the French broadened their interest with the first *Institut français d'Afrique noire*, opened in 1938 and also open to research in most of the social sciences.

In Europe as well, special institutions were devoted to colonial research problems. The *Musée Royale du Congo Belge*, the creation of Leopold II, ranged in activities from zoology to economics. The Natural History Museum in London was in 1909 the selected site for a new Entomological Research Committee. A *Kolonial-Wirtschaftliche Komitee* in Berlin directed its attention to pure and practical research and was particularly supportive of cotton-growing projects in Africa.[56]

Of all the organizations devoted to "scientific colonization," none seemed more effective or better coordinated than those of the Dutch in the East Indies. There were geological, agricultural, and plant disease institutes; there were agricultural information services and horticultural and fishery services. There was a major botanical garden and an aquarium. Many of these agencies and their activities were coordinated after 1928, with the establishment of the Council of Natural Sciences, which had the additional responsibility of advising the government in matters of scientific inquiry. Given this array, it may not be surprising that David Ormesby-Gore, British undersecretary of state for colonies, remarked after a trip to the Far East in 1929: "The island of Java affords the most remarkable example in the world today of the application of science to the development of the tropics."[57]

The substitution of scientific and rational organization for haphazard commerce in colonial economics was neither dramatic nor widespread. It simply cost too much, and it did not square well with the old Victorian rule that colonies should be self-supporting, not a financial burden to the mother country. Nevertheless, there was growing consideration in the early twentieth century of the need for direct state intervention in colonial economic development.

The first notable sign was registered in 1916 when a private, self-appointed Empire Resources Development Committee announced its existence in Great Britain. The committee's purpose was unalloyed, if not noble: the removal of the dreadful war indebtedness, about to crush the population and the government, by means of colonial development. As the committee membership announced in a circular of January 1917: "Their plan is for the *State* on its own account to develop some of the immense resources of the Empire" and so be able to pay both the interest and principle of the national debt from this colonial income.[58]

Nothing came of the committee, its suggestions being unreasonable and untimely. But, then, nothing came immediately of a more properly proportioned proposal, one made by the Dominions Royal Commission, sitting in 1917 to discuss future empire policy. This commission urged the creation of an Imperial Development Board, which would be charged with the responsibility of investigating and studying all matters relating to empire resources and their development. The board was to encourage scientific research, publish statistics, and "watch and report on the changing requirements of the Empire" in matters of raw materials and production. The board remained fixed on the printed page, an idea rather than an institution.

It was left to one man, not to commissions and committees, to find a way to obtain governmental support for colonial economic development through research. This man was the energetic imperialist, Leo Amery. His method was indirect, through the founding of an Empire Marketing Board. Created in 1924 and remaining in existence until 1933, the Empire Marketing Board was outwardly concerned with the promotion of empire goods in Great Britain. However, through Amery's efforts, much of the budget was redirected to scientific research. The former German research center at Amani was refurbished; aid went to the new agricultural college at Trinidad; and research in fields as diverse as entomology, soil content, wool raising, and pasturage was supported both in England and various parts of the empire. Amery acknowledged that most of the subsidized research centers were already in existence, "but we tried, wherever possible, to link them up and co-ordinate them with stations engaged on similar work in every part of the Empire."[59]

Amery was at one with his French counterpart, Albert Sarraut, in regretting the sparse and scattered efforts at scientific research. When Sarraut wrote that he wished to see a coherent empire policy that would replace the "small packages" by which previous research and development had been carried out,[60] he was saying just about what Amery stated several years later before a London meeting of representatives of the colonial governments:

I am sure that the case for pooling our resources sufficiently to create some sort of unified service . . . is one we ought to give the fullest and most earnest consideration . . . it would be a pity if we separated without finding at any rate some solution to the problem which would enable us to create a more effective instrument for the scientific development of our almost unlimited resources.[61]

Amery's listeners were no more persuaded than were Sarraut's readers. Both men had big dreams but little came of them. Development, notably in the form of financial aid, would be a major activity only after World War II, in those declining imperial years when the technocrat and planner replaced the politician and administrator. Even the first two development plans that actually bore that label are generally dismissed in a few lines by historians examining the interwar vagaries of empire. Perhaps this is all the attention they do merit because these plans were much more desperate responses to dire economic problems at home than they were long-range schemes for economic betterment in the colonies.

In 1929 the British Parliament passed the Colonial Development Act. The act, defined as having "the purpose of aiding and developing agriculture and industry in the colony or territory and thereby promoting commerce with or industry in the United Kingdom," contained a list of fundable projects that included harbor, transportation, and communication improvements; the development of mineral resources; and the promotion of scientific research. A maximum sum of £1,000,000 for these purposes would be annually available, and this money might be advanced either in the form of grants or loans. Before the outbreak of the Second World War, the act had led to the dispensing of some £8,000,000.

The French development proposals were, in effect, only belated implementations of a plan proposed by Sarraut in 1921 and defended at length in his *Mise en valeur des colonies françaises*. Aside from some modest port improvements in Dakar, Senegal, little initially came of Sarraut's ideas, but later the deepening world economic crisis heightened interest in them among French politicians. In 1931 legislation was passed by the French parliament that authorized loans for colonial undertakings that would make the local economies profitable. Yet only about half of the allocated sum of 1,750,000,000 francs was ever used, and a considerable portion of this money was consumed in overhead expenses such as management, transportation, and crating of equipment.[62]

The French did make one grand and concerted effort to consider the wide-ranging problems of colonial economics. The *Conference économique de la France métropolitaine et d'outre-mer*, generally called the "imperial conference," brought more than 300 representatives of various colonial interests together in Paris between December 3, 1934, and April 13, 1935. The intention of the conferees was to provide the French colonial empire with an overall plan for development, one that would be ensured by the establishment of a national fund directed to the provision of the colonies with modern equipment. However, the minister of finance did not implement this proposal and the conference, like the Sarraut Plan before it, had no measurable effect on economic development. Critics have complained that the French never readjusted their old vision of economic relations between homeland and colonies.[63] The new imperial arrangements proposed were merely variants of the old ones that assumed a dualistic economic situation consisting of an industrialized core and an agricultural periphery. Commenting on this "complementary economy," one critic described it as "a more or less deodorized synonym for autarchy."[64]

Autarchy, whether deodorized or not, seemed to offer the only possible sweet smell of success to the colonial powers at that time. Everything else had a musty quality about it. Domestic unemployment, declining traditional markets abroad, unsettled currencies, obsolescent industrial equipment—here were the signs of age and neglect and, at the same time, the reasons to seek the satisfaction in empire that was apparently denied elsewhere. "If we cannot look to the development of the Empire to lift us out of that trough [the Depression], we do not know where to turn for immediate assistance," lamented an editorial in *The Spectator*.[65]

The particular editorial was entitled "The Rationalization of Empire." The key term "rationalization" was thus popular enough to be immediately comprehended by a general readership, proof of the widespread awareness of the need for economic reordering, both at home and in the colonies. For the imperialist nations, now faced with the adverse effects of the Depression, empire acquired new economic meaning. Even though individual colonies suffered as miserably as did the metropolitan regions—the paddy quotations for Indochinese rice, for instance, fell from 7.15 piastres per 100 kilograms in 1929 to 1.88 in 1934[66]—the Depression encouraged tighter trade relations with the empires. By the end of the interwar period Great Britain and France had remarkably augmented their colonial trade: 44 percent for Great Britain in 1938 and 27 percent for France in the same year.[67]

By many contemporaries, empire was imagined to be the basis for a new economic order, one which—retrospectively—seems to have fallen between the national units of production and sale and the multinationals that currently satisfy the desiderata of "economy of scale."[68] The possibility of such new economic dimensions was precociously considered by an editorial writer of the London Times in 1930. A "practically unexplored way of promoting imperial economic co-ordination," he argued, "is to encourage the creation of imperial-wide industrial units."[69]

Such units were already appearing. The *Times* saw Imperial Chemical Industries as one, but there was also Unilever in the soap and merchandising business and Dutch Shell in the oil business. The Americans, above all, seemed to have entered empire commerce with a zeal and success that both dazzled and dismayed. The Nairn Brothers used motor vehicles manufactured in Pennsylvania and Indiana for their cross-desert bus service in the Arabian peninsula. By the late 1930s Australia was importing more American than British automobiles. The United States Rubber Company had developed, as early as 1919, a 900,000-acre plantation in northeastern Sumatra, a rubber plantation considered the largest in the world at that time.[70] In 1929 Neville Chamberlain, then British chancellor of the exchequer, spoke about the uniqueness of the American situation and the need to defend against it by some form of imperial economic unity. "Alone, the United States of America are vast enough and contain sufficient resources within their own limits, to stand on their own feet."[71] The country did more; it strode across continents and hence aroused the admiration and apprehension that Chamberlain's remarks implied.

American efficiency inspired some colonial visionaries to seek change. Articles in the *Round Table*, for instance, praised American industrial management and made the work of Frederick W. Taylor familiar, if not widely accepted.[72] Taylor's emphasis on "scientific management" was considered a fine complement to Henry Ford's practice of rationalization of industry. However, these practices were slow to be realized in Europe because, as one British commentator cynically remarked, "our grandfathers got on without them."[73]

Contemporaries nevertheless considered their possibility. There were several major conferences at which "rationalization" was defined and considered, as at the International Economic Conference of 1927 and the Advisory Committee of Management meeting of the International Labor Organization in 1937. In 1940 the subject arose in the course of discussions held by the Textile Labour Inquiry Committee of Bombay.[74] Despite such talk, there was only one notable example of rationalized use of land at the time, and it was a most notable failure. This was the French Niger "scheme," perhaps best compared to the American Tennessee Valley Authority plan, but compared only loosely. The idea, an outcome of the Imperial Economic Conference, was to irrigate a large area in the colony of Niger and then make it a cotton growing region of importance. The plan came to naught, with soil erosion its principal and unwanted development. But the structural importance of the project must be emphasized: the state here played an active and direct role in planning and directing a major aspect of the colonial economy.[75]

This said, one must also recognize that the old ways persisted everywhere. The colonial mentality, like the pith helmet that shielded it from the sun, was a matter of well-worn habit in the interwar period. Even when the new economic vocabulary was employed, it was often taken out of its modern context. Gabriel Hanotaux, addressing the French Academy of Colonial Sciences in 1923, remarked that "we ought to prepare and combine in order to reach a kind of Taylorization in our colonial effort. The French and other Europeans will furnish the money and organization; the natives will work the land."[76]

Here was the Victorian appraisal of the world reiterated, without its blatant racism, however. The dualism that Hanotaux suggested persisted and prevailed. A German author, writing in 1928, called Africa "an immense plantation," to be exploited by the European industrial powers.[77] The Dutch colonial authority Kat de Angelino declared tropical dependencies indispensable to the "world economy" and insisted that they ought be directed by organizations built "upon a modern and scientific base" so long as the indigenous population lacked the ability to do so.[78]

A new set of antonyms was introduced to define the perceived global relationship: "modern" and "traditional," "developed" and "backward," "dynamic" and "static." (The currently popular code letters "LDC"—for "less-developed countries"—owe their existence and acceptance to this Western-inspired distinction.)

The detrimental psychological effects of this division are not difficult to ascertain. Even where Europeans gave evidence of some respect for the qualities of mind and spirit of the indigenous population, they were still very hesitant to turn over control of management and administration. Certainly such a bias affected the officials who established the admissions requirements for the Royal Indian Engineering College—a college that was not even located in India! Paid for by funds from the government of India and created to prepare individuals for assignment "in the superior ranks of the Public Works Department in India," the college required that its candidates be "British subjects of European race"—except for two "natives of India," admitted only when vacancies existed in each entering class.[79]

As India industrialized in the early twentieth century, it did so in face of British contempt and indifference, attitudes only slowly altered in the interwar period. The Royal Commission on Labour in India found in 1931, for instance, the persistence of racism in appointments in the Indian Railway system. Among the 800,000 employees, there were 8,757 subordinate officials drawing a salary of 250 rupees or more a month. (408,000 drew less than 20 rupees a month.) Of this number of 8,757, 2,045 were Europeans and 3,777 Anglo-Indians. One member of the commission insisted that the railway board had abolished "racial discrimination in name," but was now trying "to discredit the whole Indian race by saying that Indians are not fit for higher posts."[80] A similar attitude of condescension affected products. Even when the Tata Iron and Steel Company, at the time the major indigenously-owned industrial complex in the colonial world, began steel production in the early twentieth century, its product was disfavored because it was Indian-manufactured.[81]

Such attitudes were further reinforced by the bilateral nature of most colonial economic conditions. Since in general the industrial products and techniques that were employed to "modernize" sectors of the colonial economy came directly from the metropolitan colonizing country, they were stamped in the colonial mind as being superior. An obvious example of this condition was the importation of British machinery for the Indian textile industry. While it is true that the "heavy Manchester bias of that technology" led to the installation of well-manufactured British equipment, that equipment was less suited to Indian needs than American or Japanese machinery, which was equally available at the time.[82]

It took a very long time for the Western world to accept the fact that the Japanese were capable of doing more than cheaply imitating Western goods.

The tendency to dismiss the non-Western did not imply indifference to the possible skills of the "natives." Development clearly implied the development of local talent. "There is no need to dispute whether economic or education development is more useful to the population," wrote one Dutch official. "The first is simply impossible without the second."[83] Thus, the wonderful remark made in 1904 by Lord Curzon when he was viceroy of India that education should be for the "business of life," actually should have read for the "business of empire."

In the twentieth century, but notably in the interwar period, the educational thrust in the colonies was in the direction of the vocational and the technical. This is not to say that the older tradition of replicating abroad, but in a much more parsimonious and socially limited way, the European educational system was completely abandoned. However, the prevalent attitude was captured in the strategic word "adaptation." The word was popularized in the report on African education prepared by the American-sponsored Phelps-Stokes Commission that made two visits to black Africa in the 1920s.[84] "Adaptation" described the policy of adjusting education to local needs and immediate concerns. But these needs and concerns were defined by Europeans, not by Africans themselves.

The adjustments made were based on matters other than pedagogy, as might be imagined. Well-articulated school systems were expensive to establish and difficult to maintain, particularly where populations were dispersed in small villages cast across a rural landscape. Furthermore, earlier efforts to educate Asians and Africans in the strict European mold had been criticized as inappropriate, culturally nonsensical and politically dangerous. Finally, higher education in European professions, such as the law or teaching, had attracted more students than the market could bear, particularly as the Depression spread overseas. At that time, the problem was of major proportions in India, where a universities conference declared:

A practical solution to the *problem of unemployment* can only be found by a radical re-adjustment of the present system of education in schools in such a way that a large number of pupils shall be diverted at the completion of their secondary education either to occupations or to separate vocational institutions.[85]

The search for the practical and the utilitarian in educational policy generally was multi-tracked. First, because it was the oldest, there was the need for trained personnel in the colonial administration, whether they were clerks or chiefs. Second, there was a growing desire in the interwar era to turn the local populations to trade, commerce, and industry. Third, and most pervasive, was the interest in "village life," an interest in the prosperity and well-being of the rural population, those masses idealized by some colonial authorities as "peasants."[86]

Clearly, the colonial system depended on collaborators, locals who would bridge the two cultures, act as go-betweens, serve the newly-imposed colonial system by making it known to the populations who would have preferred to ignore it. In the beginning, therefore, Africans and Asians entered the system as interpreters.[87] Then they became clerks and thereafter lower-level administrators. Literacy, or more specifically, literacy in a European tongue, was the vehicle by which to enter the system and, moreover, to enter that psychological compound in which European colonial officialdom was resident.

It was a topsy-turvy world, indeed, this world where many millions learned a foreign language because a few thousand never progressed very far—and never saw the need to—in the tongue of the demographic majority. All too many Europeans were like Mrs. Turton, the wife of the Collector, in *A Passage to India*, who "had learnt the lingo . . . but . . . knew none of the politer forms and of the verbs only the imperative mood."[88]

This matter of indigenous literacy worked in a peculiar way to frustrate some of the efforts made in the interwar period toward vocational education. Most of this training still followed European patterns, used European texts, and, often, was presented in European languages. The obvious result was a class of students as adept, and perhaps more so, in the foreign language as in the techniques that language instructed. "In theory," wrote a Dutch author, "trade schools are meant to produce workmen [but] a person who can read and write . . . wants to start at once higher up."[89]

The unanticipated outcome was not the result of particular individual ambitions that the colonial system had aroused but of the peculiar economic conditions that colonialism had imposed—or allowed to exist.

The Europeans clearly perceived the need for vocational education, but these same people had done little to generate a real demand for it.[90] The few industrial and technological activities in the colonial economy were dominated by Europeans. That the Belgians trained Congolese to help run the rail system in that colony, and that the Anglo-Iranian Petroleum Company provided its indigenous employees with training and with promotions into some managerial positions were occurrences viewed as quite unusual.

A number of technical and vocational schools did begin to dot the colonial landscape, but they seemed to be situated in economic wastelands. Perhaps the most notable exception was India. As early as 1904 the Association for the Advancement of Scientific and Industrial Education had been established by Indians themselves, and this was soon followed by the Society for the Promotion of Technical Education. No doubt the most impressive advance was the Jamshedpur Technical Institute, opened in 1921. Its graduates moved into key managerial and technical positions in the Tata Iron and Steel Company, to the extent that English personnel in high positions were almost all replaced by the end of the interwar period.[91]

An East African Education Commission, reporting in 1937, unintentionally spoke for all colonial administrations when it stated that the major educational concern "must for the present be the improvement of agriculture, animal husbandry, and health."[92]

It was just such a conclusion that explains the favorable reception accorded to the Phelps-Stokes Commission to Africa in the 1920s. Sponsored by the fund of the same name, an endowment set up to enhance black education in the United States, the commission came into being as a response to a request made in 1919 by a group of American missionaries in Africa who wanted a survey of educational needs.[93] The guiding figure on the commission was Dr. Jesse Jones, a Welsh émigré with a Ph.D. from Columbia and a particular vision of what "Negro education" ought to be. As an instructor at Hampton Institute, he accepted the principle of racial harmony through compromise. His philosophy was akin to that of Booker T. Washington, which was memorably described in the metaphor of the keys of the piano. Jones was assisted by J. E. K. Aggrey, an émigré from the Gold Coast, educated at Livingstone College in North Carolina, and associated with Jones at Hampton.

Both these individuals and the other members of the commission were imbued with a philosophy of rural democracy, of the value of hard work, craftsmanship, and good citizenship. Their interpretation of "industrial education" centered on the importance of instruction in crafts, on an appreciation of agricultural techniques, and on knowledge of household mechanics. Not surprisingly, therefore, the Phelps-Stokes Commission recommended for Africa an agrarian education, which would lead to economic self-sufficiency and a sense of local pride. The tone of the report was a familiar one to many colonial administrators and much appreciated by them.

In Africa and elsewhere the colonial administrator and entrepreneur were both generally hopeful of converting the "native" into a "wage earner." Schools, therefore, might become "nurseries of usefulness," to employ the term of French Governor-General Brévié.[94] Through them, a productive consumer population might be trained and thus incorporated into the colonial economy.

The major education effort was to find the means by which to create a qualified and reliable labor force. With the extension of the colonial economy into the world economy, with the development of agricultural and mineral enterprises, labor needs accelerated. Most evident in appearance was a modern plantation system, encouraged by the growing worldwide sugar and rubber consumption. Moreover, the system was necessitated by the lack of European settlers. Metropolitan efforts to induce migration had been greeted with failure; of the more recently acquired colonial territories only Kenya and Libya attracted large settler populations.

From the European point of view there was a clear and pressing need for many field workers. Nowhere was this more obvious than in the rapidly growing rubber industry after World War I. In Indochina alone, the number of field workers increased markedly: from 3,500 yearly to 18,000 between 1926 and 1929.[95] The figures, however, do not reveal the method of recruitment. Modern practices were not far removed from earlier techniques that had followed a bleak path from slavery to indenture.

It is true that forced labor was in decline in the interwar period, but it had not yet been abolished. The International Labor Office, an agency of the League of Nations, passed a convention in 1930 that urged the abolition of forced labor as quickly as possible wherever feasible. However, this convention did not deter the Belgians from continuing their practice of *travail éducatif*, a form of forced labor disguised as a means of forming good work habits. And the French on Madagascar, to cite one notable example, created a *deuxième contingent* in 1929, a "second regiment" of youth of conscript age for work on public projects. The construction of the Congo-Oceana Railroad in French Equatorial Africa has frequently been cited as one of the most brutal consumers of men. Of the nearly 150,000 used from the initiation of the railroad in 1922 to its completion in 1934, approximately 120,000 were actually recruits, impressed through quotas established in each province.

More common than this obviously crude and cruel method was the use of labor contracts, called "coolie ordinances" by the Dutch.[96] Many economic ventures begun by Europeans called for the displacement of the working population over long distances to regions that were still primitive and unsettled. The newer plantations outside of Java in the Indonesian Archipelago were one example. Moreover, the profitability of agricultural enterprise depended on regular labor prepared to work long hours under severe conditions. European owners and managers therefore enlisted administrative assistance to ensure these conditions. The result was the passage of contract laws, which defined the working arrangement—usually for a three-year period—by which owner and worker were bound. Violation of such a contract was met with penalties ranging from fines to imprisonment. Defenders of the system insisted that it provided guarantees to the worker as well as to the manager: health and nutritional care, housing, return passage home at the end of the contractual period.[97] The system, nevertheless, worked to the benefit of the Europeans. Frequently, unsuspecting and unschooled indigenous populations entered a contract they hardly understood, to perform tasks for which they were ill-prepared.

This system of labor recruitment was further extended by means of immigration. Greatly stimulated at the turn of the twentieth century, when the colonial economy was turning toward large-scale agriculture and mining, and when the colonial administration was making its first attempts at major improvement of infrastructure, migration seemed to be regulated by a "coolie principle," the desire to obtain cheap labor tolerant of poor working conditions. "The time has come for the yellow to take the place of the black," one appalled critic argued,[98] and it did seem that the end of African slavery was followed by exploitation of the Chinese. The British, for instance, began importing Chinese into Mauritius in 1829 in anticipation of the abolition of slavery. The French used Chinese coolies as porters during their campaign against the Hovas in Madagascar in 1895. And Lord Milner toyed with the idea of importing large numbers of Chinese to assist with railroad building in South Africa. However, most of the Chinese émigrés remained within the confines of Southeast Asia, where the dramatic increase of land devoted to the newer cash crop of rubber made their presence attractive. Malaya is certainly the most striking example of this particular economic-demographic combination: the newly begun rubber industry attracted so many laborers that the Chinese were almost as numerous as the Malays in 1939. A random selection of Chinese population figures in the colonial world of 1931 shows the impact of this migration. (See accompanying tabulation.)

Burma	194,000
Indochina	418,000
Indonesia	1,233,000
Philippines	72,000
Madagascar	2,500
Jamaica	4,000

There was no other population that matched the Chinese in peripatetic behavior, but other demographic movements were obvious and important. Indians moved to Burma, East and South Africa, Ceylon and Jamaica. Javanese were enlisted to work on the plantations in Cochinchina. Lebanese migrated to West Africa and, in the interwar period when Lebanon was a French mandate, they began to people cities like Dakar and Conakry in considerable numbers. The South African diamond and gold mines and the famous "copper belt" in the Rhodesias attracted migrant labor from within the continent.

As important as the demographic shift, of course, was the socio-economic effect. The émigré became the "hyphen" between the European and indigenous populations.[99] Engaging in forms of trade, commerce, and some small industry, which were alien to the local population or unappealing to most of the resident Europeans, the émigré acted as a special middleman between a rather self-sufficient local economy and a dependent colonial one. For some critics, the émigré community performed the functions of a local bourgeoisie, without which the economic development of the colony would have been gravely impaired.[100]

It is true that most of the émigré communities did exhibit a certain entrepreneurial spirit which occasionally surprised the colonial governments as much as it aggravated local populations. The Chinese in Indonesia had, in 1923, produced 55,000 tons of the total of 137,000 tons of rubber exported that year. It was estimated that four-fifths of all the domestic trade in Indochina was controlled by the Chinese before 1939. The Syro-Lebanese in Senegal were so numerous by 1922 that the local chamber of commerce called this situation perilous for French merchants.[101] A decade before, in 1911, Europeans were disturbed by the intrusive role of Indians in the East African economy. "The Europeans are now beginning to see that the one way of getting rid of the Indian," commented a Scottish minister, "is to train the native to take his place."[102]

One more factor—albeit a major one—in the increasingly complicated colonial economy, the immigrant helped to generate capital, increase the range of small businesses, support new industries, and provide needed labor. The immigrants were thus integrated into the commercial system but were seldom assimilated into the social one. Less outsiders than the Europeans, they nevertheless complicated and aggravated the civil order. They were frequently viewed with distrust, apprehension, and antagonism by the indigenous populations who borrowed and bought from them, and competed with them in the small retail and trading outlets. The social situation was particularly aggravated in Southeast Asia when commercial diversification according to ethnic groups ceased as members of the local populations entered the same businesses as the Chinese. Commercial rivalry was then overcast with ethnic intolerance. Such tension was first noticeable in Java, but it was in French Indochina that demonstrations against the Chinese business community resulted in both the loss of life and property, in Saigon in 1919 and in Haiphong in 1927.[103] Across the globe and for somewhat different reasons the Lebanese shops in Sierra Leone were looted and destroyed on November 11, 1919, in the face of a serious food shortage and accompanying rumors that the Lebanese were making enormous profits from rice that they had purposely hoarded.[104]

The "plural economy" that some observers had seen as the colonial one was tenuous at best.[105] Any confederation of economic interests was ultimately held together by the military arm of the colonial occupant, and such a confederation only made sense and endured as long as local politics were inconsequential. As nationalism grew in Asia and Africa, the immigrant community suffered its effects. This community was, after all, a creation of colonialism and so it suffered the consequence of being a victim of colonialism. Nowhere was this outcome more tragically evidenced than in Uganda in 1972, when the government forced the Asian population of 45,000 to leave the country. A diaspora took place, with 27,000 individuals going to Great Britain, 6,000 going to Canada and India respectively, 1,000 to the United States, and the rest in small numbers to other countries.

The demographic pattern formed by the movement of colonized peoples within and across the several European empires gives some demonstration of the far-reaching implications of colonial economic development. Yet the pattern does not figure at all in the grand schema that the modern academic mind has designed to explain that ever-perplexing phenomenon that is ever-redefined and renamed: earlier, "Westernization"; later, "modernization"; more recently, "dependency," and the "world capitalist system."

What the average colonial administrator neither perceived nor would have been interested in is today a major consideration in the history of overseas colonial expansion. In the thought of many critics the West's global domination has been made a part of a vast and ever-intensifying economic network that now provides imperialism with a symmetry and order that mystical British writers a century ago would have more easily and elegantly attributed to divine inspiration.

Cast in global terms, the colonial economic situation is an integral part of this world capitalist system that has been growing for centuries.[106] First Holland, then Great Britain, thereafter Germany and the United States have assumed dominant positions, but the general characteristic has been the outward movement of capitalism. The result has been described as tri-modal: three concentric circles, with the central core being the highly industrialized West; a semi-peripheral area in which some industry has been developed and capitalist forms defined; and a periphery that is essentially agrarian, the source of raw materials and the location of the Third World. The system is inner-directed, with exploitation or drainage of wealth and resources toward the core, for the benefit of the dominant capitalist classes located there.

This argument dismisses both modernization and development as false concepts that deny the reality of the situation. What has occurred is "the development of underdevelopment."[107] The peripheral areas have been set back economically by the imperialist experience. European capitalist efforts, which established export economies by reducing colonial regions to the function of suppliers of primary materials, "de-industrialized" these regions. India has been taken as the best example of an economy set back, a country "de-industrialized" to satisfy the needs for raw—not finished—cotton by the manufacturers in Lancashire.

Furthermore, underdevelopment continued to be a colonial problem even when mass marketing and industrial techniques were introduced. Because of imperialist domination and its trade regulations, the colonial economies never forged enough of the linkages by which modern manufacturing expanded.[108] These economies only engaged in slow production of consumer goods—forward linkage—and seldom found the occasion to introduce heavy capital, or producer, goods—backward linkage. The imperialist economic chain grew longer, while the colonial one hardly extended. An appropriate example of this condition would be the automobile, imported into Asia and Africa because the heavy machinery necessary for its manufacture was located in Coventry and Detroit, not in Jakarta and Cairo.

Critics supporting the twin arguments of the "development of under-development" and economic dependency also note the social disruption these conditions provoked. A "proletarianized peasant" appeared,[109] uprooted and often city-bound because of the large-scale, export-market farming imperialism introduced, and because of an alliance formed between indigenous land-lords and colonial overlords that ensured the economic interests of the former and the political interests of the latter.

Were this not enough, the "technology gap" further widened the disparity.[110] The most obvious characteristic of the technologically structured economic system is its intensifying need of more capital because of the high expenses of ever-more complicated systems. It certainly is true that when the first phase of the European industrial revolution occurred, the disparity among the world's economic systems was not exceedingly great: all were labor-intensive; all were small-scale in scope ("cottage industries"); all had, at their most advanced, machine-supported worker activities.

"Developed" and "underdeveloped" would have been inappropriate adjectives; the degrees of difference were inconsequential. However, as machines took over the work of men, as factories became industrial and their activities more functional and specialized, the necessary capital investment in the establishment of any new industrial enterprise increased. The cost of technology rose in proportion to the increase of productivity. "Efficiency" guaranteed large returns, no doubt, but it was also predicated upon large outlays.

The capital shortage that characterized the colonial economy and would be a major problem in the Third World that replaced colonial empires meant that technological improvement, even when desired, was difficult to achieve. Again, critics speak bitterly. Capital that was originally generated in the colonial regions was treated as if it were an "export product." The headquarters of large firms, like Unilever and Firestone Rubber, were not located in the countries or colonies from which their raw materials came. Managerial salaries, outlays for research laboratories, and major purchase orders were sources of wealth to the "home country," even though the initial materials that provided that wealth had been extracted or harvested from the colonial soil. Add to this situation the existence of tariffs and export taxes imposed by and for the colonial administration, and the burden of the colonial economy was further weighted.

There are other, more local, reasons for the slow generation of capital in the colonies. First, a dual-scale of salaries for professional services denied much capital formation by personal savings or investments. Europeans were paid much more than indigenous personnel for work of comparable quality. In the Gold Coast, for instance, a European civil servant in the 1930s received an average salary of 40 pounds a month, while an African received four pounds. Similarly, Moroccans and Algerians at the same time were paid only 16 to 25 percent of the wages that French workers doing the same job received.[111]

Second, the small-scale businesses through which an indigenous bourgeoisie was being created, notably in black Africa, were swept away by new European commercial combinations. Large trading companies like the United African Company (a subsidiary of Unilever) and SCOA (Société commerciale ouest africaine), moved rapidly and effectively into the local commercial and trading fields after World War I. In the instance of Senegal, a region submitted to close historical analysis, the results of this change were disastrous for the indigenous population.[112] Over the several centuries of French coastal occupation, Senegalese had developed family businesses in which European goods were traded and sold for useful agrarian products, of which gum rubber and peanuts were the most important. Now, with the advent of the large commercial combinations, these local merchants found themselves faced with competition and price-cutting that they could not match.

The two general factors just considered partially explain a unique development in much of the colonial world: the emergence of a bourgeoisie quite removed from the commercial and managerial activities that had led to European entrepreneurial skills. This administrative bourgeoisie entered comfortable residences on the basis of governmental salaries, not on the basis of profits accumulated.[113] The decline of commercial activity, both because of the intrusion of large European-based companies and, later, the ill effects of the worldwide depression, diverted the talent and interest of the young from the market place to the government square.

In terms of economic stratification, the colonial world had a heavy and thus unbalanced tertiary sector: large numbers of underpaid and underemployed individuals engaged in domestic chores (usually as servants) and a smaller number, but an important salaried group, in the capacity of bureaucrats or professionals. The service sector was large; the productive (industrial and commercial) one was small. The agricultural sector remained the largest and yet the least well-integrated into the world economy.

Whether this is as it would have been had the capitalist West not intruded with its banks and gunboats is the question prefacing the ethical aspects of the debate over the economics of imperialism. The critic's eye sees cultural as well as economic debasement: the colonial world was one robbed of dignity as well as of resources. Conversely, the farther vision is a rather romantic one, of well-integrated agrarian societies, of family industries, working harmoniously. The spinning wheel, which Gandhi included as a political party symbol, represented that mythical world; the basic elements of African Socialism were derived from the same source.

The imagined contrasts between a self-developing world with its well-integrated parts and a selfish world with its intrusive, disruptive activities makes the question of "development" a sensitive one. The sides are drawn. Those analysts who see imperialism as a modernizing force, liberating vast portions of the world from their fixed and tired ways, are in conflict with those analysts who see imperialism as an oppressive force, creating dependency and subservience.

The available fact sheets allow both sides to claim some of the historical truth. If 1700 is taken as a base year, a time when the differential in development and wealth between Europe and the rest of the world was minimal, then the following differential ratios occur:[114]

	Europe	The Third World
1860	1.9	1
1913	3.4	1
1950	5.2	1

Also the export figures for primary materials sent from the Third World to Europe during the colonial period bear noting. Again, in 1700, about 100,000 tons of goods made their way by sail to Europe; in 1910, approximately 30,000,000 tons were moved by steamboat and steam train; this figure rose to 85,000,000 tons in 1936.[115] The economic pull of the industrializing West, with its every increasing GNP and, hence, its ability to command the world's wealth, is easily measured. Yet, interestingly, the colonial world, both as a source of raw materials and as a market, never counted much in the European global scene. Between 1800 and 1936, about 18 percent of the European manufactured goods worked their way annually to colonial (or Third World) markets. The energy dependency of the West is also a very recent phenomenon, with minerals (other than the precious ones that have long dazzled the human imagination) and fuel amounting to only 2 percent of Third World exportation between 1928 and 1931 and no higher than 16 percent from 1936 to 1938.[116]

The economic dependence of the West on raw materials and the Third World on technology is much more a postcolonial phenomenon than a colonial one. Yet even when this fact is taken into account, one must recognize that the conditions that led to global disparity were largely determined in the colonial period. As far as can be determined, between 73 and 78 percent of the world's manufactured goods in 1750 were produced by regions later grouped under the rubric "Third World." By 1900 the percentage had been drastically reduced, with the same regions then only accounting for 6 percent of that production.[117] Some of this difference is certainly due to "deindustrialization," but much more is due to the technological advantages that the West had acquired. By the late nineteenth century a textile worker in England and a mill hand in Germany were capable of turning out hundreds of times the daily amount that their counterparts in India or Malaya could. The productive capacity of the world had increased, and most of it was situated in European and American industrial cities.

The thesis that proposes the "development of underdevelopment" cannot be lightly dismissed, nor should it be allowed to blanket the colonial world so that the activities, intentions, and ambitions of the many little makers of that one big history are unseen. Imperialism, as practiced by late nineteenth- and early twentieth-century Europeans, was haphazard, careless, and poorly directed. The good and bad effects were more the result of accident than of calculation. Few administrators were well-trained to cope with modernity; few were even interested in it. Ormsby-Gore worried about the backgrounds of British colonial recruits. "The examination," he stated in 1928, "seems still to attract in the main those who have specialized at the university in classics or pure mathematics. In the tropics, especially in tropical areas in process of rapid economic development, sound basic knowledge of natural science . . . is of ever-increasing significance."[118]

No doubt his observation was correct, but the men in the field saw them- selves as administrators, not technicians; chiefs, not managers. They felt a certain uneasiness with modernity, born of unfamiliarity with technique, but also of a condescending familiarity with local populations. They were all there, after all, to "hold the ring," not to reorder the universe. This hesitancy toward change, toward the endorsement of development, was best expressed by the French administrator Robert Delavignette. "We are already wit- nessing an Africa dominated not by administrators, but by engineers. In order to protect Africa from America will we 'Americanize' Africa?"[119]

No, the French did not "Americanize" Africa. The coca-colization of the world, as some wit termed it, would come later, after yet another world war and still another phase in industrial development. In the meantime, which is to say in the interwar period, the colonial world went on much as before. There were signs of change, of course. "It is, in fact, no uncommon occur- rence," announced one observer of the Asian scene, "to see natives who a few years ago had not a rag to their back now driving from village to village in Ford cars."[120] Airfields were built; wealthy sons were educated in Europe; newspapers appeared daily in most major colonial cities. Yet the colonial sys- tem still seemed fixed in time—but not because of the persistence of Asian and African traditions. The cause is to be found primarily in that special com- bination of European doggedness and lethargy which was called colonial rule.

CHAPTER 4

Colonial Cities

The decision made by General Hubert Lyautey in 1912 to establish the official French residence in Rabat, Morocco, was dramatic in setting and gesture. As he halted his horse on the heights overlooking the future city site and, beyond, the ancient villages of Rabat and Salé set against the Mediterranean, he declared that there, and nowhere else, would the French capital be situated. The three fig trees that marked the spot were made the center of the patio of the residence.[1] From this magnificent and spacious building, with its administrative offices clustering around it, the modern city of Rabat later unfolded below. Lyautey supervised it all, determined that the view would remain unimpaired and that the capital city would be a credit to his rule and to the genius of the nation that supported it.

The urge to build, to etch in stone a statement of historical presence, has been an imperial sentiment since Caesar Augustus found Rome a city of brick and left it a city of marble. Yet urban form was of keen interest to so few colonial administrators in the twentieth century that architectural structures and masses, which were obviously the most durable part of modern empire, will not be found illustrated in art histories or architectural surveys today. Even visitors who entered the urban scene at high noon of empire were less than inspired. Aldous Huxley described the Victorian facade of Bombay as looking "like a collection of architectural cads and bounders."[2] Another English critic viewed interwar Dakar with comparable deprecation. "The greater part of the buildings," he wrote, "look as if they had been made after models confected by a pastry-cook on one of the luxury Italian boats who had

114

paid a hurried visit to the French Colonial Exhibition."[3] This particular comment more grandly echoed the words a Frenchman voiced in 1912: "Alas, we have not yet taken the trouble in Dakar to maintain our reputation as patrons of the arts."[4]

In contrast to the somber and often derisive comments that described so much of colonial urbanization are the strikingly enthusiastic responses to the Italian effort in Libya. During the governorship of Count Guiseppe Volpi di Misurata (1921–1925), and, more particularly, under the energetic governorship of Italo Balbo (1933–1940), Tripoli was redesigned along appealing lines. Parks and promenades, and a well-articulated esplanade running along the sea front provided the setting for the modern architecture, which was originally Neo-Moorish in motif but evolved into a pleasing variant of Fascist Modern: simple lines, rectangular forms, and white facades.[5] The overall effect, the blend of the old Arab city and the modern Italian one, was enthusiastically appraised. "It takes very real genius," one tourist commented, "to combine ancient charm, modern efficiency, and what a grand job they've made of both in Tripoli."[6]

For sheer grandeur, however, the imperial city of New Delhi commanded the most attention. This new capital of British India, commissioned in 1911, was of monumental proportions. Its Viceroy House was more spacious than the Palace of Versailles. Its ceremonial boulevard, Kingsway, was longer and wider than the Champs-Elysées. Herbert Baker, a major colonial architect himself, was naively enthusiastic when he wrote Sir Edwin Lutyens, the architect of this imperial city, that "in 2000 years there must be an Imperial Lutyens tradition in Indian architecture as there now clings a memory of Alexander."[7]

Nothing of that sort occurred. Lutyens was unimitated, his buildings and avenues, while used for other purposes today, are really empty reminders of the scope of the imperial dream. Modern empire generated no meaningful architectural styles, and few colonial administrators were at all versed in urban planning or supported by governments willing to make outlays necessary to ensure any variation of the City Beautiful. Yet the growth of the urban environment in the interwar period and the efforts to control it were of such an order that colonialism at the time may largely be considered an exercise in urbanization carried out in a predominantly rural setting.

The urban phenomenon that had changed the social pattern of European life in the middle of the nineteenth century started to do the same for the rest of the world one-half century later. The first great leap in urban population

The governor-general's palace at Dakar, illuminated for the visit of the
French president, Vincent Auriol, 1947. From the National Archives.

in that vast area today called the Third World occurred when the city became
the locus of European colonial power. The military and mining frontiers,
where European activities and personnel were grouped earlier, gave way to
the urban scene. That scene may not have been cluttered with Europeans, but
it was dominated by them. In the East Indies 80 percent of the Dutch lived
in urban areas in 1938; in French West Africa 33 percent of the Europeans
lived in nine urban agglomerations in 1931.[8] Their collective presence, more
than their individual numbers, stimulated urban growth. Old cities like Calcutta and Algiers expanded; new ports like Casablanca and Abidjan came into
existence. Primate cities like Singapore and Freetown dominated their hinterland, while new capitals like Rabat, New Delhi, and Lusaka reseated power
and influence. The tempo of these changes in cityscape was well-described
by Isak Dinesen when she made reference to the Kenyan city she frequently
visited. "Nairobi is a lively place, in movement like running water, and in
growth like a young thing, it changes from year to year."[9]

The city was the environment in which the transplanted culture and its participants flourished—or languished. Within the city, the business of empire was conducted. From it, administration radiated outward—both in command and personnel—to the hinterland. Toward it, the produce and labor of empire moved, arriving in railroad station, market place, or port. The city was the falsely dazzling location of all that was modern; in that condition it seemed to conflict with the countryside and to cause, in Africa, "detribalization," according to earlier anthropologists observing the setting.[10] Much of modern African fiction is a narrative of the movement of the young from the bush to the boulevard. Much of the current radical interpretation of modern imperialism is city-centered.

What distinguishes this newly imposed cultural context from the older, organic one is not the advent of cities, but the establishment of an urbanized social order. The "cradle of civilization" consisted of the city states of Mesopotamia and the city kingdoms of Egypt, areas later incorporated into European colonial empire. Timbuktu was a major city long before its "mysteries" were discovered by the Frenchman René Caille in the early nineteenth century. The Yoruba cities of Nigeria, of which Ibadan was the most important, date back several centuries. As if further historical evidence were needed, there is Bangkok, the primate city of Thailand, a country never officially colonized, which came into existence at the end of the eighteenth century and grew in significance before the British presence in Southeast Asia was felt. Even in those regions colonized during the first phase of European overseas expansion, the Americas, newly established cities had become integral parts of the regional culture by the nineteenth century and thus were distinct from their European counterparts: Montreal, Lima, and New Orleans, for instance.

It was the change, the new geographical tilt, in the rural-urban relationship that was the most noticeable factor in early twentieth-century colonial culture. Granted that the major and overwhelming urbanization of the world occurred after World War II, the tendency and the pattern were dramatically, perhaps inexorably, established in the first half of the century. Describing this phenomenon of urban growth, one analyst asserted that "existing urbanization appears to have begun under colonial interest and sponsorship."[11] Compared with the remarkable increase in the American urban population of the same period, that of the colonial world may not have been statistically impressive, but it was nevertheless significant—an augury of conditions to come, a prefatory statement of some of the most persistent problems left behind by the imperialists. The rhythm of urbanization is evident in Indian increases, where the rate of population growth in centers of 20,000 or more was nearly double that of all urban settlements in every decade since the first of the twentieth century.[12] In the Philippines, where Manila quickly emerged as the primate city, the increase in urban population jumped from 1.7 percent annually in the period from 1903 to 1918 to 5 percent annually from 1918 to 1939.[13] Even though the history of Africa until independence was characterized by what one author has clumsily labeled "non-urbanness,"[14] the urban effect on this vast continent of widely dispersed populations was also noticeable. According to a world demographic survey, the total percentage of African people living in large cities (100,000 and more) was 0.3 percent in 1880, 1.1 percent in 1900, and 5.2 percent in 1950.[15]

Of equal importance to the statistics, and a condition that they do not reveal, was the changing nature of urban employment and settlement. Where it existed before the European presence, as in Yorubaland, the Middle East, and India, the city had seldom dominated the countryside; it did not pull the surrounding resources into it or the population away from the land. Generally, the city served as a residential complex around which farming activities took place. Thus, in sharp contrast to the American rural pattern of homesteading, or its South African equivalent practiced by the Boers, most of the colonized portions of the world in their earlier established patterns had formed agrarian communities in which the village or the town was integrated as a place of residence, not as a social unit distinct from its surrounding environment. As late as 1877, for instance, about 57 percent of Cairo's working population was involved in farming. Yet by 1907 that portion of the population had fallen to 10 percent.[16] As these simple figures show, the economic structure of cities was changing, principally because urban life was enmeshed in the colonial system.

That system acquired one of its most easily determined and persistent forms in the new space economy of which the city was a unit. The symbiotic relationship that the precolonial city had so frequently formed with the countryside—and that the colonial city never acquired—was replaced by a network of transportation and communications in which the relationship of each city to other cities—its economic linkage—grew in importance. The graphic appearance of this system would resemble a molecular structure, with cities as nodes strung together by regional communications lines.

One of the most striking examples of the new colonial space economy was Malaya.[17] An unurbanized region before the British occupation in 1874, Malaya grew within one century to be among the world's regions with highest urban density. Its older, small-scaled village settlements withered as new colonially formed ones took shape. Its major city, Singapore, was really a British colonial creation of the early nineteenth century; its federal capital, Kuala Lumpur, began as a rough-hewn mining camp in the middle of the century and became a British-created administrative center by the end of the century. The urban clusters that came to characterize the Malayan countryside and have been described as "surface settlement" were all the result of an expanding mining frontier determined by the extraction of tin in a social environment remarkably like the American and South African "boom towns" in gold rush days.[18] This urban scene, first established in the state of Perak, was somewhat contrasted by later urban development in the state of Selangor, where large populations were concentrated in few urban centers—hence the descriptive term "point settlement"[19]—of which Singapore and Kuala Lumpur were the dominant.

The dimensions of this urban growth can easily be appreciated by a brief review of statistics for two urban centers. The mining village of Ipoh in Parak had a population of about 3,000 in 1891. That population reached 27,978 in 1911; 36,860 in 1921; and 53,183 in 1931.[20] Equally impressive in its ratio of increase was Kuala Lumpur in Selangor. Its population remained at about 2,000 throughout the 1870s, but rose to 25,000 in 1895, the year before it became the federal capital. By 1911, its population reached 46,718; by 1921, 80,424; by 1931, 111,418.[21]

The fundamental characteristics underlying Malayan urban development were replicated in most colonial regions. The colonial city was a commonplace. Focal point of regional agro-extractive industries, administrative capital of colony or federation, and ocean-fronted commercial center for international trade, the colonial city directly served European needs and only incidentally those of the inhabitants whose land felt the city's thrust.

The true colonial city, the locus of competing cultures, the place where goods flowed, labor headed, and Europeans stood transfixed in awe and disappointment, was the port. The port was the gateway of empire, the point where those imaginary shipping and naval lines converged with the real lines of railroads. Emblematically, the great arch of Bombay defined this function of gateway. Considering this particular arch, the Scottish physiologist and urbanist Patrick Geddes suggested that "each of the great ports between London and furthest Australia and New Zealand" be supplied with just such an arch.[22] His suggestion was not acted on, nor need it have been, for the port required no special definition.

Quayside was alive with activity when the passenger liner or mail steamer

Raffles Place—the heart of the business district,—in Singapore, 1936.
From the National Archives.

was nudged in. New troops, returning administrators, anxious businessmen, canned foods, motor cars, medical supplies—all were disgorged among the stevedores, taxi drivers, servants, porters, and beggars who were the underemployed and unappreciated of the colonial city. However, it was the mail that regulated the imperial system.

A British business house then had its main contact with head office through the weekly mail steamer, and its whole routine centered around the P & O mail days. It rose to a climax from Thursday morning, when the mail came in, till Friday evening when it was posted for the westbound mail boat on Saturday. After that business returned to its ordinary tempo, quickened occasionally by a cable, till the next Thursday rush.[23]

This account of interwar Bombay is in stark contrast with the reports submitted by the administrator for Dakar in the 1870s. On May 1, 1877, he wrote: "The natives are as usual, quiet and lazy. No commerce, no industry, no new residents."[24]

Dakar was not alone. The modern colonial port city, the one that provided the kaleidoscopic effect that has colored many novels and films of mystery and intrigue, was only well-defined at the turn of the century and in the early years of the twentieth century. As it grew to accommodate intensifying trade with its hinterland and to transship goods to a larger world regulated by Europe, the port city invariably became the primate city, the one that dominated the economy of the region and overshadowed any other urban complex. Singapore's rapid growth in the early twentieth century dramatically demonstrates this condition. With a population of 137,722 in 1881, the city grew to 226,842 in 1901, and increased to 418,358 in 1921.[25]

The antecedents of the port cities were the "factories" or trading centers, which had been scattered along the coasts where the European appeared over the course of the last several centuries. These small settlements were large neither in space nor in population, but they did appear in abundance. On the west coast of Africa, extending about 2,400 miles, there were approximately 150 of these as late as the nineteenth century.[26] Such entrepôts were seldom interconnected, and their economic influence seldom extended into the hinterland. What altered these conditions was the establishment of penetrating land transportation systems: first the railroad at the turn of the century; then the motor roads in the interwar period.[27]

As the colonial trade intensified and was more easily managed because of the new communication lines, the number of ports declined, and the size of those that remained increased impressively. However, the phenomenon was not simply local. It was part of the emerging global economic system, which witnessed the diversification of goods and the importation of primary materials by a Western world undergoing a new phase in its industrial revolution. Just as the Malayan centers grew with the tin mining industry, so did Hong Kong and Cairo grow with the establishment of the Suez Canal, Stanleyville with its role as railhead for the Belgian Congo, Saigon with the exportation of rice, and Aden on the southern tip of the Arabian peninsula as the spigot of the oil lines. The French novelist Paul Nizan saw it with his own eyes:

Not so long ago Aden was a coaling station. Oil brought with it offices, docks, the black tanks of the Anglo-Persian and Asiatic petroleum, and intrigues that arouse the emotions of little native potentates who have become sellers of oil and buyers of gasoline for automobiles. A little war for concessions is spreading all around.[28]

The construction of port facilities became a major colonial enterprise and

Singapore seen from the sea, 1936. From the National Archives.

expenditure in the early twentieth century. From the west coast of Africa to
the east coast of Australia, new wharves, warehouses, loading equipment,
and jetties were built, and harbor dredging was widely done. Lagos, hitherto
a port hampered by seasonally shifting sandbars, was converted into a deep
water, year-round port by the construction of two moles between 1907 and
1917. The Customs Wharf, originally 300 feet long, was extended another
344 feet by 1913.[29] Yet this wharf seemed small when compared to Victoria
Dock in Melbourne, which had been opened in 1893 and then enlarged in
1916 so that the central pier was 1,600 feet long and had 21 ship berths.[30]

Dakar, long a source of derisive commentary because of its sleepy commercial appearance, also became lively by the interwar period. A visitor to
the city at the end of the nineteenth century commented:

I have heard people say, "Dakar has really grown in the last ten years." What must it have been like before then. Take away the barracks, the maritime agency, the sheds of the Saint Louis railroad, and what is left? Two or three stores, cluttered bazaars where everything is sold, useful and trade items, marmalade and boots, parasols and accordians.[31]

With the improvement of port facilities at the beginning of the twentieth century, when the French government decided to make it a major Atlantic naval station as well as a commercial port, Dakar's economic tempo accelerated. By 1931, 803,000 tons of merchandise went through the port; by 1938 that figure had increased to 2,390,000 tons.[32] The population also grew:[33]

1914	22,833
1926	33,409
1932	69,102
1936	92,634

Such figures give no hint of the ethnic composition of this city. Like port cities around the world, it was heterogeneous, bringing together immigrants from a variety of backgrounds to perform the labor-intensive activities connected with the transshipment of goods. Unlike New York or Liverpool, however, a colonial port city like Dakar was in, but not of, the country. A later critic called Dakar a "foreign extrusion."[34] Perhaps the term might be generally applied; both in economic purpose and social structure the colonial city was initially forced out of the land, not cultivated within it. No doubt the Malayan mining towns were most unusual in their particular alien social composition. They were, quite simply, not Malayan. Rather, they consisted of a small European population in entrepreneurial capacities and a large number of Chinese performing as "coolies." Moreover, the Chinese so employed came from great distances and from an agrarian, not an urban, background, thus suggesting that theirs was a double adjustment to a foreign land and cultural environment.[35]

Few colonial cities were so unusual in their social makeup, but migration from long distances was a common characteristic, as was, therefore, a rude cosmopolitanism quite different from the precolonial environment. Only with independence did urbanization begin to be a more distinctly national process, marked by a considerable influx of neighboring, as opposed to distant, peoples. In the major Algerian cities, for instance, the dominant elements in the urban population had been French and Jewish. Arab migration altered this balance, not before, but after independence.[36]

Whatever their ethnic diversity, the populations of the colonial city did share a common quality in the early days of urban development: they were predominantly male and celibate. Both colonizer and colonized looked upon their stay in the city as a temporary one. Both were there primarily for the purpose of making sufficient money to return home, each anxious to re-assume a previous life-style but with a little more panache. The Chinese, more readily than any other foreign group, settled into the new urban ways, as they frequently used their savings to bring their families with them. How-ever, the Europeans assigned to the commercial houses located in West African cities were, in the late nineteenth century, very young men, generally between 18 and 20 years of age upon their arrival. They stayed only a few years. Even colonial administrators were like birds-of-passage, posted every two or four years to new locations. The exception to this general rule of social mobility was the Far East. The Dutch in Indonesia, the French in Indochina, and the English in India were longtime residents, primarily engaged in plan-tation or large-scale commercial activities. The French in Algeria, the Dutch-origin Boers in South Africa, and more recently the British in Kenya and the Italians in Libya were settlers in the full sense of the word. But, by and large, the European colonial population was in transit, doing a tour in an en-vironment that was generally viewed indifferently, when not hostilely.

There were modifications primarily introduced in the interwar period. The social pattern of European demography changed. Medical improvements, particularly the control of malaria and yellow fever, made life less precarious and, hence, the risk of family relocation less severe. The widespread distri-bution of canned or tinned foods and the increased quality of sanitation facilities—running water and enclosed sewage systems chief among them—meant that the amenities associated with the modern European city were to be found in some degree in the colonial city. Finally, the economic depres-sion of the 1930s inhibited travel between colony and metropolitan country so that the health leave or annual vacation declined in practice. All of these factors contributed to new family residency patterns in the colonial city. More women and children arrived, a social condition that particularly altered the colonial city in Subsaharan Africa. Its rudimentary nature was trans-formed; those cultural attributes captured in the word "urbanity" began to appear: theaters and movie houses, shops and good restaurants, suburbs and villas.[37] As the African chronicler Isak Dinesen said of interwar Nairobi, " . . . big hotels grew up, great impressive agricultural shows and fine flower shows were held, our Quasi Smart Set of the Colony from time to time enlivened the town with rows of quick melodrama."[38]

Seldom did the colonized peoples enter this special domain of the colonizer other than in the capacity of domestics. But they did respond to the urban environment for a number of reasons, all nicely summarized by the phrase "push-pull." The "push" was the result of the disruption of traditional agrarian patterns. Forced or crowded off the land because of new European land-uses, such as the plantation, segments of the rural population moved toward the city, which absorbed them, if it did not gainfully employ them.[39] Others still, probably more numerous, went to the city to gain the wages necessary to pay newly imposed money taxes.   ·

Most critics think, however, that the "pull" element was much stronger than the "push." It is the "bright light" theory that—even by its very name—neatly explains all. The novelist Chinua Achebe best allows the outsider to witness this urban appeal by having one of his characters in *No Longer At Ease* describe Lagos:

There is no darkness there because at night the light shines like the sun, and people are always walking about, that is, those who want to walk. If you don't want to walk you only have to wave your hand and a pleasure car stops for you.[40]

Achebe wrote these words in 1960, but well before then the "pull" of the city as a magnet of new opportunities and attractions, as the source of advancement in the colonial economy, brought the young inward.

Such an influx was never successfully absorbed. It might have appeared outwardly that the colonial city was a center of growth; it was more accurately a place of stagnation for the many who lived in "shared poverty," not comfort.[41] By a process of social fragmentation in which more people did less work individually, the new arrivals were shabbily integrated into the system, or, more accurately, into one aspect of the system. The colonial urban system has been defined as dualistic. A bazaarlike economy was juxtaposed with a firmlike economy.[42] The former was labor-intensive, capable of absorbing, by way of seemingly infinite division of labor, large numbers of individuals. Like a chain, this economy was stretched by adding new human links.[43] The bazaarlike economy was small-scale in operation, its stock limited in variety and quantity, its principle of success being one of rapid turnover. Centered in the marketplace, or stretched out along the curb of the street, this indigenous sector of the urban economy included hawkers of fruits and vegetables, vendors of sandals, enamel pots, shoelaces, combs, and mirrors, and merchants displaying cooked meats and vermicelli.

The firmlike economy was generally European-directed, with management handled by individuals from abroad and general policy established there. Members of the indigenous population working in the firm served in subordinate capacities, usually as clerks, with little authority or room for initiative. Describing the functions of his first day in Unilever of Bombay, an Indian commented:

The clerks were all men: South Indians, if they were stenographers, Christians and Parsis, if they did general work. . . . The younger Europeans wore all whites, the seniors usually palm beach in light shades. The clerks wore anything that went as shirt and trousers. . . . At eleven the sahibs had their tea. The office boys, who were called sepoys because their forerunners were soldiers who guarded the East India Company offices, and who still wore some kind of uniform, took tea on trays to the managers.[44]

The new occupational distribution ratios in the colonial territories were marked by the importance of the city. The highest percentage of the population still worked in the primary sector, of which traditional agriculture was the most important activity. The smallest percentage (seldom over 20 percent) was employed in the secondary sector, where the mining industries were predominant, followed by other industrial development, such as Indian steel. Most telling was the increase in the tertiary sector, now the second most important location of employment (sometimes as high as 40 percent), with the greatest concentration of individuals found in the commerce of the great port cities. Singapore's unique role as international entrepôt is reflected in its occupational ratios: 66.6 percent of the population was gainfully employed in the tertiary sector in 1921.[45]

Such an analysis should not be allowed to provide a false arithmetic cover: the urban centers were heavily populated with the unemployed and the underemployed, this urban mass haphazardly gathered in congested areas. The most serious and insufficiently attended problem in the colonial city was the slum. The term was European, but it was widely applied to those densely populated sections in which, at best, housing was flimsy and sanitary conditions barely adequate. A special housing committee, investigating the urban condition of Madras, India, in 1933, defined slums as "hutting areas with squalid surroundings."[46] The suggestion was that of the wretched placement of traditional housing forms in an ill-prepared urban site. However, even where housing was more suited to the urban environment, it was regularly

Tunisian merchants during the interwar period. From the National Archives.

overcrowded by the constantly incoming population, which imposed on relatives and countrymen who had earlier arrived. In interwar Singapore it was not unusual to find ten families living in a dwelling designed to accommodate one.[47] The situation was repeated elsewhere. In Dakar, Africans had constructed some 285 houses of brick between the years 1903 and 1908. Yet these buildings did not enhance the quality of life as they had been intended to. "Many of these durable homes are badly maintained," wrote a French critic, "because they are transformed into interloping hotels where the floating population of blacks, drawn to the city in hope of finding work, are squeezed during the night."[48]

Beyond this core congestion spread the peripheral slums. The growing unavailability of center city property—land speculation was a major problem in most colonial cities—along with the "infilling" of courtyards and alleys with barracks and shanties denied the new migrants space in which to locate. The result was the encircling shantytown, what the French called the *bidonville*, a haphazard housing development raggedly made of cartons and cans, pieces of corrugated iron, old siding, and any other object that might be forced to serve temporarily as a chunk of wall or a piece of roof. In North Africa bidonvilles became an integral, and unwanted, feature of the city-scape. Algiers, Casablanca, and Cairo were marred by them. In Tripoli, the bidonvilles formed a semi-circle between one-half and two-and-one half miles from the city center and stood as a dreadful contrast to the Italian portion of the city, elegantly wrought soon after World War I.[49]

Whether shantytown, bidonville, bustee (the Indian term), or *ciudad perdida* (the "lost city" outside of contemporary Mexico City), the new urban slum grew as swiftly as the city and explains that otherwise curious condition, "urban involution," whereby the city seems to absorb a greater population than it can possibly sustain.

The obvious sanitary problems generated by such overcrowding were badly aggravated by other environmental factors. The most expected was what had been called "the contagious disease" by the British in Malaya.[50] Fire ravaged the poorly and flimsily constructed portions of the colonial city with frightening regularity. In Lagos alone approximately 40 major fires broke out between 1859 and 1882.[51] In Malaya in 1893, three major urban concentrations were victims of fire.[52] The severe fire hazard soon led to the introduction of more solid building materials. Brick was used widely. Brick kilns were established in Dakar and Lagos by the middle of the century, and Kuala Lumpur alone had 15 such kilns by 1884.[53] In 1901 the colonial government in Hanoi began offering financial advances to Indochinese who would build their homes of brick and roof them with tile.[54] Roofing material had hitherto been a major fire hazard. In Ibadan the substitution of iron for thatch was a major improvement, initiated by missionaries in 1854.[55]

Modern building materials appeared in the colonial city just about as quickly as they did in the European metropolis. The farsighted French minister of war, whose department then had the responsibility for the ad-ministration of Algeria, recommended in 1849 that iron be employed in place of wood as a basic structural material. His research showed, he stated, that the new material would even be cheaper.[56] After a major fire in Kingston, Jamaica, two British architects developed plans for rebuilding the city, plans that included the use of reinforced concrete for public buildings. The project was impressive enough to be displayed at the 1909 Town Planning Exhibition in London.[57]

Fire was not the worst scourge of the colonial city, however, nor did the possibilities of new building materials occupy official attention regularly. Disease was; disease did. Smallpox, malaria, and typhoid epidemics were nearly commonplace. Most appalling and dramatically moving was the third great wave of bubonic plague that afflicted the colonial world in the late nineteenth century. Begun in China, this ancient urban disease—described by the Greek physician Galen and memorable in European history as the "Black Death" of the fourteenth century—worked its way through the colonial empires at the turn of the century as it followed the maritime routes established by the European powers. Hong Kong suffered from it badly in 1894, Bombay in 1896. The Portuguese towns of Lappa and Macao succumbed to it in 1897; Sydney, Adelaide, and Melbourne did likewise in 1900. In 1901 the disease severely affected Cape Town and Port Elizabeth in South Africa. It reached Morocco in early 1914 and was transported to Dakar shortly thereafter.[58]

The mortality rates were high, the fears commensurate. In Bombay during the four-year period from 1896 to 1899, there were 51,840 cases of plague and 46,023 deaths, for a mortality rate of 85.4 percent. In Dakar in 1914, where the proportions were just as appalling, the statistics added up to a grim total of 1,391 deaths from the disease in a population of about 26,000. However, the disaster had more than medical implications; it became the source of racial segregation.[59] In Port Elizabeth and Cape Town, where there was a long-standing desire to isolate the African population, the plague offered the justification for the removal of thousands of Africans, although this measure turned out to be only temporary. In Dakar the matter was somewhat more complicated and, indeed, the results more enduring. The plague hit that city just after a bitter political campaign in which the first black African deputy, Blaise Diagne, had been elected. As officials moved to the relocation of the African population, Diagne and others saw the move as vindictive and accordingly protested. Strikes and other forms of civil disturbance occurred, causing the French colonial administration to be fearful. The turbulence was controlled, nevertheless, and the population was relocated to a new quarter named the "Medina" in 1916.

Elsewhere, remedial action was not so dramatic in effect, but, perhaps, equally effective in hygienic benefits. Housing and residential patterns were widely modified, with the detached house with ample space between its neighbors now widely recommended.[60] In the new extension of Bangalore, India, "Frazertown," stone foundations and stone or tiled floors were introduced as standard in construction methods. In Indonesia, the medical budget was suddenly increased greatly, from 3.4 million florins in 1910 to 11.1 million florins in 1915.[61]

However health-providing these activities may have been, they were frequently informed by strong cultural and social biases. The "sanitation syndrome" worked to encourage or reinforce the general European desire to put distance between colonizer and colonized.[62] Treating the indigenous population as if it were particularly susceptible to disease because it was less heedful of proper health standards, hinting that this population did not require the treatment that the white man did because it was less advanced, European colonial administrators and medical officers assumed a condescending attitude toward African and Asian that was remarkably similar to that which the upper classes and their medical physicians assumed toward the urban poor. George Bernard Shaw satirized this attitude in his play *Pygmalion*. The aristocratic pastime of "slumming" resembled the later tourist's behavior of photographing the "natives."

To stand above and apart from daily commerce with the indigenous populations became a medical recommendation as well as a social posture that most Europeans assumed. Urbanists frequently suggested putting "green space" between the European and native sectors of the colonial city in part to serve imagined health needs, these being derivative elements of the popular nineteenth-century assumption that diseases were most commonly communicated "aerially," an assumption fixed in the word "malaria," or "bad air."[63] Belgian planners in Leopoldville and Elizabethville in the Congo placed the indigenous quarter of these new cities 500 meters from the European so that the new residential location would not be a "foyer of possible epidemics."[64] Similar medical considerations led to the establishment of the famous Indian "hill stations," those retreats well above sea level and far away from "noxious" air and summer heat.

These medical considerations blended in nicely with other cultural assumptions, of which the new interest in comparative anthropology was the most obvious. Just as "native policy" was now characterized by the indirect approach that left the colonized the facade and trappings of their political system, so urbanists were now disinclined toward imposing European grid systems on the seemingly helter-skelter pattern of indigenous urban quarters. No one was better intentioned and perhaps unwisely romantic in this matter than Hubert Lyautey, the first resident general in Morocco. That he considered "native policy" and urbanism his two chief interests helps explain his impact on Moroccan urban development in the early twentieth century.[65]

Lyautey was enamored of Islamic culture, notably its artistic characteristics. He appreciated the craftsmanship, the timelessness of the styles, the remarkable blend of artifact and environment. He sought to rehabilitate local crafts that had fallen into desuetude, and he was careful to respect what stood from the past.[66] His charge to his team of architects and urbanists was the need to separate the European from the indigenous sectors, in effect to juxtapose two distinct cities. His two basic principles, as summarized by Jacques Marrast, an architect on his staff, were: "1) respect for the artistic and social integrity of the old cities; 2) application of the most modern rules of urbanism to the new cities."[67] This two-city approach, applauded at the time, would soon be denounced.[68] Such a "nativist" appreciation of what existed might be seen as culturally racist, leading to the denial of modern advances in technology and urban design to a people who needed them as much as any other. In defending Lyautey against such an accusation, Marrast said that it was out of respect for cultural differences and not for "any motives of racial segregation" that this policy was established. The local populations, he continued, "were free to live in the new cities if they were tempted by the European style of life."[69]

This was easier said than done. Even though the French, unlike the Boers in South Africa, practiced no officially sanctioned policy of racial segregation, movement into the European residential citadel here, as anywhere else in any colonial empire, was not easy. Few Africans or Asians were financially able to build or buy there; few were engaged in those professions that made social contact easy or desirable. It is a small irony of imperialism that there were better relationships between colonizer and colonized in the European countries than in the colonial regions. That this was so is directly attributable to the "enclave mentality" of Europeans abroad. As one British urbanist wrote in 1925: "The European may live for years at a place and never once visit the Indian city, endeavouring as far as possible to ignore its existence, if he is not concerned with it in some official capacity."[70] This comment makes reference to the most well-known example of de facto segregation, that which had been practiced in Anglo-India.

Whether in a metropolitan center, a "civil station," or a military "cantonment," the English who were on the subcontinent usually sought to deny the local environment as much as possible and to recreate the home one as completely as possible. The sentimental tales found in diaries and reminiscences about the importation of flower seeds and their forced growth in flower pots are obvious examples of transplanted domesticity. Spatial patterns of European residency were frequently out of keeping with the local environment as well, as the following commentary on the cantonment suggests:

Every European likes to isolate himself in a large compound so as to secure privacy, but such large compounds are far too extensive for cultivation of gardens; at their best they simulate a park, at their worst a desert.[71]

The most exclusionary colonial institution, and yet also the most British, was the club. Subject to later critical analysis and derision, the club was the foundation of the British urban existence in the colonies. Or as George Orwell described it in *Burmese Days*, "The European club is the spiritual citadel, the real seat of British power."[72] However exaggerated Orwell's assessment may have been—it actually was cynical—the club was the center of entertainment and social life; it was the place to be seen, the place to be counted, the place to gossip and to drink, to carp and to complain, to recall and to forget. Membership in the club was seldom casual; it was rather an act of imperial citizenship. "It was considered obligatory to join," one Englishman said of his interwar experiences.[73] Another asserted that "I regard it as a duty to go to the club at least every other night."[74]

Such clubs were notoriously discriminatory. Few Indians were ever offered membership in them, a fact that aggravated the debate over racial discrimination in the interwar era when Indianization of the civil service increased. The debate "almost split the Empire," one contemporary melodramatically stated.[75] However, as with most colonial debates, this one went no further. Both empire and club survived until after World War II.

Thus, like a tableau at some patriotic pageant of the time, the verandah of the club remained traditionally arranged with wicker furniture and white-clad people holding glasses in their hands. The rest of the urban scene was not so fixed, however. The layout of the colonial city was being scrutinized and reworked, at least by those individuals, both within and without the colonial service, who saw the imperative need for colonial planning.

Wherever and whenever such planning occurred before the twentieth century, it was most unusual, the inspiration of a gifted colonial administrator or a determined sanitation engineer. Generally, the invisible hand of commerce and the heavy hand of the military had arranged—or disarranged—the city site. Only in the older settlement colonies, where towns were dominated by European residency, did a semblance of urban style and grace appear. Vancouver and Capetown, Point à Pitre in Guadeloupe and Willemsted in Curaçao proved that human needs and natural settings could be harmonized in a colonial environment. These settled places, however, stood apart from the newer urban centers, which were initially characterized by the haphazard growth of the "boom town." Here, the lack of well-defined ordinances on building, the scarcity of qualified architects in colonial service, the absence of a citizenry concerned with urban amenities, and the obvious precedence that "pacification" took in colonial thinking ensured little more than urban mediocrity. What Cecil Rhodes defined as the "Doctrine of Ransom," which proposed that those who defiled the earth by extracting its wealth should provide compensation through subsequent beautification, was not widely followed.[76]

Nor was the doctrine ignored only in the colonial world. Urban blight spread widely as a characteristic of industrialization, with Coketowns in the Western world more real in fact than realistic in the fiction of Charles Dickens. That magnificent seat of empire, London, was infamous for its slums long before Admiralty Arch was constructed to glorify a monarchy whose sceptered power reached far east of Suez. Urban planning was an exceptional practice before the end of the nineteenth century. Then, German and Austrian interest in urban form quickly developed and was extended by the town planning movement in Great Britain, which influenced the colonial world as quickly as it did at home.

The London Planning Act was passed in 1909, and the first French omnibus town planning act was written into law in 1919. It is worth noting that this latter act was actually inspired by regulations earlier imposed in Morocco. There, a Central Service for City Planning had been established in 1914, which was only a short time before similar colonial regulations and institutions appeared elsewhere. A Town Planning Act was approved for Bombay in 1915; in the same year a Town Planning Board was established in Nova Scotia, followed by similar developments in other Canadian provinces. In the 1920s such acts and agencies were frequent:

> South Australia: Town Planning and Development Act, 1920
> Federated Malay States: Town Planning Act, 1923
> Madagascar: Higher Council of Urbanism, 1926
> Singapore: Town Planning Ordinance, 1928
> Northern Rhodesia: Town Planning Act, 1929

There were other activities throughout the interwar period: special commissions, individual city plans, new ordinances, architects and urbanists individually sent on investigative missions, even a special congress on colonial urbanism held in conjunction with the International Colonial Exposition in 1931.

No person more energetically championed the cause of colonial urban development than Patrick Geddes, who drew up 15 plans for 30 cities in India and Ceylon during the period of 1914 to 1920.[77] His overseas career began when the governor of Madras invited him "to enlighten municipal authorities and others in India upon the subject of town planning."[78] He did so in his detailed reports, which addressed every conceivable aspect of city development. Geddes came to his calling from a career as a physiologist. It was this indomitable and imaginative Scot who created the first major philosophy of modern urbanism.

As he assessed urban problems in India, Geddes urged careful planning, a "diagnostic survey" that would follow the lines of a city's previous growth to determine the best directions for its future thrust.[79] He wished a fusion of old and new, with both understanding and respect given to indigenous culture through "folk planning," the careful consideration of where and how to locate rural people in an urban environment.[80] His sympathetic attitude was such that "he had natives come to him and talk pure Geddesism, which seemed to suggest that his ideas had not been too far removed from their comprehension."[81]

A further penetration of the older precincts of colonial thought with new planning ideas occurred on July 14, 1930, when Professor Raymond Unwin, one of the leading figures in the British Town Planning Institute, wrote the secretary of state for colonies, Lord Passfield (the Fabian Socialist Sidney Webb), the following note:

Would it be possible for you, while at the Colonial Office, to give a little encouragement to the greater use of town and regional planning as a guide in the development of territories, where such guidance may be most effective? . . . That the town planning Department as a newcomer should be regarded by the Resident Commissioners as a Cinderella of the Services is not surprising. . . . I think some advice as to the proper function of town or regional planning, and the proper time for consulting any planning officer available does seem to be needed.[82]

Lord Passfield responded by sending a circular to all colonial administrators requesting that "you give your sympathetic consideration to this subject."[83]

More than sympathy was needed and some regions of the colonial world did get more. A few of the new planners saw their overseas domains as open, untried environments where "the sun and natural riches work in conjunction" to allow bold urban development.[84]

The political climate as well made the challenge appealing. There were no municipal councils or special interest groups that might complain about urban reform or restrict it. The interests of the resident populations could be largely ignored because the "rights of conquest" prevailed. Furthermore, the interests of the national government were removed by hundreds, even thousands of miles of ocean voyage and, hence, of scrutiny. It has, for instance, been said of Lyautey that "he was perhaps of all the great leaders of the world the most obvious holder of absolute power . . . " from 1914 to 1916, when France was obviously concerned with more pressing needs on the western front.[85]

Openness of environment and freedom from restraint did not mean that the opportunity for the construction of the ideal city was readily at hand. Some new major urban centers were created, and more old cities were reworked or provided with new extensions, but most urban sites remained without either a well-articulated plan for development or the individuals needed for such development.

The exceptions may prove the rule; they also added a dramatic setting to more mundane colonial activity. Their number was not small. The American Daniel Burnham, chief architect of the World's Columbian Exposition of 1893, designed the new Philippine summer capital at Bagiuo in 1905. S. D. Adshead, professor of town planning at the University of London, was commissioned in 1930 to design the new capital of Lusaka in Northern Rhodesia. On a lesser scale, but with impressive results, the new government buildings of Pretoria were decked out in an obviously imperialist architectural idiom by the English architect Herbert Baker shortly after the Boer War. Total planning, in the manner defined by the British "Town Planning" school of thought, was anticipated for Heliopolis, a suburb north of Cairo, initiated by the Belgian industrialist Baron Empain in 1905. Not colonial, and certainly not imperial, but yet a part of the British empire, was the new capital of Australia, Canberra. The designs for this city were derived from an international competition, which was won by the Chicago architect Walter Burley Griffin in 1912. Griffin recognized that this was "the greatest opportunity the world has offered for the expression of the great democratic civic ideal."[86]

The greatest opportunity the world then offered for the expression of the imperial ideal was New Delhi. No city began with more theatricality. On December 11, 1911, the king-emperor George V suddenly announced during his coronation trip to India that the capital of British India would be relocated from Calcutta to Delhi. "Seven Delhis had come and gone," declared a contemporary observer who was also a member of the city's first planning commission. "At his command [the king's] an eighth was to rise, the creation of the British Raj."[87]

The political reasons for the new city have been variously discussed, but there is no doubt that George V, the one truly imperialistic monarch in recent British history, was anxious that imperial authority "move in a setting of proper magnificence and that in India the temporal power shall be hedged with the divinity of earthly splendour"—these words of a sympathetic architectural critic.[88]

New Delhi was a grandly planned city, even though its execution was first impeded by the war and then made hesitant by British imperial reform and growing Indian nationalism, both of which threw into question an enterprise of these proportions. Placed on Raisina Ridge and initially planned to encompass ten square miles—the size of the original Washington, D.C.—the new city was sited along two large roads, both of which led to Indian historic sites and formed a 60-degree angle that provided "the geometrical key" to the design worked out by Edwin Lutyens.[89] It was the layout, with its spaciousness, its well-sited large buildings—in brief, its monumentality—that commended the city.

There was little that was original or unusual in the buildings themselves, and they have therefore been the subject of as much criticism as praise. That they were magnificent in scale no one has ever questioned. That they ignored local architectural idioms is a fact that immediately aroused expressions of disappointment and anger. But Lutyens, who designed Viceroy House, and Herbert Baker, whom he hired to design the twin secretariat buildings that stood on either side of it but at a distance, were imbued with the European classical tradition or, in the harsh words of one critic, they followed "a couple of worn-out European examples."[90]

Lutyens was definitely without much sympathy for Indian architecture. "But India has never had any real architecture," he announced, "and if you may not graft the West out here, she never will have any."[91] Still, he did add Indian elements to Viceroy House so that it resembled, or so someone said, a vast bungalow.[92] Of course it was no bungalow in ideological purpose.

Viceroy House was a grand palace designed to be the focal point and the emblem of the raj's power. The two-mile-long ceremonial roadway, Kingsway, reached its culmination in the great dome of the house and the two thrones that were situated directly below it. The effect has been favorably described:

Viceroy House, New Delhi, India, 1931. From the National Archives.

The climax, the shout of the Imperial suggestion is the dome, reared blind and sudden from the middle of the house. . . . Not a window nor a door, not a hint of utilitarianism, interpolates upon the monumental affirmation of temporal power.[93]

Lutyens's architectural vision was abstract, geometric, above the mundane and the masses who trafficked in it.[94] He created for a patron who thought in metaphysical, quasi-sacred terms when imperial matters were discussed. His king-emperor and the viceroys who represented that power still antici- pated a duration of British rule that might have justified a modern variant on Imperial Rome. But hardly had the new buildings been completed before the times had changed. The then-current viceroy, Lord Irwin, was seen confer- ring with Mohandas Gandhi in Viceroy House in 1931. The modest garb, the near nakedness of Gandhi's form, contrasted with the building's imperial adornments. Yet Lord Irwin said that Viceroy House was a "liveable-in" house,[95] a statement that Lutyens probably did not consider when he laid out the 40-foot master bedroom.

    If the British seemed determined to outdo the French by building an of- ficial residence larger than the Palace of Versailles, the French did not bother to repeat their regal tradition in the one major capital they designed. Rabat, a result of the genius of the soldier-urbanist Hubert Lyautey and the architect-urbanist Henri Prost, was a thoroughly modern city, an exercise in cultural appreciation, academic restraint, and environmental consideration.

As the French administrative capital, Rabat was situated primarily for geographical reasons. It was midpoint between Agadir and Ouidjah, where the major "pacification" efforts were then taking place. Moreover, it was sufficiently removed from the frenetic development of Casablanca not to be enveloped by it.[96] Sentiment also entered the picture. Lyautey had been taken by the "poetry of the place," when he had first seen it in 1907. His team of experts were enthralled by the town villages of Rabat and Salé, their buildings appearing as white, cubelike gems brilliantly illuminated by the Mediterranean sunlight.[97]

Under Prost's direction an urban plan was drawn up for Rabat. The original conception was to form the city along a single, monumental axis that would "go from the main gate of the native village to the doorway of the Resident General"[98] and thereby seemingly serve as a statement of French colonial policy as much as of French urban design. At midpoint in this route the central railroad station would be located, but placed underground. Beyond the city itself the route would continue to the new airport, servicing planes outbound from Toulouse. Although a secondary transaxial road, the main coastal one, was later built, the monumental one provided the elegance and architectural thrust that Prost had anticipated.[99]

Of major importance was the administrative effort to control the appearance of the city. Initially all of the architects, and Lyautey himself, had been fascinated by the Hispano-Moorish traditions and therefore cast the public buildings, the residence included, in a modification of that style. These were later criticized as too heavily romanticized, but they do well represent Lyautey's desire to respect the local artistic tradition and to enhance it by working it into different and modern uses. Somewhat later, in 1924, an official regulation, or *dahir*, required that all buildings fronting on public routes or appearing around public squares would have to be submitted for architectural review and approval. Most critics consider this legislation to have been beneficial, not restraining, to the urban development of Morocco.[100] Certainly it helped prevent shabby construction and the pastiche of Dakar's cityscape. Moreover, it ensured the simplicity and honesty of line that was so characteristic of modern architecture.

Rabat, among all of the cities in Morocco developed by the French, ac-

View of the French residence and garden in Rabat, Morocco, 1927.
From the National Archives.

quired an appearance that seemed consonant with the modern principles only
recently enunciated in Europe. "Unity, simplicity, purity, these are the three
terms in the new French architectural formula in Morocco," remarked one
of the French colonial urbanists.[101]

Prost had left Morocco and Rabat long before the commendation of the
new urban style was made. The individuals responsible for this architectural
evolution were part of his team, however. It may therefore be correct to assert, as one of Prost's colleagues did, that "Prost opened the era of contemporary French urbanism."[102]

If he did, it was Le Corbusier who dominated that era.[103] Born Edouard
Jeanneret in Switzerland, Le Corbusier had made his mark as an intellectual,
if not a practicing architect, with his urbanist manifesto, *Towards A New
Architecture*, published in 1923. The work was characterized by comparisons
between modern machinery, oceanliners, and airplanes and outdated architectural practices. Le Corbusier insisted that "henceforth the problem is in

the hands of the technical expert,''[104] a declaration he respected when he was called to Algiers to advise the city on future urban development. He drew up seven plans for the city between 1931 and 1942. With the first of these, rather melodramatically entitled *Project Obus*, he shattered past thought on African urbanization and caused the mayor of Algiers, his sponsor, to remark, ''But these are designs for the next century.''[105]

Le Corbusier planned boldly. His original design called for a *cité de'affaires* and a *cité de résidence*, separate in location but joined by an elevated roadway which presaged the contemporary freeway. The *cité d'affaires* introduced the monolithic skyscraper to French Africa, while the *cité de résidence* consisted of curved structures described by an architectural historian as ''having the 'organic' qualities of the Crescents of Bath.''[106] Le Corbusier later told a group of students that what he was attempting to do was to relate architecture to its natural site. But he was also experimenting with the immense technological advantages now available to the imaginative architect; these he put on paper in the form of ribbon-like roadways skirting the sea and supported by a continuous apartment complex several miles in length. Through its several mutations Le Corbusier's plans had sketches of buildings that retained their striking, original characteristics. These were grandly scaled slabs, models of the curtain wall skyscrapers and high-rise residential complexes familiar to any city today.

The real possibilities for new urban form through the combination of reinforced concrete as a building material with technocratic planning as a *desideratum* were first demonstrated by Le Corbusier in his plans for a new city called Nemours, Algeria, which he put on paper in 1934.[107] There, an impressive administrative complex would face the sea, while a set of 17 apartment buildings, similar to that later realized in his famous *Cité radieuse* erected in Marseilles after World War II, would house the population. Nothing came of Le Corbusier's grand Algerian designs, but they remain statements of what might have been if empire had continued its course.

This brief tale of several cities was contrived to suggest some of the bolder steps taken in colonial architecture and urbanism. The more tried and successful planning of the interwar era was predicated on compromise, on embellishment of what was in place, and on an effort toward correspondence between the old and the new.

Perhaps the key term and concept in colonial urban thought and practice of the interwar era was ''garden city,'' modifications of which appeared on the maps of every colonial power. The new capitals of Rabat, New Delhi,

Lusaka, and Canberra had, on more than one occasion, been called "garden cities" or cities that responded to "garden city" principles. New sections of other cities, such as Cairo, Tananarive, Semarang, and Dalat, were called "garden villages" or "garden cities." Older cities like Colombo and Madras were belatedly labeled "garden cities." The profusion of plans and appellations led one critic to exclaim in 1933: "The term 'Garden City' has been applied, even more abroad than at home, to enterprises which are not in accord with the full principle."[108]

There was no full principle, however, but a collection of ideas and concepts, all of which can be traced back to the seminal work of Ebenezeer Howard, *Tomorrow, A Peaceful Path to Real Reform*, first published in 1899. The book suggested a reworking of the urban situation by taking the city to the country. Howard wished to create new communities in the rural areas of England that would offer a "third alternative," harmonizing the other two social alternatives: the urban and the rural ways of life.[109] He envisioned a carefully planned model community, radial in form, restricted in size, and verdant in appearance. From its central core, which would be a central park of 145 acres and the setting for communal services, "six magnificent boulevards—each 120 feet wide" would radiate outward until they ended at circumferential agricultural land that would serve as a buffer against the encroachment of other cities. Space within the city would be ample enough to accommodate "garden-surrounded homes" and to ensure, even with continuing growth, "the free gifts of nature—fresh air, sunlight, breathing room and playing room."[110]

It would be difficult to estimate how many of the colonial urbanists who labeled their blueprints with the words "garden city" had seriously considered Howard's work and the tone of social reform in which it was expressed. But the aesthetic principles had great appeal: the wide boulevards, the "garden-surrounded houses," the tree-lined streets, and the general spaciousness were in contrast to the crowded and sinuous streets of the "native city."

Most of all, Howard's concept of the "third alternative" must have been very attractive because, if slightly reworked, it suggested a means of harmonizing African and Asian reality with European ideals, the two joined or separated—this depending on one's angle of vision—by green space.

Where it was directed to the perceived needs of the indigenous populations, the concept seemed the means of allowing for easy and effective adaptation or continuation of urban development along lines that were consonant with local culture. Thus, plans for the regional development of Tananarive, Madagascar, drawn up in the 1920s, called for the creation of "garden cities" for the Europeans and "garden villages" for the Malagasy, with this arrangement seen as consistent with the "ruralism" that the French administrators considered an essential part of their "native policy" on the island.[111] In his report on town planning for Colombo, presented in 1920, Patrick Geddes remarked:

Here in Colombo people seemed to preserve their rural spirit, and to express this in a love of gardens and flowers . . . and for that, Colombo cannot be too carefully guarded as 'The Garden City of the East' so that the ever-dominant influences of the capital may here, better than elsewhere, preserve the rural spirit.[112]

More, perhaps, than in the national background of any other colonial power, the English ideal of the countryside with its small hamlets added a romantic and somewhat utopian aspect to modern town planning. As one urban historian has written, "The English ideal remained the village."[113] The French economist Charles Gide would not have disagreed, for he attributed to John Ruskin the origin of the garden city ideal, with its emphasis on man in harmony with and hence enhancing the value of nature.[114] It was the imperial architect Herbert Baker who most clearly recognized Ruskin's influence, particularly on Cecil Rhodes. In his biography of Rhodes, Baker wrote that Ruskin thought the beauty of a natural site would diminish if it were not enhanced by villages, fields, and other human additions.[115] Claiming for Rhodes the titles of architect and urbanist, Baker praised him for this particular vision of the South African landscape and the reverence he showed the old Dutch farmhouses that dotted it.[116] In a slightly different context, he stated that Rhodes was "in advance of his age in the art of garden cities in South Africa," as evidenced by the layout of the mining village he had constructed at Kimberley.[117]

Whether conscious or not, there was a direct correlation between the concerns that upholders of the English garden city movement had for the worker and the colonial urbanist's concern with the indigenous population. The issue was derived from the broader one that occupied late Victorian reformers: how to provide the urban poor with decent housing and satisfactory health conditions. One author, who might have been writing of Manchester, said of India that "Garden Suburbs offer the best remedy for the housing of the industrial poor."[118] As a means of combating the plague, of ensuring "the perflation of air," and of generally enhancing the well-being of the indigenous population, the garden city or its derivatives was happily recommended. In the 1930s when the British were seriously disturbed by the increasing slums in Lagos, the "Yaba Estate" was established, some 700 acres of land "acquired by the government for the purpose of making a 'garden suburb' to which it was hoped that some of the congested population of the slums on the Island of Lagos could be persuaded to move."[119]

For all the discussion of the practical benefits of the garden city approach to planning, no colonial realization succeeded in achieving what Ebenezeer Howard considered a major benefit: the use of green space for agricultural and recreational purposes. Patrick Geddes had seen the garden city ideal as one that matched the rural emphasis dominant in India and Southeast Asia; he hoped that land surrounding individual residences would indeed be gardens with "agricultural productivity." He found, however, that the "garden villages" were merely "urban suburbs."[120] As for recreational benefits, they too were few, if they existed at all. The English architect H. V. Lanchester had planned a green belt for Madras in 1916 that would provide small parks "needed in order to provide playgrounds near the homes of the people."[121] Such provisions were principally made on paper, not on the surfaces of the developing colonial cities.

Seldom did the garden city concept actually get translated into benefits for the indigenous community, but it enhanced the residential situation of the Europeans and most strikingly embellished the improvements made in public space. New Delhi, for instance, was described as a garden city—and Lutyens himself had considered it such.[122] One of the original members of the planning commission for the city depicted it in 1930 as "a sea of foliage" out of which the grand governmental buildings arose.[123] A more recent appraisal offers a similar assessment: "The geometry of hexagons is blurred by the continuity of the landscape which forms a blanket of green over the city."[124] This verdure and the architectural forms it enclosed did not extend beyond the imperial city.

Just as the desire for social reform, which had driven Howard to the realization of his plan for the first garden city, disappeared in the intentions of most garden city planners in interwar Europe, so did it disappear in the colonial world of the same time. The green-enrobed villa, not the garden-surrounded bungalow or hut, became both the ideal and the reality. Thus, the new garden cities of Sumatra were described as consisting of "villas encircled by their green gardens, constructed along wide avenues whose magnificent trees enhance the impression of beauty."[125] Rabat was described as a garden city also, primarily because its many private villas were "drowned in greenery and flowers."[126]

This shift in purpose has been interpreted as a cultural twist, another sign of the cultural arrogance or racism of the colonial rulers. One judicious critic of colonial urbanism has interpreted the garden city movement as producing little new in social relationships between colonizer and colonized. It "represents a rationalized application of the underlying values which had characterized conceptual models of settlement in colonial society at least since the eighteenth century."[127] The effect certainly seemed to be the same. The two-town approach to urban design, in which the garden city principle of green space offered an attractive line of division, can be seen as segregationist.[128] The Congress on Colonial Urbanism, held in 1931, recognized this possibility and at least warned against it in principle. The second resolution of the Congress read

that the creation of satellite communities be planned, these separated by screens of greenery, with the prohibition of all arrangements intended to prevent contact or cooperation among the races.[129]

Perhaps as important as the admonition included in this resolution was the endorsement of open space as an integral element in colonial urban planning. Medical, cultural, and environmental considerations had weighted the argument in favor of what the French called a *zone non-aedificandi*. Modern transportation, particularly the automobile and tramway, made the ample use of space seem practical, not wasteful.

More than such immediate conditions were at work. The apparent availability of vast space occasionally turned the urbanist's imagination from the rabbit warrens which European cities seemed to be to the geometric forms that Versailles and Washington had stunningly become. Some colonial urbanists did have grand visions that focused on the large unit, so that Howard's plan for small towns with a spirit of community were distended to become large cities with tree-lined boulevards, monumental buildings, and broad parks. In the process, the social purpose of the garden city movement was forgotten, if it had ever been learned. No one detected much incongruity in the description of Lutyens's New Delhi as a "Garden Capital."[130] Nor was Adshead's plans for Lusaka, defined as a "generous, gracious city" based on garden city principles, criticized at the time. Only on the eve of independence were the many disadvantages to the African population seen and negatively assessed: the distances to be traversed, the land squandered, and the lack of sufficient public housing.[131]

In all of colonial urban development very little serious attention was paid to the peculiar needs and interests of the indigenous population. This population was occasionally given what was considered best for it; it was more frequently simply removed from the central scene. It was most often the victim of insufficient budgets, which did not provide for public housing or for sufficient public housing. Such funds established for urban improvement as the Calcutta Improvement Trust of 1911 and the Singapore Improvement Trust of 1927 used their monies primarily for road and sanitation improvements, not for housing. No doubt the boldest scheme of the interwar era was the Office of Low-Cost Housing (Offices des habitations économiques), established in Dakar in 1925. Modeled after a metropolitan program begun in 1922, it was designed to encourage the construction of good African housing by making loans available to builders and buyers. The interest rate initially established, 10 percent, was too high.[132] Moreover, the earliest models of the two types of structures to be built were found unsatisfactory by the African politician Blaise Diagne, who raised pertinent questions about the suitability of the designs for African social needs and financial resources.[133]

Perhaps it is inappropriate to inquire why more was not done about slum clearance and public housing improvement when these matters were badly attended in contemporary European urban centers. Yet more could have been done to examine and calculate local needs intelligently and sympathetically. Patrick Geddes's idea of a "diagnostic survey" might have been the right tool. However, urban planners in colonial service or employ were more interested in the modern blueprint, not the historical antecedent, more concerned with roadway than folkway. In India the common British method was described as simple and direct; roads were cut through congested areas, and then building sites "were allocated wherever they could easily be found."[134] Lutyens did not do this at New Delhi; he had a rather clear field of action. Nevertheless, his approach to urban planning was the opposite of Geddes's. The grandly proportioned public space was laid out; whatever had preceded it was ignored.[135]

Patrick Geddes, the culturally concerned urbanist, wrote the following in 1915, when urban planning was just beginning to become a part of colonial policy:

Without entering unduly into imperial politics, it may be recalled that city planning has ever been a part of imperial policy. But this is not permanently linked to the expression of the powers and glories of the ruler or the state as on the whole form imperial Rome to modern Paris or Berlin, and now from

Whitehall to New Delhi. The people, in all cities alike, must increasingly ask, with homely directness, "Where and when are we to come in?."[136]

The question was seldom asked in the early twentieth century, and when it was, it was seldom heard.

CHAPTER 5

Voices of Protest

The American press took notice when Marcus Garvey addressed approximately 25,000 of his followers in New York's Madison Square Garden in the evening of August 2, 1920. The event was spectacular, in part made so by the vivid green, purple, and gold academic regalia in which Garvey was dressed, but even more by the tone and content of his speech. After the five-minute ovation he received upon appearing at the speaker's lectern, Garvey began reading aloud the telegram he had sent to President Eamon de Valera of the Irish Republic, which stated in part: "We believe that Ireland should be free even as Africa should be free for the Negroes of the world. Keep up the fight for a free Ireland."[1]

Although personally removed from the geographical centers in which colonial protest was then most strongly forming, Garvey was able to see the politics of the moment in grand historical perspective. He therefore made the connection between the old "Irish Question" and the newer one of African independence. That he did so rather melodramatically, by telegram, in the form of a greeting from "25,000 Negro delegates . . . representing 400,000,000 Negroes of the world" was Garveyesque, that remarkable combination of political activism, showmanship, and sheer vanity.

A black Jamaican, largely self-schooled but profoundly committed to giving blacks a collective sense of dignity and pride, Garvey followed a meteoric career that converted his name into an "ism" that long endured after the single decade in which Garvey himself was a figure of international importance—inspirational to large numbers, bothersome to some colonial

147

administrators in Africa, and embarrassing to many American blacks of the middle class. Garvey generated adoration, aroused suspicion, and courted contempt. His ideology was as mixed as the opinions publicly offered about the man.

Garveyism ranged far in ideas and in the activities it proposed. Singularly devoted to the establishment of "race pride," the ideology was diffuse and eclectic, containing something for everyone, particularly everyone in the black world who had been ignored or isolated from hope and authority. Garvey wished to create a community, to have blacks speak with one voice, work to one common end—their own destiny. He spoke romantically of the African past, and he provided a vision of a wonderful African future. He even attempted a back-to-Africa colonization movement, which was not well-received by either American blacks or Africans. He believed in entrepreneurship, and he would have blacks beat whites at their commercial games. Furthermore, he believed in racial purity and acknowledged this common interest he had with the Ku Klux Klan. He was a popular leader who affected monarchical airs and had the temerity to style himself "provisional president of Africa." He was confused, and he was controversial. Nevertheless, he moved resolutely in one direction: to the future when the colonial system would be gone and Africa would be independent. "It is in the wind," he remarked of Africa's redemption. "It is coming. One day, like a storm, it will be here."[2]

He did not live to see that storm. He died in London in 1940, all but forgotten in a European world at war. But in the brief span of years in which he harangued and agitated, Garvey created a remarkable organization and engendered a sense of community and purpose that inspired blacks as they had not been before.

Basically, Garvey wanted blacks to bootstrap, to do for themselves what others would not do or sought to inhibit anyone else from doing. Yet it was not rugged individualism but fraternal cooperation that he declared to be the way to a successful future. To achieve this objective, he founded the United Negro Improvement Association, first in Jamaica in 1914, and then in the United States in 1917, where it became an influential force. The founding statement listed the many purposes for which the organization was to stand, but its two most significant charges were "to promote the spirit of race pride and love" and "to conduct a world-wide commercial and industrial intercourse."[3]

Garvey was a modernist who would redeem the past by moving quickly into the present and on to the future. Commercial and industrial enterprises would generate both the revenue and the spirit to give blacks the authority they needed and yet still lacked in world affairs. To this end Garvey established the Black Star Shipping Line, which would create commercial and cultural ties among the black people on three continents. As advertisements for stock purchase in the line boldly proclaimed: "Let us guide our own destiny by financing our own commercial ventures." The Negro Factories Corporation, another Garvey undertaking to be capitalized at $1,000,000, was designed to "build and operate factories in the big industrial centers of the United States, Central America, the West Indies, and Africa to manufacture every marketable commodity."[4]

Garvey's enterprises were enthusiastically supported by large numbers of blacks in the United States, and the Black Star Line did enter into international trade. But the line was soon bankrupt, its activities marred by poor management and the careless purchase of unsatisfactory ships. The ships could barely stay afloat; the commercial enterprises they represented were not even able to do this. Garvey's reputation sank with his business ventures. He was eventually jailed on unsubstantiated charges of fraud and deported as an unwanted alien. His business sense was at fault but not his integrity. Even in his own lifetime he was recognized as an exceptional leader, winning the title of a "Negro Moses" from the novelist Claude McKay.

Garvey was without doubt the most flamboyant of those leaders who protested the oppressed condition of colored peoples around the world and the colonial system that seemed to maintain that condition. He certainly was a remarkable contrast to the best known of the protestors and the mildest in personal demeanor, Mohandas Gandhi.

Gandhi is today remembered as that fragile-looking little figure, sparingly dressed in a white *dhoti*—the traditional fakir's costume—and sandals. The staff he used in old age gave him a particularly timeless, pastoral appearance, but his steel-rimmed glasses were a sign of his Western training. A lawyer by profession, although one without a university degree, Gandhi began his first protests against colonial rule in South Africa, where in the early years of the twentieth century he advocated the principle of *satyagraha*, usually described in English as "passive resistance," but defined by Gandhi himself as "soul-force." Its opposite, in his interpretation, is "body-force," physical force by which colonial oppression was met on its own terms.

In interwar India Gandhi practiced *satyagraha* religiously, and he even persuaded the ever-increasing number of his followers to do likewise. His public life was an erratic progression of imprisonments, fasts, releases, and further protests. Throughout it all, he remained remarkably convincing in his assertion that the only way to combat the power of the Raj was to defy it morally and, if necessary, to succumb to it physically. The British were truly perplexed by Gandhi's behavior, but not always disrespectful. Lord Reading, then viceroy of India, wrote Prime Minister Lloyd George in 1922 that Gandhi "preaches—and I verily believe with all sincerity—that non-violence is the most powerful weapon in the hands of men against those who, like the Government, exert force and violence."[5]

Gandhi, who never held political office and who never led a political party as such, won over many Hindus and Moslems with his demand for *swaraj*, or home rule. It was by force of his personality that the Congress party, founded in 1887, moved from its established base as a parliamentary party abiding by British political practice to a mass party protesting British rule. When Gandhi went to London in 1931 for the first set of "Roundtable Talks," which were designed to redefine the nature of British rule in India, his humble appearance belied the powerful force he then represented, a force that the Raj was not able to contain.

Between Gandhi and Garvey there was no communication, nor should it have been expected. Their political styles and personal manners were at variance. However, in broad terms they both defined the same ideal of independence and dignity for the people they represented. They approached that ideal with different interpretations of the modern Western world and of its usefulness as a model from which they might shape the future. Garvey registered no complaint about modern civilization; he wished to appropriate its techniques and assure its advantages to his people. Gandhi, on the contrary, had severe reservations about any value that might be derived from the modern West. *Swaraj*, or home rule, was for him more than independence from the British Raj; it was freedom from modernity, a return to the "home rule" or domestic order that he imagined previous generations of Indians had enjoyed when they directed their lives according to their own customs.

Were modern imperialism to be made the subject of a morality play, Garvey might be cast as flamboyant "modernity" and Gandhi as muted "traditionalism." Yet these terms would have to be qualified historically, for the matter of modern civilization was seriously questioned in the interwar period, at a time when the virtues of the West were no longer self-evident—as they certainly had been considered to be before the Great War, by both Westerners and those they dominated. In the interwar period technology and the rational-

Mohandas Gandhi speaking to a crowd at Bangalore, India, in March, 1920.
From the National Archives.

ism upon which it was premised were not seen as humanizing qualities by many critics around the world. The adjective "mechanical" was charged with a negative meaning; the ability to "run things" was not necessarily deemed an admirable trait.[6] "Machinery is the chief symbol of modern civilization," Gandhi lamented, and "it represents a great sin."[7]

Years later, after yet another world war, the Martiniquan poet Aimé Césaire also condemned the ill-effects of the machine:

And when you speak of the machine, do you not see there in the heart of our forests and fields, spitting out its cinders, the hysterical and overbearing factory, producing automatons—a prodigious mechanization, but of men . . . the machine, yes, always present, the machine; but in order to crush down, grind up, brutalize the people.[8]

Such words were echoes of similar denunciations expressed by Westerners from at least that precisely dated moment—July 27, 1844—when Nathaniel Hawthorne wrote in his notebook that the shriek of a suddenly appearing locomotive produced such a harshness "that the space of a mile cannot mollify it into harmony."[9] The fear of the renting effect of the industrial process on the countryside and on its local inhabitants, who were posed as local variants of the sturdy English yeoman, was to become an international sentiment among writers who looked longingly back to a recent past, which they quickly fantasized into those noble proportions that mark an ideal social order.

Much of the intellectual opposition to the machine was founded in the pastoral myth, and that particular myth had its most fertile setting in the older colonial environment of the New World where the Noble Savage roamed, where Crèvecoeur wrote his letters, and where Chateaubriand dramatically situated his romantic novel, *Atala*. In later, and somewhat more exotic hues, the myth was transported eastward where it appeared in the writings of Pierre Loti and in the paintings of Paul Gauguin. Even Tarzan demonstrated, with flexed muscles, the benefits that the scion of a titled British family might obtain, if not forced to wear an Eton collar.

These visions of unspoiled nature or, better, of human beings living in a state of harmony with nature were in strong contrast to the urban and industrial situations described by nineteenth-century realistic novelists, among whom Charles Dickens and Emile Zola figured large. But only the early science fiction writers could imagine—and then only vaguely—the brutal reality the machine might produce if harnessed for military purposes. The world war shelled out of existence the greatest of popular nineteenth-century myths, peace through industrial progress. Immediately after the war, and as at no time since the early eighteenth century, many European intellectuals looked out, away from the carnage of their own continent, in a search for meaning or wisdom. André Malraux, in his *Temptation of the West*, published in 1925, has his Chinese protagonist say of Europeans: "You have offered up your lives to power. . . . You have weighted the universe with anguish."[10] This certainly was the mood and frequently the criticism that informed so many popular books of the time, among which Sigmund Freud's *Civilization and Its Discontents* acquired historical prominence.

In this moment of despair and self-examination Asia was once again discovered or, more accurately, remade in the European mind. Its civilization now became one of balance and serenity, of mystery accepted, not analyzed until disintegrated into nothingness. This interpretation appeared in novels such as Herman Hesse's *Siddharta* and E. M. Forster's *A Passage to India*. The imagined contrast with the contemporary West explains the remarkable

A gasoline pump in the Sahara desert, 1925. It was called the most isolated in
the world. From the National Archives.

words of the French novelist Romain Rolland, which are contained in a letter
he wrote to the Indian philosopher-poet and Nobel Laureate Rabindranath
Tagore in 1919:

After the disaster of this shameful World War which marked Europe's failure, it has become evident that Europe alone cannot save herself. Her thought is in need of Asia's thought, just as the latter has profited from contact with Europe's thought. They are two hemispheres of the brain of mankind.[11]

The metaphor is attractive and befitting the effort of Rolland to rise above the inhumanity caused by nationalism. Tagore was in general agreement, but, as with many intellectuals in the colonial world, he was also disquieted by the soulless nature of modern Western civilization. Tagore and others challenged the earlier, tacitly accepted assumption about Europe's "civilizing mission."

The issue was no longer one of imperialism disregarding its vaunted principles; now the principles themselves were seriously questioned. A new generation of novelists, for whom the colonial situation was an appropriate theme of artistic expression, created characters and plots in which old ways and new methods were in competition and conflict, and in which the new was not necessarily the bright or the right. Mulk Ray Anand, a major Indian writer of the time, has a character in *Untouchable*, one of his major novels, speak mockingly of "greater efficiency, better salesmanship, more mass production, standardization, dictatorship of the sweepers."[12] Claude McKay, the Jamaican writer, causes the missionary in his novel *Banana Bottom* to ponder and question the meaning of the self-assumed responsibilities of white people:

Who knows but that many of those natives whom they were seeking to advise as mentors and ministers might prefer their own particular patterns of life and living and do better in the simple way perhaps than many of their guardians and teachers?[13]

René Maran, the black novelist from Martinique, went further and was more direct in his sensational work, *Batouala*, published in France in 1921. In the preface, he turns the French metaphor of civilization as illumination into its opposite: "You are not a torch, but a fire. Whatever you touch, you devour."[14]

Redefined in colonial terms and reconsidered in light of indigenous cultures, many of the arguments that European and American critics had raised about the corrosive effect of industrial, rationalized society on the human being now supported a form of anticolonialism that was essentially cultural in mode. But it was not only belletristic. In fact, one of the first expressions of this mode was made by Mohandas Gandhi. His early essay "Home Rule," written in 1909 as he was returning from England to South Africa, was a strong protest against the ill-effects of imposed Western values and institutions. Gandhi put the matter bluntly: "It is my deliberate opinion that India is being ground down, not under the English heel, but under that of modern civilization."[15] Above all, Gandhi objected to the materialistic aspects of modern civilization. These sapped self-reliance and hindered personal development; furthermore, they removed morality and religion from the forefront of consideration. To make this point, Gandhi prepared what, at first glance, seems to have been an odd cluster of characteristics of modern Western civilization, but which were in fact among those most evident in India. Railroads, lawyers, and doctors were all denounced. The railroad carried disease and spread human depravity. "Bad men fulfill their evil deeds with greater rapidity," thanks to the railroad, he asserted. Lawyers generated dissension. Rather than reconciling quarrels, they stirred them up in order to have clients and therefore make money. Doctors made vice easy. Rather than making the indulger suffer for his intemperate acts and hence reform in order to avoid their recurrence, the doctor provided medicine that relieved pain and hence weakened the moral lesson that might be learned.[16]

These activities falsified life as they also adulterated it. True civilization, Gandhi insisted, was predicated upon the principle of good conduct. "Our ancestors, therefore, set a limit to our indulgences," he contended. They eschewed technology, prevented the creation of large cities, and avoided competition for wealth and power. "They saw that our real happiness consisted in a proper use of our hands and feet," he wrote in one of his most telling phrases.[17] For Gandhi the good life was that of the family in the small town where manual labor was dignified and where religion was practiced. It was a world he imagined to be without discord, a civilization that respected the human being by praising modesty in all things.

These differences in proportions and purposes between the two civilizations were also the concern of Tagore, who singled out the nation as the institution that denied humanity. A nation, according to Tagore, is "that aspect which a whole population assumes when organized for a mechanical purpose."[18] There was nothing particularly British about the nation; "it is an applied science and therefore more or less similar in its principles wherever it is used," he wrote.[19] As in the argument of Gandhi, Tagore did not condemn the British so much as the civilization that they had imposed on India. The mechanical organization—Tagore's term—of the West is what distinguishes its domination of India from that of all its other conquerors. All of the previous tyrannies had been essentially human, in the sense that they were flawed or open-textured, thus "leaving big gaps through which Indian life sent its threads and imposed its designs."[20] To use a term that was foreign to Tagore, but appropriate to his thought, Western civilization seemed totalitarian, intrusive into all aspects of Indian life. He described this complaint in many metaphors but nowhere does he better express his sentiments about modern civilization than in the following statement:

In the West the national machinery of commerce and politics turns out neatly compressed bales of humanity which have their use and high market value; but they are bound in iron hoops, labeled and separated off with scientific care and precision. Obviously God made man to be human; but this modern product has such marvelous square-cut finish, savouring of gigantic manufacture, that the Creator will find it difficult to recognize it as a thing of the spirit and a creature made in his own divine image.[21]

In Tagore's assessment the perfection of the West was in its power, not in idealism, and in a power that was lifeless, mechanical. This basic criticism, a variation of Gandhi's, was one that was not restricted to Indian men-of-letters. It found expression in Africa, particularly in the early poetry of protest. If not the first, then certainly one of the first forceful statements was that of the Zulu poet Benedict Vilakazi in his poem "In the Gold Mines," wherein he commented bitterly on the mining experience his countrymen suffered in South Africa:

> Roar without rest, machines of the mine!
> Our hands are aching, always aching,
> Our swollen feet are aching too. . . .
> Well have I served the rich white masters,
> But, oh, my soul is heavy in me!
> Roar less loudly, let me slumber,
> Close my eyes and sleep and sleep
> And stop all thinking of tomorrow.

And then the poet expresses his hope of leaving this overbearing environment:

> Let me sleep and wake afar,
> At peace where my forebears are
> And where, no more, is earthly waking!
> Let me sleep in arms long vanished,
> Safe beneath the world's green pastures.[22]

This final return to the pastoral, away from the harsh sounds and forms of a Westernized environment, was a spiritual movement that many writers celebrated, but that received its most profound expression in that near-epic poem of the Martiniquan author Aimé Césaire. *Return to My Native Land* was composed as Césaire prepared to return to Martinique in 1939 after an educational stay in France. The mixed feelings that surged through Césaire's mind and heart created sentiments of nostalgia and bitterness, according to André Bréton, the surrealist poet who discovered Césaire. Césaire knew, Bréton claimed, "the anguish felt by a black for the condition of all blacks in modern society," just as he realized the need "to finish with this moral disassociation of the human spirit" that Western civilization caused.[23]

The poem that Césaire wrote stresses the cultural dichotomy between what is European and what is African, or Afro-American, if that term may be extended to Césaire's Martinique. The European qualities that Césaire perceived and criticized were those that Gandhi and Tagore had already considered. Césaire saw them all meaninglessly assembled in the city:

At the end of the dawn, the city—flat, sprawled, tripped by its own common sense, inert, winded under the geometric weight of its eternally renewed cross, at odds with its fate, mute, baffled, unable to circulate the pith of this ground, embarrassed, lopped, reduced, cut off from fauna and flora.[24]

Césaire, one critic stated, was so sufficient a Marxist that he did not indulge in pastoral dreams,[25] but he did champion the cultural protest against colonialism as an urban and economically explosive process, one that disregarded human needs. In so doing he added the strength of his voice to that outspoken ideology of blackness—known in French as *négritude*—that glorified the cultural conditions that blacks shared as a result of their common African heritage and their separateness from the dominant civilization in which they found themselves after they had been forced from their African homeland.

The component elements that gave this ideology structure were gathered in three continents, the oldest source being found in the Caribbean. Although black authors writing in the three major European languages in the region had described their people's condition for nearly a century before *négritude* emerged, the most obvious expression of discontent occurred in Haiti, on the occasion of the occupation of the country by American marines in 1915. The troops and the administrators who accompanied them deprecated what they saw and sought to impose alien institutions, with a shift in educational policy away from the classical to the technical being a matter of particular local concern.[26] In direct response to this double political and cultural imperialism, a Haitian literary renaissance began, defined rather eloquently by the *Griots*, a group of writers assuming the traditional African function of troubadors, who enthusiastically turned to the Haitian past and the physical environment in which it had been staged.

We others, Haitian Griots, must sing of the splendor of the countryside, the sweetness of April dawns . . . the beauty of our women, the exploits of our ancestors.[27]

It was one person in particular, a medical doctor and self-educated folk-lorist, Jean Price-Mars, who strongly defined the movement. In his *Ainsi parla l'Oncle*, a collection of speeches that he had given in Haiti between 1922 and 1923—but published in 1928, Price-Mars lay his own culture open with surgical skill. The particular role of the black in that broader category of "human nature" was his chief concern and, like his later Caribbean compatriot, the Martiniquan Frantz Fanon, who also analyzed the anguish of the black in a white-dominated world (Fanon's book bears the remarkable title *Black Skin, White Masks*), Price-Mars serenely stated that, despite all the difficulties and pressures placed on him "the African negro has maintained . . . his position as co-heir of the eminent dignity of human nature."[28] The analysis that Price-Mars followed to this conclusion was made through an ethnographic study of Haitian folklore, both oral tradition and its system of beliefs, notably that of voodoo. With care and caution, Price-Mars followed his "scientific inquiry with the serenity of someone undertaking a laboratory experience." Yet Price-Mars's real purpose was inspirational: to arouse an appreciation and a pride among the Haitian people in their African past and in its influence on their daily behavior. Like Garvey, then in New York, Price-Mars aspired to create a sense of "race pride."

Price-Mars did find one element in the black's character, an element he thought had reached the quality of being genetic, that would later form a controversial aspect of négritude. He stressed "the office performed by music and dance . . . in [a black's] spiritual life" and declared that "their power over the organism takes on a clearly biological character."[29] Whatever the significance of this remark, it seems in retrospect to have been timely. The moment of Price-Mars's thoughts was also that of the celebration of what Langston Hughes called the "soul world", which took form in the Harlem Renaissance. "In Harlem," wrote the young Howard University professor Alain Locke, "Negro life is seizing upon its first chances for group expression and self-determination."[30] The mood, literary forms, and—above all—the musical idiom were carried abroad where they inspired Caribbean and African blacks studying as colonial students in Paris. That old city accepted the new cultural tempo with considerable enthusiasm. Langston Hughes recounts a "jam session" offered in 1924 by a group of blacks in *The Big Sea*, and his description lyrically captures the spirit of the moment, shared by both blacks and Parisians:

Blues in the rue Pigalle. Black and laughing, heartbreaking blues in the Paris dawn, pounding like a pulse-beat, moving like the Mississippi.[31]

Speaking of this "pulse-beat," Léopold Sédar Senghor, Senegalese poet and future president of that country, remarked that "Negro-American music made a world tour. . . . For song and poetry are the same thing for the negro, whether he comes from America or Africa."[32] Senghor acknowledged on several occasions the importance of the American black cultural idiom to Africans; he declared the "Negro Renaissance," that the Americans inspired, to be the result of a desire for "fertile" cultural difference.[33] He, like many other young students then in Paris, participated vigorously in this renaissance. They created a flurry of "little magazines" that appeared in the early 1930s, magazines that ran for a limited number of issues and then disappeared—but not before being read feverishly. *La Revue noire* was the first, and it seized as its themes both Pan-Africanism and racial harmony. *Légitime défense* was the next, but its purposes were avowedly more political. Then came *L'Etudiant noir*, to which Senghor contributed, a publication both rhapsodic and revolutionary in mood. As outlets for the thoughts of black Americans and Africans, these publications were expressions of protest against the rationalism and materialism of the modern West. The appeal of the then popular French artistic movement, surrealism, to the authors of the articles in these journals is easily understood.[34] It, too, railed against rationalism and bourgeois culture, sought the deeply recessed in the mind, praised the subconscious, and explored the emotional.

This revolt of the spirit against the Western world and the colonialism it supported was not the means to topple empires or even to seriously disconcert colonial administrators, most of whom did not subscribe to any literary review. However, it was a significant refutation of the nineteenth-century thesis that Western civilization was superior and ought be conferred as a "blessing" on those countless souls Kipling sweepingly described as "the lesser breeds."

It was more than this as well. It was an effort at intellectual freedom, a means to escape from the Western prison of the mind and the social inferiority it imposed. As one writer contributing to the *Revue du monde noir* described this need: "So long as our conscience is dependent on that of the foreigner, our bodies will succumb to that special form of slavery which necessarily follows from particular ways of thinking."[35]

This effort to create a black consciousness, one steeped in the African past, was later criticized for its romanticism, its diversion, however unintended, from many of the harsh realities of colonial rule and the class system that it imposed. In asking,

> What does Africa mean to me?
> Copper sun or scarlet sea.
> Jungle star or jungle track,
> Strong bronzed men, or regal black
> Women from whose loins I sprang
> When the birds of Eden sang?[36]

the romancers of Africa ignored, where they did not disdain, the effects of the intrusion of Western modernity. For other critics the major issue was as much functional as it was cultural: how could local populations and local cultures make the best use of what had been thrust upon them by the West and from which poetic flights were hardly the appropriate means of evasion. Jawaharlal Nehru, Gandhi's closest collaborator, put the matter simply when he expressed his dissent from Gandhi's backward-looking future:

Certainly most of us were not prepared to reject the achievements of modern civilization, although we may have felt some variation to suit Indian needs was possible.

Then Nehru added a comment that clearly defined him as a modern:

Personally, I have always felt attracted towards big machinery and fast travelling.[37]

Nehru was more than attracted to the qualities of the new technology; he considered the impact of the West on India to be a necessity, if an unpleasant one.

Science was the great gift of the West; India lacked this, and without it she was doomed to decay. The manner of our contacts was unfortunate and yet, perhaps, only a succession of violent shocks could shake us out of our torpor.[38]

Variously expressed, this interpretation was a widely shared one. Indeed, it had accompanied Western civilization even as it marked its ascendency in the world. Long before the airplane and telephone had changed the sense of time, Arab authors had considered how Islam, as a civilization, might adjust to the technological thrust from abroad. The great original force in Egyptian nationalism, Jamal al-Din al-Afghani (1893-1897), presented the situation as clearly as possible in a now often-quoted statement: "The very existence of the East depends on acquiring scientific knowledge; it is an instrument with which it can crush the power of the West."[39] A long time later and in reference to another civilization, the founder of modern China, Sun Yat-Sen offered an identical thought: "A few hundred years ago, Europe could not compare with China so now if we want to learn from Europe we should learn what we ourselves lack—science."[40]

Sun's statement concluded with the assertion that the Chinese had nothing to learn from the West about political philosophy. Yet the lecture in which these remarks were made was entitled "The Principles of Nationalism," a subject as modern and as Western as the steam engine. Sun ignored this fact, or purposely skirted it, and argued that Chinese nationalism was an age-old quality. Here was one of many instances throughout the twentieth century in which Asians and Africans allowed rhetoric to prevail over history in order to create a sense of nationhood.

Nationalism and technology were outgrowths of the modern secular spirit, and they appeared in close alliance as they went abroad. Empire was, of course, set out in the name of the nation, and the symbols of the nation were the most visible forms of Europe's temporary dominion over the world. The nation appeared resplendent in flags and anthems, in insignia on uniforms and camp gates, in the smoke of gunpowder following a military salute. Looking into the mirror of their own mind, European imperialists concluded that the non-European was most frequently dazzled by the panoply of power. "Power, might, majesty, and dominion appeal to all who need support and protection," wrote an English observer of the Durbar of 1911, at which occasion George V was crowned emperor of India in Delhi.[41] "The Eastern mind requires something more than a verbal symbol. . . . It requires the living presence of the Crown," wrote another.[42]

In truth, what attracted the "Eastern mind" was not what the Europeans grandly displayed but what they said and how they organized their thoughts. Nationalism in the colonial world was the result of European ideology and education, both modified to suit local needs. Protesting European rule, a new generation—or a segment of it that qualifies to be called an intellectual elite—made reference to Rousseau and to Marx, to self-determination and to sovereignty. They did so in English, French, and Dutch. Europe was denounced in its own language, attacked with its own ideas. As one of the leading African nationalist theorists stated toward the end of the colonial era, "African nationalism is a political feeling manifesting itself against European rule in favour of African rule."[43] If the geographical setting is changed, the statement serves as an appropriate one for all colonial nationalist movements. They were more immediately concerned with the ejection of the foreigner than with the establishment of the nation.

Of course such sentiment found expression primarily in the press. The growth of local newspapers and the intensifying spirit of nationalism are closely related. An early Turkish nationalist writer, Ziya Gokalp, assessed the importance of the press in this way:

The newspaper, which has spurred the feelings of honor and sacrifice in the masses merely to increase its circulation, has consequently aroused a consciousness of national traditions and cherished ideals.[44]

Gokalp's statement is worthy of consideration because it is at such variance with the facts. The major characteristics of the colonial newspaper were the opposite of those that made "yellow journalism" such a successful enterprise in the Western world.

As the colonial newspaper moved from a weekly to a daily status in the early twentieth century, it struggled against the difficulties of poor printing facilities, ill-trained personnel, and frequent official pressure to control what was written. Moreover, circulation figures were small in populations still highly illiterate and poorly paid, where the newspaper was not the daily convenience the European found at his breakfast table.

However tenuous its development, the colonial press is as old as the colonial act. An American black, Charles L. Force, began the *Liberia Herald* in 1829 on a small handpress that had been the gift of the Massachusetts Colonization Society of Boston.[45] The first English-language newspaper in Hong Kong was the *Canton Register*, begun in 1828, and later followed by the first publication in Chinese, *Chung Ngo San Po*, started around 1860.[46] By the interwar period newspapers were abundant in number, if not in copies circulated, throughout the colonial world. Moreover, they were frequently voicing strong opinions against colonial rule. A striking example of this mood appeared in 1925 in *La Cloche Fêlée*, which described itself as an "organ of democratic persuasion." Its young editor, Nguyen An Ninh, denounced French colonialism as an act perpetrated by incompetents and resulting in "unbridled exploitation" that he considered contrary to the principles of French civilization.[47]

Such protest against colonialism was not only found in the indigenous press but also in the newspapers edited by Europeans. Dr. Annie Besant, a sturdy English critic of imperialism who caused the Raj some anguish, acquired the *Madras Standard*, renamed it *New India*, and used its columns as the means to make heard her demands for dominion status for India.[48] The young André Malraux, headstrong and idealistic, created his own newspaper in Saigon, *Indochine*, which had a press run of 5,000 copies when it first appeared on June 17, 1925. Malraux marked the colonial administration as corrupt and incompetent. During the eight months of the publication's life, Malraux and his collaborator, Paul Monin, brought a quality of literary excellence and trenchant argument to the newspaper that made it unusual in the colonial world.[49]

The newspaper assisted some political careers and inspired others. Mohandas Gandhi had founded *Indian Opinion*, while he was in South Africa; and soon after his return to India in 1915, he took over two weeklies, *Young India* and *Navajivan*, the latter published in an Indian dialect.[50] Dr. J. B. Danquah, the leader of the first political party in the Gold Coast, had previously acquired fame as the founder of the *West African News* in Accra in 1931. More famous as a journalist-politican was Dr. Nnamdi Azikiwe who in 1934 took over the *African Morning Post* upon his return to the Gold Coast from the United States. Azikiwe went to Nigeria in 1937 where he began the most influential of all black African publications, the *West African Pilot*. Azikiwe's commitment to the press is measured by the statement he wrote in a small booklet entitled *Renascent Africa*: "There is no better means to arouse African peoples than that of the power of the pen and of the tongue."[51]

Despite press laws that imposed fines, imprisonment, and even exile, the colonial newspaper continued to extend its influence over the European-educated elite and thus helped arouse a sense of common interest and define a set of common goals. However ambiguous nationalism may have been in the interwar empires, there is clear evidence that political sentiments against colonial rule were galvanizing, and this occurrence was largely attributable to the activities of the newspapers. "We are a Nation," the Reverend Attoh Ahuma had affirmed in a column of the *Gold Coast Leader* in 1911.[52] This brief line is the summary statement of much editorial opinion of the interwar period, when the conversion of colonial administrative units into sovereign states was being planned, at least on paper.

If press activities were any measure, the statement made by the Turkish nationalist Gokalp, that "the most powerful force over the mind of this age is the ideal of nationalism" has considerable validity.[53] Moreover, the sweep of nationalism did not only disturb colonial governments; it was bothersome to the most powerful anticolonial force as well, the newly created Soviet Union. The history of Soviet relationships with the colonial world during the interwar period is one of confusion and compromise in the face of rising nationalism.

As a Western ideology directed toward the problem of industrialization, Communism immediately had no particular interest in the colonial question and, obviously, no policy that accommodated the regions of the world still in a preindustrial state. Marx certainly had acknowledged the expansionist tendencies of modern capitalist industrialism. "The need of a constantly expanding market for its products chases the bourgeoisie over the whole surface of the globe," he announced in *The Communist Manifesto*.[54] Others later developed this idea, but no one with greater appeal than Nikolai Lenin.

Lenin's little tract, *Imperialism, The Highest Stage of Capitalism*, completed only a year before the October revolution, has been one of the most influential political works of the twentieth century. It is logically structured, even though it is neither eloquently argued nor respectful of historical fact.

Lenin arranged the history of modern capitalism according to stages characterized by increasing complexity of organization and range of activity, but also by intensifying control. Imperialism occurred during the phase of finance capitalism when interlocking directorates and "monopolist combines" dominated the European economy. In this world of precariously balanced giants, colonial possessions alone gave "complete guarantee of success to the monopolies against all risks of struggle with competitors."[55] Both as a source of raw materials and as a place for investment of surplus capital, the colonies were essential to the continuation of advanced capitalism.

In simple terms, imperialism provided capitalism with a stay of execution. How to revoke that stay was the question frequently asked in interwar Communist debates. The most significant and dramatic encounter over the issue was the one between Lenin and a young Indian Communist, M. N. Roy, which occurred during the Second Congress of the Third International in 1920.[56] The debate that they engaged in was concerned with direction: should the revolution come primarily "from above" or "from below." The two possible strategies, or so it appeared, were (1) cooperation with the bourgeois democrats leading the nationalist movements, and (2) enlistment and grouping of the peasants and workers into distinct Communist revolutionary movements.

Lenin adhered to the first strategy because he believed that an initial phase of cooperation would be necessary and because he was convinced that the nationalist movements were at least progressive. Roy heartily disagreed.

Roy was one of the most ardent Communists of his day, and an individual who briefly served in many capacities, until he incurred the wrath of Joseph Stalin.[57] During his moment of intense involvement, he helped shape Communist policy toward the developing world in a lasting way. His interest began when he was converted to Communism in 1920, during the checkers games he played in exile with M. M. Borodin, a Soviet agent, then in Mexico City.[58] Roy quickly became an ardent adherent to the new order, and he turned his eyes to the prospects of Communism in the East, where he saw it as the means of unseating the British empire and also the Indian bourgeoisie which he predicted would eventually occupy the places the British had vacated, once nationalism was successful. It was his fear that the nationalist movement would effect no fundamental social changes that drove Roy to protest any Communist policy of accommodation or cooperation. In short, he was opposed to revolution "from above."

Roy offered a series of "Supplemental Theses on the National and Colonial Questions" to the membership of the Second Congress of the Comintern. His position was clearly stated in the seventh thesis, which read as follows:

Two distinct movements which grow farther apart every day are to be found in the dependent countries. One is the bourgeois-democratic movement, with a program of political independence under the bourgeois order. The other is the mass struggle of the poor and ignorant peasants and workers for their liberation from various forms of exploitation.[59]

Not only did he want to encourage the latter and be done with the former, but also he hoped to make the point that colonial revolution was a necessary element in the overthrow of the capitalist regimes in the Western world. This particular argument did work its way into the final, revised theses that the Congress transmitted. It then read: "The breaking up of the colonial empire, together with a proletarian revolution in the home country, will overthrow the capitalist system in Europe."

Even with this said, it was Lenin's interpretation that really prevailed. Revolution in the colonies would come "from above." In the words of the revised theses, this condition required that "all communist parties must give active support to the revolutionary liberation movements in these countries."[60] The acceptance of a two-stage revolution—national liberation to be followed by Communist domination—by the Third International largely determined Communist policy in the interwar years.

Nowhere was this more easily observed than at the Conference of the League to Struggle against Imperialism and Colonial Oppression. This conference, important in that it was not a Communist-sponsored one, took place in Brussels in 1927, and has been frequently called the congress of oppressed minorities. Its honorary leadership included Albert Einstein and Romain Rolland, Upton Sinclair and Maxim Gorki.[61] The 174 delegates came from around the world. They debated and resolved the colonial question, this done under a banner bearing the words "National Freedom, Social Equality." The general debate was assessed by the correspondent of the *Berliner Tageblatt* in terms that suggested its agreement with the "two-stage" theory of revolution:

Evidentally, the great idea is first of all to win national independence and the allying of the international movement with the proletariat movement comes second. To put it in other words, internationalism cannot be realized until self-determination is an actual fact.[62]

The necessary preliminary state—the "actual fact" of national independence—did not widely occur until three decades later, and, even when it did, the sequence described above was not frequently followed. In the interwar period the Soviet leadership waged a rhetorical assault on colonialism but pursued no constant policy toward its perpetrators. The initial idealism and enthusiasm, apparent in Lenin's 1919 statement that "the victory of the proletarian revolution throughout the world is assured," quickly vanished.[63] After 1921 the regime behaved more like a traditional nation-state and less like the vanguard of world revolution, as it sought diplomatic support and negotiated economic assistance from the Western powers.

Henceforth the colonial issue was generally cast in terms of the Soviet Union's own strategic needs, not in terms of a new world order.

The consequence of these developments, when combined with local colonial conditions, usually resulted in communism counting as only a minor political factor in the European empires, except, perhaps, in the imagination of colonial administrators.[64] Even though the proliferation of Communist parties in North Africa, the Near East, and Far East was remarkable in the period immediately following the Russian success, few of these organizations gained much hold on the local populations.

Communism seemed to be both misplaced and mistimed: it remained doctrinally an industrial ideology in which the peasantry and the countryside were still secondary factors; it made little adjustment to the particular social environment of the colonial city, where a regimented, factory-located work force was all but non-existent. If this lack of appreciation of local conditions had been the only weakness, Communism might have had more effect. However, the leadership and even the membership of the parties were often removed from the local masses. The Egyptian Communist party, for instance, is estimated to have been made up of 80 to 90 percent foreigners in the interwar period.[65] The Communist parties in French North Africa were primarily composed of Frenchmen. The Communist party of South Africa was exclusively made up of white workers, with its chief delegate to the Fourth Congress of the Comintern, Sydney Bunting, placed on a special "Negro Commission" because he so requested.[66]

None of these parties was numerically significant. Few ever enlisted more than several hundred members. Even the Chinese Communist party, the one that the Soviet Union most strongly courted and supported in its early days, had only 1,000 members in 1925. Membership suddenly jumped to 25,000 as the result of a general strike in the port cities, which met with severe British resistance—and which forms the plot of André Malraux's first novel, *The Conquerors*. Malraux's narrator claims that he understood "this new kind of warfare, with cannons replaced by slogans, with defeated cities not sacked and burned but occupied by the great silence of the Asian strike."[67]

He also understood the chagrin of failure, for the silence of the strike was not followed by any cheer of victory among its participants; nor did the Communists, who immediately benefited from it by a surge in their numbers, long have reason to be jubilant. By 1927 Chiang Kai-shek had brutally frustrated all efforts at Communist domination in that Asiatic country.

The Far East had earlier seemed susceptible to Soviet advances. The geographical stretch of the Soviet Union in that direction and the long continuous borders with China suggested a geopolitical imperative that was not ignored by the Soviet leadership. Moreover, Joseph Stalin, who was the figure principally concerned with such matters in his capacity of commissar for nationalities, viewed all of Asia—"the East" in his terminology—as "the most reliable rear base for world imperialism.'' He added that ''the imperialists have always viewed the East as the basis of their prosperity.''[68]

Black Africa was all but ignored by the Soviet Union in the interwar period and Latin America assumed no major role, but the East, from Near to Far, was given special attention. In an effort to enlist support for their own solution to the Eastern question, the Comintern called a conference at Baku in 1920, with attendance primarily made up of representatives of ''the enslaved peoples of Persia, Armenia, and Turkey.''[69] This conference was followed by another, The First Congress of Toilers of the Far East, which was a reply to the Washington Naval Conference, perceived by the Soviet government as an imperialist gathering on problems in the Far East. The First Congress of Toilers of the Far East met in Moscow in January 1922 and was told by a Soviet Far Eastern specialist named G. I. Safarov that ''we support . . . bourgeois nationalists . . . because Japanese, American and English imperialism is the most reactionary force.''[70]

While the Comintern thus ranged across Asia in its plans and negotiations, its activities were most concentrated on China, the one land that offered some promise of raising the red banner.

China had long been on the sensitive edge of world affairs: it was intruded upon by Western imperialism in the nineteenth century, and it was trampled shortly thereafter by Japanese imperialism. Its semi-colonial status, ensured through economic domination, was further aggravated by internal political unrest. The republic founded under Sun Yat-Sen in 1911 had yet to assert its authority over the entire land. As the postwar era opened, the warlords held the north of the country, while Sun was attempting to rearrange a disheveled republican government in the south, with its capital at Canton.

In this atmosphere the Chinese Communist party quickly flourished. Founded in 1921, the Party had accepted the Leninist interpretation laid down at the Second Congress of the Comintern and therefore prepared for a two-stage revolution by beginning to cooperate with the ''bourgeois nationalist'' Kuomintang, Sun's political organization. By 1926 the Communists had made excellent progress and enjoyed strong representation on the Central Executive Committee of the Kuomintang. Moscow expected triumph; the unexpected happened. The right-wing faction of the Kuomintang was worried by the Communist success, and Chiang Kai-Shek, the most effective military leader in the Kuomintang, was gravely disturbed. Chiang set out to deprive the Communists of political power, and he succeeded through forceful action in achieving this objective by 1927, even to the extent that the Chinese Communist party held its 1928 party conference in Moscow, a safe distance from Chiang's armies.

Both Soviet ideology and policy had failed in China, and the activities of the Chinese Communist party were reduced to insignificance for some time. Only Mao Tse-tung stood resolute, chiefly because he had stood aside during the controversy within the Kuomintang. Mao had amassed a truly popular following, approximately 2,000,000 in the province of Hunan. He had done so because he recognized and acted on the principle that "the national revolution requires a profound change in the countryside."[71] Mao was thus influential in reworking Communist theory so that it became something more than another export item from the West.

When Communism was finally adjusted to meet environmental needs, when its field of action was moved from the city to the countryside, and when the basis of its struggle was reordered so that the peasantry was invited to play a more forceful role, then, and only then, did Communism become a powerful force in the colonial world. This "revolution in the revolution" was primarily achieved after World War II.[72] In the preceding period Communism was but one element—often an undifferentiated and unimportant one—in the various expressions of protest against colonial rule.

The interwar era was not yet a "time of troubles," but disturbances were frequent enough to raise doubts about the resiliency of empire. Colonial governments were challenged by mountain and desert warriors, by student demonstrations and urban strikes, and by opposition political parties and representatives in colonial councils. The response to this challenge was fitful, occasionally bold and fierce, occasionally conciliatory, but never undertaken with long-range objectives in view. Uncertain of the future, the colonial leadership seemed directionless in the present.

Part of the problem was with the concept and practice of empire itself. Empire was never much more than a nominal term. It was the stuff of school textbooks and political speeches. It was dream and sentiment. Empire was gratefully praised immediately after World War I, and empire was regarded with comfort as World War II appeared. A French wartime slogan, "We Shall Win Because We Are the Strongest," appeared on a poster that showed the British and French empires and the more modest geographical extent of Nazi Germany.

Semanticists and politicians alike groped with the term. When Field Marshal Smuts first popularized the new title, "British Commonwealth of Nations," he declared:

We are far greater than any Empire which has ever existed, and by using this ancient expression, we really disguise the fact that our whole position is different, and that we are not one state or nation or empire, but a whole world by ourselves, and all sorts of communities under one flag.[73]

The key phrase is "all sorts of communities under one flag." There were no measurable or memorable bonds. Neither commerce nor geography, neither politics nor traditions brought the colonial units together to form an empire. Governance was most often haphazard and ad hoc, unsupported by empire-wide institutions, and unorganized at home by any single unit of the national government. That wonderful term, "The United States of the Britannic Empire," which federationists at the end of the nineteenth century thought might, like a shibboleth, allow empire to pass easily into the new century, was never employed. The French used the term "union" officially in 1946, and then they struck upon the romantic word "community" in 1958 when General de Gaulle came to power.

Logically, therefore, one cannot say that the colonial empires collapsed or fell apart; such a condition presupposed some coherence, some unity. The unity would later come from the other side, in the opposition that was universally supported by national liberation movements in the last days of colonial empire.

The interwar period was one of testing, of determining how resilient the imperial systems were, of how accommodating they might be. If there was a common indigenous concern, it was to benefit more from the existing situation to achieve better wages and living conditions, to exercise more authority in governmental councils, and to be treated more equitably by the colonial overlord. Direct opposition was generally of modest proportions, still not yet popular. The colonial administrators tended to discount it, when they did not badly misread it. They saw a world of cunning conspirators and inchoate masses; they seldom recognized the potential of discontent.

In no instance was there a worse or more tragic misreading of such events than in the Amritsar massacre of April 13, 1919. This occurrence was no doubt an unusual and dreadfully intemperate use of force during the era of the British Raj, but it was later interpreted as proof that empire was only maintained by the sword.

The massacre had its beginnings in the Rowlatt Acts, passed in March 1919 and containing measures of wartime stringency that the Indians rightly interpreted as being politically oppressive. Gandhi called for peaceful demonstrations and *hatrals*, or strikes. Unexpectedly, the response became violent;

one upsetting incident was the assault of an English schoolteacher in Amritsar, Punjab. General Reginald Dyer decided to play a heavy hand and therefore forebade all demonstrations. When a crowd estimated at 100,000 gathered in defiance of his order at Jalliamwallah Bagh on April 13, he initiated a sharp reprisal. Ninety soldiers expended 1,650 rounds of ammunition in ten minutes, killing 379 Indians and wounding another 1,200.

The official reaction to Dyer's action was favorable both in India and at home. As the event was later placed in perspective, a sense of horror filled the Indian people, and a sense of doubt spread over the English. The matter was made more grave by Dyer's bold admission that "if more troops had been present, the effect would have been greater in proportion."[74] Nehru heard words of a similar nature. While on the night train from Amritsar to Delhi at the end of 1919, Nehru occupied an upper bunk and found in the morning that he was in a car of military officers, among whom was General Dyer. Overhearing some of Dyer's conversation, Nehru later commented: "He pointed out how he had the whole town at his mercy and he had felt like reducing the rebellious city to a heap of ashes, but he took pity on it and refrained."[75]

Nehru further noted that Dyer got off the train in Delhi "in pajamas with bright pink stripes and a dressing gown." Dyer did not appear again in India, so dressed or otherwise.

An investigating committee later condemned Dyer's action and he was forced into retirement. However, a public subscription fund undertaken in England raised a large sum of money in his behalf, some measure of continuing British belief that the general had done the right thing. Gandhi was distressed and infuriated. He returned to the viceroy a gold medal he had earlier received from the British government, doing so because the British responses to the incident "have filled me with the gravest misgiving regarding the future of the Empire."[76] Gandhi now prescribed "a remedy of non-cooperation" with the government, and this policy, which he henceforth followed, gained in popularity.

Gandhi also regretted that the Indian people had reverted to violence; he considered that they were not yet quite ready for the *satyagraha* that he wished practiced and that he considered the only viable response to British rule. But other participants and observers, away from the Indian scene, concluded that violence was the only effective means of protest against military-bound colonial rule. This particular position was worked into a historical principle some time later by Frantz Fanon, in his now famous, *The Wretched*

Hindu demonstration in Detroit, 1931, to protest Gandhi's imprisonment. The protest was supported by local members of Sinn Fein, the Irish nationalists. From the National Archives.

of the Earth. Because the colonial act was itself one of violence Fanon argued that its removal required the same means. Violence would be a form of catharsis. "Violence is a cleansing force," he wrote. "It frees the native from his inferiority complex and from his despair and inaction; it makes him fearless and restores his self-respect."[77]

Fanon was observing the national liberation movement in Algeria of the 1950s when he made these comments, but by that time the principle of violent action was well-established as the most effective means to unhinge colonial rule. Whether violence was inherent in colonialism, whether it was a global characteristic of the later twentieth century, whether it was a new expression of old behavior—these are interesting questions, but ones without facile answers. The one certain historical condition was this: colonial rule was minority and alien rule; therefore, when threatened, the colonial administration's usual response was a trigger response, to bring forth troops to dispel the crowd. The response seldom worked in the long run, but it usually had immediate, positive effects. General Dyer thought that he had saved the Punjab from anarchy and revolt when he ordered his riflemen to fire on the masses at Jalliamwallah Bagh. He was wrong.

The test that Dyer failed was one of many. The first half of the twentieth century, down to the global violence unleashed by World War II, was the time in which Europeans were trying to consolidate what they had so recently gained, and indigenous peoples were trying to determine how they might regain what was lost—or gain something new. The forms of colonial protest were direct reactions to the problems of colonial rule. They seldom went beyond this to the modern terms of nationhood. As many historians have argued, this was the time of "proto-nationalism," when freedom was desired but when the "free" nation, the sovereign state, was still ill-defined or not yet contemplated.[78]

There is a certain irony to be found in the fact that the *pax colonia* was a *casus belli* of sorts. With the establishment of administrative empires peopled by individuals anxious to stimulate commerce, build roads, and collect taxes regularly, the effects of European modernism penetrated far into the countryside. Money taxes replaced taxes-in-kind; the corvée became a widespread means of creating the necessary infrastructure; new lands were put into cultivation and older ones were replanted to suit the needs of an export economy. All of these activities disturbed the old order and placed heavy burdens on populations that neither understood nor desired the European presence. Popular protest against these economic pressures was frequent in the early twentieth century, as evident in the famous Hut Tax War in Sierra Leone in 1898 and in the far-reaching riots in Indochina in 1908. One demonstration in that colony resulted in 13 dead or wounded out of a crowd of 800.[79]

Within the colonial city protest also developed dramatically and for reasons of the same nature as those provoking agitation in the countryside. The general problem was again one of disruption caused by a socio-economic system that exploited local populations. However, the urban problem was particularly aggravated by the vicissitudes of the international economy. With the outbreak of World War I, city life increased its economic tempo. Raw materials and manufactured goods were required in war-torn Europe and, therefore, port commerce rose as did wages and the cost of living. When the war ended, the local economies slipped precipitously because the national economies sought to recoup what they had lost during the war. Then, of course, the Great Depression worked its effects overseas as well as at home. The

instability of the global economy resulted in a number of strikes. Approximately 700 cloth dyers struck in Cholon, Indochina, over low wages in 1922.
The great Chinese seaport strikes of 1925, described by Malraux in *The Conquerors*, were provoked by matters of wages and labor exploitation. The
French possessions of North Africa and the mandated territories of the Near
East were all strike-ridden in the 1920s and 1930s. Cairo was the center of
a series of strikes that culminated in a general strike of 1924. In South Africa
a strike called by white miners to protest the possible use of black Africans
in the mines was broken by Prime Minister Smuts in 1922, but he lost his
position in 1924 largely as a result of this action. The Nationalists won
power, a development that moved South African politics away from the British empire.

However frequent, the strikes at this time were less disturbing to the *pax
colonia* than the rebellions that erupted into major warfare. Most famous was
the Rif War in the Atlas Mountains of Morocco, waged between 1921 and
1926 by Abd-el-Krim against the imposition of Spanish rule there. The
Spanish were supported by the French in their effort to crush this rebellion.
To the East, the Italians in Libya encountered Omar Mukhtar, a Sanusi leader
who, even though over 60 years of age, led a wily campaign that embarrassed
the Fascist regime in the 1920s.

Of all the uprisings none was more obviously the result of the forced
modernizing policies of the Europeans than the Druze rebellion of 1925–27.
It had its origin in the energetic and despotic leadership of one Captain
Carbillet, who assumed the position of governor of the Djebel-Druze area
upon the death of the Syrian incumbent.[80] With a spirit that matched that of
Lyautey and a tact that did not, Carbillet began his own *mise en valeur* of
the territory. He initiated economic and administrative reforms as well as the
construction of roads and schools. The intensity of his activities was matched
by the severity of burdens on the local population. Tax receipts were
insufficient to pay for the desired economic progress and hence the
population was forcibly enlisted to work. The Druze leaders demanded
Carbillet's recall. The French acted obstinately and imperiously; the Druze
rankled under the foreign rule they already detested. Tension mounted, and
violence erupted. A colonial war then occurred, with Damascus badly
bombed by the French, and with the insurrection lasting until the spring of
1927.

In another ten years the Syrian war was pushed back in memory by the sounds and sights of the Italian preparations for war in Ethiopia. Here was a war of colonial conquest, protested primarily by the single voice of the emperor, Haile Selassie. The war dramatically highlighted the entire question of colonialism and stood as proof of the fact that the old imperialism had not vanished in the face of protest. Mussolini unleashed his cumbersome force on October 3, 1935, regularly urged his hesitant generals on, and finally rejoiced in victory on May 9, 1936, when the Italians occupied the capital city of Addis Ababa.

The Western world was stunned, if not shocked, by Mussolini's behavior. Yet the aggrieved Haile Selassie received very little sympathy personally, and his country's plight was treated more like a legal problem than a moral one. It was not Italy's demands, but its methods, that were bothersome. The author of an article appearing in *The Round Table* shortly before the war began put the matter this way: "If there is to be peace, a more ample 'place in the sun' must be found today for Germany, Italy, and Japan than they obtained in 1919." Such an adjustment, he continued, ought be made peacefully through the League of Nations. "The significance of the Abyssinian question is that it brings the issue nakedly to the front," he concluded.[81]

The broader issue of imperialism as white domination was also brought to the front by the intensifying Pan-African movement. According to George Padmore, both chronicler of the movement and a very active participant in it:

The brutal rape of Ethiopia combined with the cynical attitude of the Great Powers convinced Africans and people of African descent that the black man had no rights which white men felt bound to respect if they stood in the way of their imperialist interests.[82]

The Italian aggression in Ethiopia occurred at the time that Garvey's movement had lost momentum and, conversely, that the Pan-African movement, chiefly directed by W. E. B. Du Bois, was gaining in strength.[83]

A new sense of common cause arose as "blacks felt it necessary to look to themselves" in the face of Mussolini's invasion.[84] In London, Paris, and many of the cities of West Africa, Africans spoke out vigorously and demonstrated angrily.[85] Given additional reason to denounce imperialism, they were also provided with the opportunity to fuse metaphysically the Ethiopia of biblical reference with the Ethiopia of Italian assault, even though the two were not at all contiguous.[86] The attack on Ethiopia was, accordingly, interpreted as an attack on African civilization.

Ethiopians sign up to fight in the war against Italy, 1935.
From the National Archives.

Mussolini paid little or no attention to the sounds of public protest. Yet he was not unmindful of the problems affecting the colonial world. Only a few years earlier, when Gandhi had paid him a visit in Rome, the dictator castigated his children with the following words, when they had laughed at the goat that Gandhi had brought along for milk: "That man and his goat are shaking the British Empire."[87]

The British control of India lasted somewhat longer than Mussolini's of Ethiopia. On May 9, 1936, the Italians proudly rumbled into Addis Ababa. On April 6, 1941, they wearily departed, defeated by the British in a minor campaign of World War II. Just a year after this event, President Roosevelt, responding to another bit of news, asked Winston Churchill why the British were unwilling to grant India immediate independence. The Cripps mission, sent to India to review the current political situation, had recommended on March 30, 1942, that steps be taken "for the earliest realization of self-government in India." To Roosevelt's question, raised by the advice of the

Cripps mission, Churchill replied that he "could not take the responsibility for the defence of India if everything else is to be thrown into the melting-pot at this crucial juncture."[88]

Everything was not. The end of empire did not occur until after World War II. Then, however, the end was dramatically short.

CHAPTER 6

The End of Empire

Nineteen and one-half hours after their departure from Heathrow Airport in London, the royal couple landed at Nairobi, Kenya, the first official stop in a planned tour of the Commonwealth, which was to cover 30,000 miles over a five-month period of time.[1] As Princess Elizabeth and her consort, Prince Phillip, alighted at Nairobi, the correspondent for *Life* magazine observed the welcoming scene and described it:

There were stiff-starched officials whose medals tinkled in the sun, proud gaunt spearmen who had done lions to death in single combat, clerks who had spent their lives doing nothing bolder than lick envelopes franked ''On His Majesty's Service.''
    These were cross sections of the British world. At the sight of Elizabeth, they loosed a surflike sound to express the great thing they had in common: loyalty to the crown.[2]

The setting and the commentary on it may seem anachronistic considering that the date was February 1, 1952. Yet here was another royal progress in lands overseas—the sort of ceremony that the British had developed into a minor art of empire. Shortly after World War I, the then heir to the throne, the popular Prince of Wales, had made his several goodwill tours. Princess Elizabeth was now doing much the same. On the surface—where bouquets were given and greetings of welcome exchanged—the political condition of Kenya appeared unchanged. But within a decade Kenya, like most of the rest of colonial Africa, would be free of formal imperialism.
    If the *Life* correspondent found the romantic rhetoric of imperialism suit-

able to his description of the airport scene in Kenya, his colleagues already had reported more soberly on the dissolution of empire elsewhere. In the short period of time between the end of World War II and the planned royal tour of 1952, the geographic dimensions of the colonial world had been severely reproportioned. In the Far East the changes were the most dramatic. The Philippines, as had been promised before the war, were granted nationhood in 1946, appropriately on July 4. India, Pakistan, Burma, and Ceylon had each gained independence from the British Crown and had been established as republics. Farther east, the Dutch colonial empire had completely disappeared. After a forceful attempt to regain control of the East Indies, the Dutch, responding to diplomatic pressure generated in the United Nations, agreed to transfer sovereignty to the United States of Indonesia in 1949. In Indochina the French were fighting what was even then generally agreed to be a desperate struggle to reassert their authority.

If, in contrast, empire in Subsaharan Africa still had the outer semblance of order, the northern portion of the continent was changing politically. Egypt, which had gained nominal independence in 1922, underwent a coup d'etat in 1952 that led to the establishment of a republic that helped hasten the departure of the remaining British guarding the Suez Canal. Even before this resolution of the Egyptian question, Libya, one of the most recently acquired colonies, gained independence—but after an administrative, not a colonial, struggle. As a European battlefield during World War II, Libya was no longer a colonial possession but a military-occupied country at the war's conclusion. The former colony was placed under United Nations control, but this arrangement, however ill-defined, was also short-lived; it ended on December 24, 1951, when the land was granted independence.

As described in a popular term of the time, empire was collapsing, as if swept by cosmic forces. Such indeed was the perception of those still concerned with colonial dominion. General Georges Catroux, Gaullist governor-general of Algeria in 1943, later wrote that "French North Africa was caught up in a wind of emancipation coming at once from the East and from across the Atlantic." Then, in 1960, Prime Minister Harold Macmillan made his now famous statement before the South African parliament: "The wind of change is blowing through this continent."[3]

Whenever the metaphor is meteorological, there is a suggestion of historical inevitability. What becomes "inevitable" in human affairs is long in forming, the "slow conspiracy of the ages," as the Frenchman René de Chateaubriand said of the French Revolution. The "collapse" of empire has been seen—retrospectively—as foreordained. Resistance movements and a sense of national awakening have been traced to those moments when Europeans first disembarked and unlimbered their cannon. Self-doubt about the colonial enterprise has also been detected from the time of its initiation, with the words of the eighteenth-century *philosophe* Turgot, "colonies, like fruit, will fall from the tree when ripe," reworked into more suitable, contemporary idioms.

What was occurring at the time Princess Elizabeth was greeted by the governor of Kenya, who was still outfitted in traditional whites and ostrich-plumed helmet, has usually been analyzed as beginning several decades before. The Indian politician and historian K. M. Panikkar argued in 1959 that "The Second World War gave the coup de grâce to a system which had already broken down and which could no longer function effectively."[4]

Although the dramatic simplicity of this statement is appealing, the condition it describes was far more complicated and much less neatly defined chronologically than the statement supposes. The colonial system had certainly not "broken down" in the interwar period. If anything, it was articulated at this time, as the preceding narrative has attempted to demonstrate. Moreover, the Second World War did not dispatch imperialism with any contrived finality.

If any metaphor is to be employed, the chemical one of catalyst is probably most appropriate. The Second World War brought together the various ingredients of discontent and dissatisfaction; it compounded the problems of rule and weakened the European will to dominate; it rearranged the economic order so that the welfare state replaced the liberal state, thus increasing the purposes and expenses of administration. These elements prompted change—but not immediately, not everywhere at the same time, nor in the same manner.

The danger in Panikkar's interpretation, as no doubt in the previous paragraph criticizing it, is in the historical treatment of the many forms of imperialism and colonies as if they did indeed form a system, as if there was some sort of structural development—organic or mechanical—that was later found to be flawed or diseased, that collapsed or was destroyed.

Overseas empires were never well integrated; they were inconstant affairs, rarely characterized by long periods of fixity or serenity. Huge chunks of territory had been gained and lost frequently during the 500 years of this political activity. French Canada and the thirteen British North American colonies are the obvious examples of previous loss, while the "scramble for

Africa'' marks the great land-grabs of the late nineteenth century. Yet even the outward appearance of masterful domination at this time was belied by internal discontent, as the French struggled through most of their history in Algeria to keep the "colonial peace" or as the British went from one African war or skirmish to another. Elsewhere expressions of discontent were not unusual. The Sepoy Mutiny of 1856 in India had shattered all British illusions of peaceful community in the subcontinent; and the bomb that severely wounded the viceroy, Lord Hardinge, as he ceremonially entered the new capital of Delhi in 1912, demonstrated that "loyalty to the crown" was not a universally appreciated sentiment.

Placed within the larger context of this turbulent history of empire, the interwar years seem to have been constructive ones—and not so conflict-ridden as to suggest the inevitable end of empire. The enthusiasm for imperialism had by then waned, but the task of colonial development was undertaken with considerable hope and spirit. The future in the 1920s and 1930s only looked bleak after empire was over. Contemporaries were cautiously confident.

Even in India, where the most advanced strides toward nationalism had been taken, the inevitability of independence was not yet recognized by the British authorities in the 1920s. Reform in the direction of dominion status was suggested but not achieved. A system of internal self-government and of dyarchy, or shared power, was introduced by the Montagu-Chelmsford reforms of 1919. "The system of autocracy has been abandoned," announced the Duke of Connaught when he inaugurated the new system in 1921.[5] In place of autocracy some of the elements of parliamentary government were arranged, and these were enhanced by the Government of India Act of 1935, which ensured responsible government throughout the provinces, extended the dyarchical principle to the central government itself, and called for a federal system joining the princely states with British India.

As usual in imperial matters, appearances were deceiving. The 1935 act was conservative in tone and designed at a time when British confidence had again grown. The fundamental federal principle was contingent upon approval of the majority of the princes for its realization, and the parliamentary expansiveness of the act was hedged by reserve powers for the Raj. Nehru dubbed the act a "new charter of bondage."[6]

Mohandas Gandhi refused even to read the act because neither he nor any other Indian leader had had a part in its drafting. However, Gandhi was a major factor in the reforms the British were initiating, because his leadership

of the nationalist movement had hurried the British on to political accommodations they had not immediately desired.

The viceroy at the time when Gandhi became a figure to reckon with was
Lord Irwin, who was tall, gaunt, and conciliatory. He recognized only two
options for Great Britain in India: forceful domination or peaceful compromise. He chose the latter and entered into negotiations with Gandhi, which
took place within the splendid spaces of the newly opened Viceroy House.
The sight was more than that archimperialist Winston Churchill could take.
He fulminated:

It is alarming and nauseating to see Mr. Gandhi, a seditious, Middle Temple
lawyer, now posing as a fakir . . . striding half-naked up the steps of the
viceregal palace . . . to parlay on equal terms with the representative of the
King-Emperor.[7]

That was Churchill out of power. Nevertheless, Churchill in power was of
the same mind. In 1942 he announced: "I have not become the King's first
minister in order to preside over the liquidation of the British Empire."[8]

Yet he did reluctantly carry out much of that unwanted responsibility at
a later time. The Second World War, which provided the occasion for
Churchill to appear as a figure of great strength, reduced the British empire
to a condition of great weakness.

Described in broad historical terms, the Second World War was the most
fierce and far-spread of all the conflicts in the era of modern imperialism.
The new empires of Nazi Germany and Imperial Japan aggressively challenged the older empires and absorbed much of their territory. Germany
dominated most of the European colonial nations—conquering France, Belgium, and the Netherlands, and making Italy a vassal state. The Nazis so
threatened Great Britain that its ability to retain its territories scattered around
the world was gravely impaired. Japan took advantage of these difficulties
occurring a continent away by seizing what the Europeans could not effectively defend. In little more than two years Japan created its euphemistically
described "Great East Asian Co-Prosperity Sphere," some 2,000 miles in
diameter and running among the islands and along the shores of the Pacific
Ocean. In the same length of time, Germany forged the largest territorial
empire that had ever spanned the European continent. Quickly amassed,
brutally administered, and crudely exploited, both empires soon spent their
expansive forces. In the spring of 1942, the Japanese suffered a severe naval
set-back in the Battle of Midway; in the winter of 1942, the Germans were
held at Stalingrad.

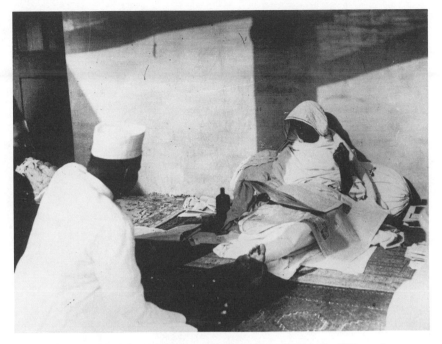

Mohandas Gandhi, in Delhi for a reception with Lord Irwin, in 1931, reads a
newspaper in the sun, 1931. From the National Archives.

Nazism was imperialism without restraint, the unfortunate extension of the
doctrine of force to obvious conclusion. Nazism was a crude mixture of racist
ideology, expansionist demands for *Lebensraum*, and militarism and severe
occupation policy. Its expansionist policy was justified before the fact by the
terms *Ostpolitik* and *Kolonialpolitik*, the first an expression of imagined need
for settlement colonies in Eastern Europe, the second, an argument to regain
the lost, overseas areas in order to ensure autarchy or economic self-sufficiency. Once expansion began, the German quest for territory seemed
insatiable, an effort to give real meaning to the words of the *Horst Wessel
Lied*: "Europe today, tomorrow the world."[9]

Only Great Britain in 1940 mustered the strength to resist the Nazi on-
slaught, but the British were badly taxed, both at home and in the desert
where war now threatened their traditional hold on the northeastern corner
of Africa.

The North African campaign, fought for and across the colonial territories
of Egypt, Libya, and Tunisia, was not a traditional colonial war in personnel

Hindu bugler, standing near the Pyramids, announces the arrival of the first
empire troops in the Near East, 1939. From the National Archives.

or execution. Europeans using modern strategy and equipment converted the desert into an ideal battlefield—a vast arena in which the military could play, unobstructed by manmade obstacles like cities, undisturbed by the problems of large numbers of civilians.[10] Mobility of action, not fortress defense, was the main characteristic of battle. The Italians, who enjoyed the initial advantage in men and equipment, misconstrued the nature of modern strategy and undertook their campaign as if, indeed, it were a classical one. The British nimbly attacked, outflanked the cumbersome, well-equipped but outmoded, Italian military machine, and soon caused the Italians to reel backward, until Tobruck in Cyrenica was taken on January 22, 1941.

As the British moved forward, they utilized Fascism's earlier effort at modernization; their motorized equipment rolled along the Litoranea Libica. According to the Australian war correspondent Alan Moorehead, who covered the campaign: "It was a strange sensation to ride here on this sound motor-road through enemy territory."[11] Providing another example of historical irony, this Italian colonial achievement became the main avenue of Italian colonial defeat—this occurrence only five years after Mussolini had triumphantly ridden its length at its opening and at the peak of his role as the modern Caesar Augustus.

Mussolini's dismay at defeat in 1941 was not matched in mood by his northern ally, Adolph Hitler, who in disgust, but with calculation of possible advantages, sent aid to the Italians. He dispatched Erwin Rommel, soon to gain renown as the "Desert Fox," to Tripoli with the necessary equipment to undertake a forceful reply to the British. Rommel's arrival on February 15, 1941 began a campaign romanticized in the annals of war, one that continued back and forth across the desert until Field Marshal Bernard Montgomery cautiously massed his own British forces and proceeded to defeat the now exhausted and undersupplied Germans at the battle of El Alamein, only 70 miles from Alexandria, on October 23, 1942.

Rommel, who had been in Germany when the battle began, rushed back to North Africa and quickly determined that the situation was hopeless. He retreated. The Germans continued to do so until they were finally repulsed from North Africa in early 1943, just a few months after the Anglo-American landings in Morocco and Algeria had been effected.

By then, however, the tracks of Rommel's heavy tanks had been covered by the shifting sands of the desert. The footprints of Napoleon's infantry had so disappeared a century and one-half before.

Rommel had his own imperial vision, one of Napoleonic proportions,

Field Marshal Erwin Rommel in North Africa, 1941.
From the National Archives.

which was expressed in the last chapter of his book *Krieg Ohne Hasse*. Had
he more equipment and more troops, he wrote, he probably could have swept
the British out of Egypt, moved on to Persia and then into the Caucasian
steppes, there to undermine the Soviets. "Who fights on a world scale," he
stated in an epigram that would have pleased the more aggressive protago-
nists of nineteenth-century empire, "must think continentally."[12]

The British certainly needed no reminder of this sort in early 1942; they
knew the difficulties of global war. Nowhere was their position more precarious than in the Pacific where a long-anticipated clash with the Japanese had
been dramatically realized on February 15, 1942, when 60,000 empire troops
guarding the fortress of Singapore, surrendered. In Berlin, Joseph Goebbels,
Nazi propaganda minister, noted in his diary entry of February 16: "For the
first time in the war the English are obliged to hoist the white flag in grand
style." Winston Churchill would later write that this was "the worst disaster
and the largest capitulation in British history."[13]

For the Japanese, however, the attack on Singapore was one of the several necessary moves against the European colonial powers to secure hegemony in the region. Moreover, the Japanese high command realized that the formidable enemy was not Great Britain, but the United States.

In the 1930s Japanese foreign policy was marked by impatience and ambition. Of paramount importance was the desire to retain the great power status only recently won. Next there was the growing anxiety over America's Pacific role and the vast potential of that nation's industrial resources. Finally, the military was seized by the opportunity provided, after Hitler's initial successes in western Europe, by the weak hold of the European colonial powers on their Asiatic possessions. The mood of the Japanese government in the late 1930s was well-assessed by an eminent Japanese statesman of the time, who said of his country:

She was obsessed by the urgency of her immediate problems. She rushed in time and again; she reverted to the methods of European imperialism of the dim, distant past.[14]

The collision of competing empires in the Far East was not unexpected. A Japanese naval officer, in a book published in English in 1936, wrote that "England is already on the down-grade; Japan has started on the up-grade. The two come into collision because England is trying to hold on to what she has, while Japan must perforce expand."[15]

Indeed the English were holding on to what they had, and they made that determination clear when they designated Singapore to be the strategic center of interwar British strength in the Pacific and, consequently, the regional emblem of British rule. Later critics would say that the formidable-appearing bastion only created the illusion of power. That illusion was graphically presented on February 14, 1938, when the prow of the governor's yacht cut the ribbon stretched across the King George VI dock in the opening ceremonies. The ceremonies, muted by imperial standards, were of sufficient grandeur to hide the fact that the naval facilities were still not completed and—far more important—that a military exercise conducted the week before had demonstrated the lamentable weaknesses of the defenses of the Malayan peninsula and of the port of Singapore.[16]

The Japanese would effectively exploit these weaknesses as they pursued their "southern advance." The decision to shift from an Asian continental policy to a Pacific naval one occurred in the late 1930s. By then the military expansion begun with the invasion of Manchuria in 1931 had been compli-

New Graving dock in Singapore, 1938. From the National Archives.

cated by the undeclared war with China, a war which became a major conflict in 1937. Victory eluded the Japanese on the mainland, and so the military acceded to the naval plan for a southward thrust that would secure for Japan vitally needed resources and, possibly, the means to resolve the war with China by getting an economic stranglehold on Chiang Kai-shek.

The first action was against Indochina, which was forced to submit to Japanese demands in July 1940. The domination of northern Indochina enabled Japan to stop the flow of goods into China by way of the Yunnan railroad, then China's principal line of external communications. However, the action against Indochina caused the American government to impose an embargo on scrap steel and aviation petroleum supplied to Japan. This decision, in turn, urged the Japanese to consider seizing the Dutch East Indies, the major available alternative source of oil.

Thus Japan's fear of the United States—of its economic reprisals and industrial-naval power—made forceful expansion seem imperative. To secure vital resources, Japan had to strike; to avoid the ill-effects of the forthcoming increase of American naval strength when, by 1943, the Japanese navy would only be at 50 percent parity of the American, Japan had to strike soon.[17] Such in sum was Japanese official thought.

On December 7, 1941, the Japanese decision was launched on the sea and in the air. The attack on Pearl Harbor was a severe setback for the United States, but the fall of Singapore in February of the new year was an even worse disaster for Great Britain. In an amazingly short period of time, the Japanese had realized their immediate objectives. But they had risked all; they lacked the reserves, both in trained men and sophisticated equipment, to carry on an extended war.

The great naval gamble that the Japanese had undertaken succeeded no more in the Pacific than had the military venture risked by Hitler on the European continent. In each instance the expansionist power was slowly forced back, its periphery diminishing until final surrender.

Colonial empire, the empire created by the Europeans in the nineteenth century, did not endure much longer. The overturned and broken statue of the famous colonial administrator Paul Bert was the sight that greeted the eyes of the French when they returned to Hanoi in 1945.[18] Here was an ominous augury of the future for the colonialists. Few expected that future to be imminent, however.

The wartime activities destroyed colonies but did not shatter the belief in empire. The colonial nations anticipated maintaining their possessions, albeit in a manner modified to suit the needs of the time. Even the defeated Italians briefly hoped to retain one segment of Libya, Tripolitania, if all else was lost.[19] The Dutch, fearful of the effects of American policy in the Far East, tried to shed the colonial image by declaring in December 1942 the creation of a Commonwealth that would bind the former colonies into a partnership.[20] The French were more hopeful yet, their hope born out of the peculiarities of their military defeat.

Hardly had the Germans finished dancing their jig over the armistice they had forced on the defeated French, then the French nation was redeemed overseas. General de Gaulle, declaring on radio from London on June 18, 1940, that a battle had been lost, not a war, and that France would continue to fight, sought support from the administrators in the colonies. A response came quickly on August 26, 1940, from Felix Eboué, governor of Chad, and himself a native of French Guiana.[21] Soon other support came from black Africa, an indication, sentimentally interpreted, of the loyalty of the empire to France. It was indeed from the colonies that de Gaulle drew his initial strength, established his provisional government for the first time on French soil, and even took the first steps to arrange the postwar colonial world. At Brazzaville in January and February of 1944 a major conference was held to determine the future organization and purposes of the French empire. There was talk of internal reforms, the introduction of local legislative assemblies and the extension of the suffrage, but the major consideration was the relationships of the colonies to metropolitan France. The statement on the matter was more nineteenth century in mood than twentieth, more a reaffirmation of France's *mission civilisatrice* than an assertion of change:

. . . the goals of the task of civilization accomplished by France in her colonies rule out any idea of autonomy, any possibility of evolution outside the French bloc of empire; the eventual creation, even in the distant future, of self-government for the colonies is to be set aside.[22]

At war's end the French regarded their colonial empire as beneficent, a major source of national regeneration and the essential factor in France's continuing role as a great power.

The British debate over the future status of their empire was conditioned and complicated by the wartime alliance, the Anglo-Saxon partnership that brought Churchill and Roosevelt together, but not in their opinions about imperialism. As the war progressed, Franklin Roosevelt became for a while intractably anti-imperialist while Winston Churchill maintained the consistency of one who never doubted for a moment that the British empire was a force for the good—and should continue to be after the war.

Between these two men opinion ranged far.[23] One thing was certain: the nature of colonial relationships would have to change. The word "partnership" was then replacing "trusteeship" in British discussions of future social relationships because the newer-found term was not so paternalistic or negative.[24] But Americans and Australians alike were talking seriously of internationalizing colonial responsibilities, of establishing "trusteeships" that would be accountable to some international body. Such talk easily upset the British who, in turn, suspected the Americans of pursuing an indirect form of imperialism that was couched in the term "strategic trusteeship," designed to cover the American naval imperative of retaining the captured Japanese island possessions as bases for a winning Pacific strategy. Under no conditions was the American navy high command interested in internationalizing this special form of trusteeship.

The debate over the new status of dependent territories crested at San Francisco, where the United Nations was established in May of 1945. A "Trusteeship Council" was created within the United Nations, the successor of the League Mandate Commission. But the functions of the council rested on a broad declaration of principle, Chapter XI of the UN Charter, which was entitled "Declaration Regarding the Non-Self Governing Territories." The particular issue that raised great concern here was independence. The British were opposed to having the idea officially stated, as were the French, and therefore recommended "self-government" as the more appropriate objective. It was Harold Stassen, a member of the American delegation, who finally persuaded the delegates to accept this terminology. He told the delegation "we . . . did not wish to find ourselves committed to breaking up the British Empire."[25]

However persistent old-vision leaders like Churchill and de Gaulle may have been in their effort to retain a semblance of the prewar colonial order, the moment was over. "The war," remarked a former Belgian colonial officer in what must certainly have been the most laconic comment on the subject, "had assuredly not raised the prestige of Europeans."[26]

It had raised doubts and created new conditions at all levels, which changed the local colonial scene. A war against forces representing brutal domination and racist thought would have been difficult to justify in the older terms of imperialist ideology. "The destruction of Hitlerism . . . must mean the end of the domination of one nation over another," commented an editorial in the Bombay Chronicle of September 16, 1939.[27] Europeans themselves expressed doubt in the face of colonial defeat. The foundation of their authority—power—and the justification of their domination—order—were destroyed by the invader. The myth of white supremacy had been dissipated before, but now the myth of uniquely effective white rule was dispelled. In a reconsideration of the British defeat by the Japanese in Burma, an English author summarized the meaning of the condition in florid prose:

The humiliation could not be washed away. No fights, no clemency, no promises, no splendid plans for rehabilitation would serve. There was only one thing that would serve—goodbye, a cordial, even an affectionate goodbye, but a quick goodbye, a goodbye for ever.[28]

More than a change in sentiment was registered by Europeans shortly after the war. The bureaucratic relationship between the Europeans and the indigenous populations was also altered so that the purposes of empire seemed cloudier than ever.

The wartime isolation of empires from their European metropolitan bases had pronounced effects. In Indochina and Indonesia, the European administrative role was drastically revised. The Japanese placed most of the Dutch in concentration camps and, because the occupying forces had few administrative personnel among them, came to rely heavily on Indonesians to fill the positions forcefully vacated by the Dutch.[29] In Indochina—nominally under French rule until the last months of the war—no French replacements for existing personnel were available. Vietnamese were therefore introduced into previously inaccessible positions. Governor-General Decoux undertook a revolutionary step in 1942 when he abolished the salary differences existing between Vietnamese and French in the civil service.[30]

The modification in administration in wartime Africa was primarily attitudinal. In Nigeria the isolation from the war front first caused a sense of uselessness among European administrators; but later, when the tide had turned in Allied favor, a sense of overwork and lack of appreciation set in, understandable in light of the fact that the administrative department of Nigeria had already been reduced to 70 percent of its normal complement in 1941.[31] A similar sense of ennui was evident in the Belgian Congo, where administrative efforts were shifted to the new, primary task of supplying raw materials to the Allies and, hence, turned away from the needs of the local population. The resultant decline in the spirit of Belgian paternalism was interpreted adversely by one colonial official who stated that previous social relationships had been altered, which caused the indigenous population to express the feeling that "the whites don't like us anymore."[32]

The most radical change occurred in India. Even before 1939, the Indianization of the civil service had begun. Talk and proposals about Indian participation preceded World War I, but the major step was taken by the Royal Commission, appointed in 1923 and chaired by Lord Lee. The Lee Commission concluded that the small number of Indians then in the Indian Civil Service should be radically increased so that parity between British and Indians would be achieved in about 15 years. This did occur; in 1940, the Service was nearly evenly divided: 597 Indians, 588 British.[33]

This caused more confusion than demoralization among the British members. The shift from rule to governance, from imperialism to accountability and shared authority, forced questions about the future of the Indian Civil Service and, more important, of the British role in it.[34] However, morale demonstrably improved as the war approached India. With Burma occupied by the Japanese, and India itself used as a major military and air base, the civil servants were charged with new responsibilities, fired-up with a sense of urgency. "There was a feeling of security under war-time conditions; officials were full of confidence in discharging their duties," one participant later reminisced.[35]

The return to peace meant no return to previous modes and moods of colonial domination. The indigenization of the civil services, quite advanced both in India and Indonesia by war's end, noticeably intensified in Africa. In 1946 the Harrigan Salaries Structure Commission in effect abolished the British racially biased class system in administration by ensuring that senior positions were open to Africans as well as to Europeans. In 1950 the French parliamentary representative from Senegal, Lamine Guèye, introduced a bill that ensured equal pay and treatment for Africans occupying positions of comparable level to those of Europeans.

Few, if any, of the European colonial administrators did not expect change. There was a realization that the colonial era would come to an end. But, as one individual put it, that knowledge was much like the awareness of old age to a person who is young; it was to be an occurrence in the distant future.[36] Because bush life presented no demonstrable change of major proportions—the mortar-and-pestle and the tom-tom maintained their regular cadence—there was little daily indication that the end could possibly be near. Furthermore, the old European conceit that effective self-rule was still beyond the capabilities of Asian and African populations persisted to the end.

The talk of change, like that of the weather, had become a regular colonial pastime, something frequently referred to if not allowed to interfere with daily activities.[37] Those serving in India had discussed it in the 1930s; those serving in Africa began to mention it in the late 1940s and to fret over it in the 1950s. This latter mood is well expressed in fiction dealing with the phenomenon of political change in West Africa. In the postwar French novel *Passage de feu*, the narrator, in reality a French colonial administrator, says of the young colonial officer who is the hero of the work: "He began his career enthusiastically, but he noticed after a few months that he was living at the end of an epoch, that he arrived too late to enjoy for long the sweet taste of absolute power.''[38] Chinua Achebe's *No Longer At Ease*, the tragic odyssey of a young Ibo living in and moving through this age of transition, contains an archetypical English colonial administrator, a Mr. Greene, out of sorts because out of his time:

It was clear he loved Africa, but only Africa of Charles, the messenger, the Africa of his garden boy, and steward boy. He must have come originally with an ideal—to bring light to the heart of darkness, to tribal headhunters performing weird ceremonies and unspeakable rites. But when he arrived, Africa played him false. Where was his beloved bush full of human sacrifice? There was St. George, horsed and caparisoned, but where was the dragon?[39]

The same thought was presented with a particular poignancy by a former district officer in Tanganyika, as he reflected on the end of the colonial era. ''We saw our chosen careers fading away when we were at our most vigorous,'' he commented; and he therefore lamented that he and his associates were ''deprived of the prospects of all the glittering prizes that young men aspire to when they enter a great service like my own.''[40]

The dispirited mood of the individual administrator in the field does not figure prominently in the list of causes that explain decolonization. Although the peculiarities of the local colonial regime, like those of the political opposition and the cultural conditions of the region, are taken into account, there has been an academic tendency to treat the end of empire in a sweeping, global manner. The political similarities and the compressed time period in which they were revealed—the ''terminal decade'' of imperialism began with India's independence in 1947 and ended with Ghana's independence in 1957—invite the search for a general theory.

The model on which most such theories are based is mechanistic, a social-science derivative of Newtonian physics. The terms ''expansion'' and ''contraction'' suggest a linear process in which opposing forces are at work. ''Decolonization,'' wrote Frantz Fanon, ''is the meeting of two forces, opposed to each other by their very nature.''[41] As they acquired empires, the Europeans seemed to be moving out along lines of least resistance. As they withdrew from empire, they appeared to be vigorously pushed back by new forces of resistance. In this interpretation, power, which is measured metaphysically as well as statistically, as a function of will as well as of bayonets, explains both domination and collapse.

The colonial scene as viewed by those who felt oppressed—by Frantz

Fanon, for instance—was one in which the only assurance of success was intensifying opposition. In Fanon's terms, the colonial act was a violent one; its extirpation would accordingly need to be violent. The national liberation movements, politically and militarily organized, weakened, if they did not destroy, the base of European power to the extent that it could no longer support the colonial system. Then the Europeans negotiated. The major counterforce to European arms was guerrilla warfare, the strength of the weak, which drained the resources of the colonial occupier, psychologically fatigued him, and deprived him of his needed collaborators.

The imperialists seemed to stand alone. On the defensive in the colonies, criticized by political opponents at home, attacked from such diverse quarters as Moscow and Washington, they either were willing to devolve power or were discouraged from trying to retain it. Whichever their attitude, they were said to have lost the will to dominate. Weakened and uncertain, they gave in. In assessing the political position of Kwame Nkrumah at the moment before the independence of the Gold Coast, Margery Perham offered a homely metaphor as an explanation of this lesson in introductory physics that decolonization seemed to have become:

Dr. Nkrumah had made an exact estimate of the fortress confronting him. It had become as light as a stage property. Two or three pushes of his strong, irreverent hands and it was over.[42]

If indeed the imperial edifice had become so fragile, its impaired condition was the result of more than internal forces, the argument continues. An outside force, often described as "world opinion," buffeted empire with gusts of verbal discontent. In a statement that has since gained historical significance, the editor of *Life* admonished the British on October 12, 1942: "Quit fighting a war to hold the empire together." His anticolonialism was a pronounced American attitude of the time, one that continued to figure in national rhetoric to the time of President Dwight Eisenhower, who remarked that the United States "has traditionally been favorable to a policy of anticolonialism."[43]

The United States was loudly joined by others. The Soviet Union needed no encouragement to denounce imperialism. Its interwar rhetoric was intensified after World War II, when communism became an attractive ideology among the colonized. The transposition of terms so that industrial exploitation—capitalist versus proletarian—became colonial exploitation—imperialist nation versus oppressed people—was easily effected and just as easily appreciated by vast numbers of people. Smaller states that had known foreign domination, countries like Egypt, Burma, and Cuba, used the United Nations and international conferences as forums for public expression of discontent with colonial nations. The Bandung Conference held in 1955 was the first major gathering of Third World nations. The 29 invited nations from Asia and Africa gathered to consider their collective role in world affairs, and found their theme in the words of Chou en Lai, foreign minister of the People's Republic of China:

. . . the days when the Western powers controlled our destiny are already past. The destiny of African and Asian countries should be taken into the hands of the peoples themselves.[44]

The Cold War added a further dimension to the international forces playing on European empires. Each fearing the other's pretensions to global hegemony, the United States and the Soviet Union sought client states and attempted to establish spheres of influence around the world. The two superpowers distributed arms and intrigue, broadcasted propaganda, fused alliances, and met occasionally in direct confrontation, as in the Cuban missile crisis of 1964. The Americans, in an effort to ring the Soviet Union with air bases, took an interest in European colonial empires, not for their own sake but for the global advantages they might provide.

In a bifurcated world the colonial nations had little room to play the old game. However, the Cold War had a greater effect on the emerging new nations than on the declining old empires. The imagined international order the *pax colonia* had provided was gone, if it ever really had existed. American anticolonialism was modified in recognition of the role the British Empire had seemed to play. "Britain, which once had the training and the capability to manage a world," declared former Secretary of State Dean Acheson in a speech given in 1959, "no longer has that capability." His conclusion was that the United States would have to assume world leadership. "However much all of us may dislike this thought," he concluded, "the requisite power does not reside anywhere else."[45]

The three forces—colonial opposition, European disinclination from empire, and international pressure—worked in various combinations throughout the colonial world to make empire unsupportable. Successful when greeted with indifference, modern imperialism quickly failed when given serious attention.[46] So long as it was peripheral to the concerns of all it affected, and so indeed it was until the middle of this century, imperialism was tolerated, if not acclaimed. It was, as critics of British military involvement in the Near East during World War I had said, a "sideshow." After World War II, however, it was out front on the stage of world politics.

The end of empire was dramatic. However, it was not as catastrophic as other world events of such magnitude. It is true and tragic that major wars occurred in some regions, with the long history of conflict in Indochina or Vietnam being the most prominent. Riots and imprisonments also marred decolonization. But all in all the European withdrawal proceeded quickly and with a minimum of actual strife. Lord Samuel described the end of empire in India as a treaty of peace that was not the outcome of a war; and he considered this event to be unique in the annals of history.

Some historians of the British empire now affirm that outward appearances did not match unarticulated intentions. The change was one of form, not purpose. Just as modern imperialism was marked by the shift from informal to formal empire, its conclusion was the reversal of the process.[47] In giving up or granting political control, the British were hoping to retain economic advantage, to maintain a privileged political position without show. This assessment is not dissimilar to an earlier one made at the time colonies were gaining nominal freedom. Neocolonialism, a thesis particularly pursued by critics of Marxist ideological persuasion, stated that economic domination continued, even though political sway had ended. Through the maintenance of currency control, foreign aid, investment policies, and "off-shore" manufacturing, the former European colonial powers and also the United States, in its new capacity as center of world capitalism, exploited the former colonial regions to their own advantage. Kwame Nkrumah described the phenomenon in theory and in great detail in his *Neo-Colonialism, the Last Stage of Imperialism*, a title that advertised historical continuity. Nkrumah saw these new trade and financial arrangements as sophisticated tactics whereby the Western world took back with one hand what it had given with the other. He asserted that "neo-colonialism is the worst form of imperialism. For those who practice it, it means power without responsibility, and for those who suffer from it, it means exploitation without redress."[48]

The last two interpretations hint at, but do not explicitly state, what may become the dominant economic explanation of the end of empire. Put simply, this explanation asserts that colonial empires had become anachronistic. All such empires were fundamentally mercantile in purpose and organization. They were coeval with an age in which humankind's propensity was to truck, barter, trade, and to take outright whenever the occasion presented itself.

Simple trade relationships, consonant with the double-entry bookkeeping that kept Bob Cratchit perched on his stool, enabled colonial administrators to function quite well in a primitive way. Empire was served by unskilled labor whose chief virtue, when demonstrated, was good will. The functions and responsibilities of local administration were minimal and carried out idiosyncratically. That the British ruled India with only 1,200 members of the Indian Civil Service and that the French had about 900 members in their colonial corps serving all of their possessions in Subsaharan Africa should certainly suggest that something other than the qualities of pluck and charisma were at work. The laissez-faire state ruled lightly and haphazardly. Its chief responsibilities were maintaining order and collecting taxes. It was essentially non-interventionist, an attitude expressed in Margery Perham's phrase for indirect rule: "holding the ring."

In a rather subterranean way, the economic disturbances brought about by the world wars and the Depression began to disrupt local economies and undermine, by complicating, the rather simple relationships established between imperial administration and regional trade.[49] Both people and institutions were hastily put to new uses for which they were not prepared. "The new breed of Directors and Controllers," wrote one member of the Indian Civil Service about the experience acquired during World War II, "dealt not only with food, but with steel, cement, petrol, etc., and with the development of war industries."[50]

The combination of political unrest and economic strain explains the end of empire.

At the risk of seeming to offer romantic speculation rather than detailed historical examination, the student of decolonization might say that colonial empires were outsized, inefficient, unintegrated organizations that suited an age of steam-driven economies and iron-bound industrialization. Empires worked as well as the *Great Eastern*, and like that massive vessel they would be out of order in an age of telecommunications. In contrast with the current fascination with the power of limits,[51] the nineteenth-century empire builders were inspired by the power of the limitless, or what appeared to be limitless, which was emblematically described by the railroad tracks laid down on a desert floor or through a jungle. To have continued formal empire would have been an expensive proposition, increasing demands on finance and on available indigenous and European talent. The colonial cadet in Kano, Nigeria, who in 1951 found that the bicycle—his primary means of transportation—"geared us down to a pace that aggravated other frustrations," was unconsciously indicating what empire had been and what it could not become.[52]

Technology and economic aid were exported in large quantities during the final days of colonialism. But they were miniscule in relation to the need for meaningful development, often poorly distributed, and all too late to change the course of political events. Issues relating to economics and technology transfer continue to be the most debated historical aspect of modern imperialism and form a major component of contemporary Third World ideology. But issues such as these were separated from the official process by which political power was transferred.

In many instances—and in most occurring in West Africa—decolonization was a matter of negotiation, a settlement reached between the alien elite that was colonial and the indigenous elite that had been Europeanized. There were no rules to the game, but the understanding reached by both parties was in part obtained from common experiences and similar personal circumstances, which generally made communication easier and mediation more effective. Both groups were usually middle class in background, educated in the same language and according to similar prescripts—although these were originally foreign to the nationalists, obviously. Jawaharlal Nehru's command of the English language was often praised by the English; Léopold Sédar Senghor's command of French earned him the honor of being the grammarian for the constitution of the Fourth Republic of France. Hastings Banda, later president of Malawi, was educated in the United States and Scotland and was a practicing physician whose brief service in Liverpool was warmly remembered. Felix Houphouet-Boigny, later president of the Ivory Coast, had served as a French representative on the United Nations Trusteeship Council. The list of professionals with experience in European institutions made up an impressive element in the composition of nationalist leadership.

An equally significant factor was the history they shared in common. They formed a special cohort group whose mature lives spanned the decades of change. Nothing like it had occurred since the revolutionary era in the Western world at the end of the eighteenth century. Many later "fathers of their country" had begun as university students, évolués who benefited in this capacity from empire and who supported it. Later they became members of the "loyal opposition" when representative government was introduced into the colonies and, at the time or shortly thereafter, they were "prison graduates," jailed and then released for nationalist activities deemed a threat to the public peace.[53]

It was only a short time, often little more than a decade, from the hour when many of them had indicated their colonial loyalty to the moment when they rejoiced in national independence. The transition was usually easy and relatively smooth because the memory was not bitter. In 1946, for instance, the Sudanese leader, Fily-Dabo Sissoko exclaimed, during the debate over the colonial provisions of the new French constitution: "We are so French that we would like to remain with you until the end of time."[54] As Northern Rhodesia approached independence as the state of Zambia, Prime Minister Kenneth Kaunda said: "It is not possible for me to over-stress the importance that we attach to our past and present friendship with Her Majesty's Government."[55] An even stronger statement had been offered by the prime minister of Nigeria on independence day in 1960: "We are grateful to the British officers [colonial officers] whom we have known first as masters and then as leaders and finally as partners, but always as friends."[56]

Finally, there were those remarkable personal contacts, those accidents of encounter in an educational or professional environment. Georges Pompidou, prime minister of France during the presidency of Charles de Gaulle and later president himself, was a schoolmate and friend of Léopold Sédar Senghor, later president of the Republic of Senegal—and it was through Pompidou that Senghor embraced socialism. Lord Mountbatten described the peculiar circumstances in which he established his friendship with Nehru. The two were in Singapore in 1945, both appearing at the Indian Troops' Welfare Center where Lady Mountbatten was working. As the crowd surged forth to greet Nehru, Lady Mountbatten "lost her footing and went down in the rush. Nehru and I formed a rugger scrum and together we rescued her."[57] Mountbatten saw this as the occasion when their friendship began, a friendship that proved most important in another year when Mountbatten was viceroy of India and Nehru was head of the provisional government.

There are no such pleasant anecdotes found in the history of decolonization that took place in Indonesia, Indochina, and Algeria, the three colonies most severely contested. There, lengthy wars preceded European evacuation. In the Far East the Dutch and the French had assumed that a strong military campaign could crush the nascent nationalism they found before it reached insurmountable heights. But both colonial nations, however modern their available military equipment, lacked the necessary effectives to achieve complete victory. As one careful observer of the Vietnamese scene wrote:

The French forces sent to Indochina were too strong for France to resist the temptation of using them; yet not strong enough to keep the Viet-Minh from trying to solve the whole military problem by throwing the French into the sea.[58]

The latter did not occur, but military victory eluded the colonialists, and, as time went on, they lost the necessary groundwork of public support or, at the very least, public acquiesence. The Japanese had aggravated the colonial situation in two obvious ways. First, they had destroyed all earlier European pretensions by demonstrating the weakness of colonial rule. The Dutch put up little resistance when the Japanese invaded the East Indies in early 1942, the results of which were not lost on the Indonesians.[59] Indochina was not directly seized by the Japanese initially, but they stationed troops there and, in effect, had ensured that the Vichy-supported colonial regime should behave like a puppet state. When the Japanese did belatedly decide to establish direct control on March 9, 1945, they "swept away in a few hours eighty years of white supremacy."[60] Second, the brutal occupation policy of the Japanese, far harsher than anything ever maintained by the Europeans, had the effect of unifying the population behind the nationalists who desired to rid their lands of all foreign oppressors.

At war's end and in the wake of the Japanese retreat, a republic was established both in Indonesia and Indochina. The returning colonial forces were therefore confronted with something of a *fait accompli*, to which they made hasty adjustments. Both the Dutch and the French briefly recognized these republics but sought to circumvent and undermine them. One action they took was the creation of client states: the Dutch established a United States of Indonesia with 15 such states in addition to the Java-based Republic of Indonesia so that the Republic would be politically outweighed. The French high commissioner for Indochina, the admiral and one-time Carmelite monk, Thierry d'Argenlieu, created a separate Republic of Cochinchina, with the same privileges and authority granted the Republic of Vietnam only a few months before.

A more foreboding parallelism in the terminal years of each colony was the intensification of resistance, the development of guerrilla forces that harassed the colonial troops, yet denied them direct military encounters. As it would later be said of Algeria, two governments now reigned: that of the day, when the colonial forces seemed to dominate; and that of the night, when the guerrillas ruled where they would.

Although it would be questionable historical analysis to press such comparisons further, the common colonial experiences at this time and in these places seemed to present another example of the Bourbon mentality. The Bourbon rulers, it was said, learned nothing and forgot nothing. Both Dutch and French in the Far East returned after the war with the simple-minded attitude that the nationalists opposing colonialism were an ineffective minority that could be militarily destroyed at no great cost. When the Dutch launched their second major offensive against the Indonesians in December 1948, they expected to crush Republican resistance in a few weeks. They counted neither on the intensity of the Republican resistance nor on the increasing popular opposition to their continuing presence. The dimensions of this resistance can be measured by the fact that only 150 of the 10,000 civil servants in the region of Jakarta worked for the Dutch after that city had been taken in January 1949.[61]

The French persisted, too, in thinking military victory possible. But the war in Indochina continued, developing into three wars; one colonial, another civil, and a third international.[62] The colonial war began in December 1946 and continued until March 9, 1949, when southern Vietnam was granted its independence. Thereafter, a civil war between the two Vietnams continued, further complicated by the internationalization of the activity in 1950 when the French struck the pose of defenders of Southeast Asia against communism—a pose made striking by the outbreak of the Korean War shortly before. The international phase of the war—like the domestic one—continued even after the French had departed. The Americans first became involved imperceptibly in 1956 but soon increased their participation into a conflict of tragic proportions, not ending until 1973—America's longest war.[63] The colonial phase, even if disguised as an anti-communist action, ended disastrously on May 7, 1954, when the isolated and battle-scarred French fortress of Dien Bien Phu capitulated to the Vietnamese who, under the meticulously laid siege of the famous schoolteacher-turned-general and great theorist of guerrilla warfare, Vo Nguyen Giap, had succeeded as the French never thought possible. Briskly and wisely, the French acknowledged the end of their Far Eastern empire and thus bowed to Ho Chi Minh, the leader who had relentlessly pursued this policy of national liberation for a decade.

The French were determined that nothing of the sort would happen in Algeria, or so they planned when rebellion broke out in that colony in 1954. Perhaps with the exception of South Africa, the Algerian colonial problem was the most acute and enduring. France ruled Algeria as if it were an integral part of the French nation—which it was in a narrow legal sense. Through a series of specially contrived political arrangements—including a two-

Nationalist inscription in English in Malang, Java, 1948.
From the National Archives.

college electoral system that ensured that the French minority would always
be the political majority—the French maintained their dominance behind a
facade of representative government. Administrative and political reforms
that were introduced in 1946 through the Algerian Statute were little more
than a reaffirmation of previous French policy.

The French in Algeria had gained the reputation, a valid one, of being able
to dictate to Paris—not the other way around. The internal political difficulties of the weak Fourth Republic gave even greater authority to the Algerian
settlers who, in General de Gaulle's term, were determined to maintain the
Algérie du Papa, an antiquated regime. The resistance to change of the
French in Algeria in turn induced the intensity of national resistance. The
reformist groups, still attempting to work within the French colonial framework, were bypassed by a small number of militants who plotted outright
rebellion.

On November 1, 1954, the revolt began. Approximately 400 men engaged

Ho Chi Minh during a press reception in Paris, 1946.
From the National Archives.

in about 70 terrorist activities that destroyed the calm of the countryside and the confidence of the French in a peaceful solution. Although the French were then negotiating with Tunisia and Morocco—Algeria's neighbors and French protectorates—about their independence, no French official entertained the same outcome for Algeria. The liberal premier Pierre Mendès-France stated that "Algeria is not Tunisia." However, the FLN (National Liberation Front) was determined to refute the notion that "L'Algérie, c'est la France." The early effectiveness of the guerrilla warfare they pursued is easily measured by the increasing number of French troops concentrated in Algeria to keep the peace:

November 1954	54,500
February 1955	83,000
May 1955	100,000
April 1956	250,000[64]

Through their own effective and frequently brutal military policy, the French were able to secure the major cities, but the war then shifted to the countryside. "The war continued its monotonous course," wrote the journalist-turned-lieutenant Jean-Jacques Servan-Schreiber in 1957. "Operations and encirclements succeeded night patrols; outrages and destructions followed their usual cycle."[65] Yet the war had been effectively won in 1957, with the FLN's fighting forces tattered. However, popular opposition to French rule continued in Algeria and public indignation over the war arose to troubling proportions in France.[66] An army revolt in Algeria against the authority of the new president, Charles de Gaulle, did not help matters in 1961. De Gaulle finally made peace in 1962, more than seven years after the revolt had begun and had, in the course of events, toppled the Fourth Republic.

No other political development after Algeria was so grim or so bitterly contested. The transition in much of black Africa was uneventful, occasionally even festive. In that part of the world the British watched with interest and in hope that the "Westminster model" of government, with its emphasis on parliamentary government and a prime minister as the effective head of state, would obtain. In the words of one analyst, writing when this transition was occurring, the Westminster model "remains the most sought after of Britain's exports to the colonies."[67] The French, with their assimilationist tendencies persisting to the last, expected that cultural bonds would hold tight long after political ones had frayed.[68] The touching scene of African leaders standing tearfully before the newly turned grave of Charles de Gaulle at Colombey-les-Deux-Eglises in the autumn of 1970, was one brief moment when that expectation was fulfilled.

The primary characteristic of the European retreat from Subsaharan Africa was its suddenness. No one was truly prepared for it. One British administrator in Kenya then realized that "there simply wasn't going to be time to achieve an orderly independence."[69] The French colonial administrator and university professor Hubert Deschamps remarked in a lecture he gave in Brussels in 1963: "We developed too late an ultimate goal policy. . . . Thus evolution, although born of our contact and our action, for the most part escaped us and caught us by surprise."[70] The last lament of the imperialists was their missed opportunity to turn colonialism into development, to modernize so that Africa would be economically and politically able to fend for itself. This need for "laying the foundation for a modern future," according to Deschamps, came too late. "We all realized this only in 1945, and a mere fifteen years of formation were not enough."[71]

Such regrets were denounced as hypocritical by many who had long questioned European colonial motives, but no one had much opportunity to linger over them. Between 1957, the year in which Ghana obtained its independence, and 1964, when Zambia became independent, 19 colonies in black Africa became sovereign states. Each appeared as a republic, with its chief of state usually the head of the political party that had most effectively led the opposition to colonial rule. Almost all of these states were endowed initially with a European-modeled constitution and also ensured of continuing European economic aid. In many instances, old colonial hands stayed on to assist the new state in its transitional period.

However, this political change was punctuated by violence in some places. Most unusual and brutal was the Mau Mau movement in Kenya. It is doubtful whether this movement ought to be called nationalistic; it was essentially a protest by members of the Kikuyu people against colonial land policy, notably the so-called "White Highlands" on which the British had settled as ranchers. The land had originally been Kikuyu territory to which was attached a sacred quality. Urbanization and economic change aggravated the resentment over this land policy and caused the outbreak of Mau Mau in 1952. Although it was finally forcefully crushed by the British in 1956, it had hastened the end of colonial rule. In 1963 Jomo Kenyatta, earlier jailed for his alleged role in Mau Mau, became prime minister of independent Kenya.

After the main wave of political independence had swept Subsaharan Africa, the southern bastion of white dominance was also destroyed. Angola and Mozambique were the settings of guerrilla warfare that finally dislodged the Portuguese in 1975, following a domestic revolt in Portugal itself, which brought to power a regime pledged to decolonization. The end of the Portuguese presence was followed by that of white settler domination in Southern Rhodesia. The colony had proclaimed a unilateral declaration of independence in 1965 to avoid sharing power with black Africans. This maverick, racist republic continued until 1976, when, through pressure primarily exerted by the United States and South Africa, the regime reluctantly negotiated a transfer of power to Africans who established the new republic of Zimbabwe. Only South Africa, which broke away from the Commonwealth in 1961, continued in the manner of a colonial regime, with the white minority denying any meaningful authority to the black majority.

To speak of colonial empire today is to speak in the past tense. The remnants of European overseas territories are so small as to be insignificant and so reorganized politically as to merit a designation other than "possessions." As colonial empire receded, it exacerbated an old problem already aggravated by the labor needs of the early twentieth century but now greatly intensified by the rising political intolerance and declining economic opportunities found in the post-colonial world. The migration of the last three decades has been matched in its proportions only by the great European Transatlantic migration of the late nineteenth century.

The movement of millions of people from all parts of the world has been the most important social fact of our current global age. The range of this migration staggers the imagination, and the purposes that prompted it compose a catalog of human aspiration and anguish. Some 419,000 Palestinians left their homeland when the Israelis took control of their territory in 1948. From Hong Kong alone, some 60,000 Chinese, enjoying the status of Commonwealth citizens, went to England in the decade between 1956 and 1965, primarily to staff the 4,000 new Chinese restaurants opened to satisfy changing British appetites.[72] Nearly 1,000,000 Vietnamese moved north or south across the border established by the Geneva Accords of 1954, as these harassed people sought some security, if not peace. In 1975 alone, 40,000 Surinamese left their island home for Holland; at that time independence approached, with the impending loss of the social benefits that were provided under Dutch law.[73]

As empire ended, people left a transitional world behind, either in hope or in despair. The latter sentiment was the one frequently expressed in testimonies of the French and Algerians, as they fell victim to the war that wracked Algeria between 1954 and 1962. The *pieds noirs*, the nickname given the French settlers in Algeria, considered the colony their homeland. They had worked its soil so long that either they had conveniently forgotten it had originally been expropriated, or they could honestly argue it had been legally acquired by due process of French law. Like their compatriots in Perigord or Burgundy, many were simple, hard-working farmers solely interested in the land. They first endured the loss of domestic security and, then, everything else as conflict swept the countryside.

One day, my wife found her chickens with slit throats, and those not so killed, were set loose in the fields. Her incubators had been destroyed, and her rabbits drowned. Can you imagine the scene? This explains her mood of depression. Yes, all of this, and then the bursts of machine gun fire . . . and that sort of life lived behind barricaded windows. And then the daily thought of the possibility of her not seeing me return from the fields one evening! We had to leave, didn't we?[74]

The departure of such individuals as these *pieds noirs* accounted for numbers that were statistically overwhelmed by the approximately 2,500,000

Arab Algerians, out of a population of 6,900,000 in 1961, who were up-rooted by the war. Among this mass were a few dozen children whose testi-monies were gathered in one of the most poignant collections of oral history to recount the end of empire. The words of one youth, not even sure whether he was eight or nine years of age, sum up the collective experience with stark economy:

I left a long time ago. France, they came one night. We were sleeping in the bedroom. Gun fire woke us up. We left the house to save ourselves. They burned our houses, and then we left the place.[75]

The plight of the Algerians in the late 1950s was later matched in despair by that of the Vietnamese. Both groups would comprise the largest number of political refugees who, discouraged or prevented from returning home, left their native land for Europe or North America. The Algerians who arrived in France in large numbers after the end of the conflict came from those regions—Kabylia, Aures, and Oran—most severely disturbed by the fight-ing.[76]

These refugees augmented the numbers of other colonial peoples who were flocking to Europe in search of economic opportunity. Like their colo-nized predecessors who had moved within empire to the labor-intensive activ-ities characteristic of economic development of the early twentieth century, these people also left home with the intention of eventually returning. They were attracted to the expanding labor-intensive industries and services that were part of the "economic miracle," Europe's economic recovery from World War II.

This population shift was assisted by several factors. First, colonial legis-lation had recently changed the legal status of many of the colonized people, affording them forms of citizenship that allowed easy entry into Europe. In 1962, when faced with the serious problems of such ingress, the British gov-ernment passed the Commonwealth Immigrants Act, a very controversial decision that imposed immigration restrictions on Commonwealth citizens—including those from the "Tropical Commonwealth"—who previously had entered freely. Second, shipping lines and airlines, like the earlier transat-lantic steamers specializing in "steerage" accommodations, encouraged such travel by former colonials. For some people who availed themselves of the seaborne route, sensations similar to those that raced through the minds of nineteenth-century Europeans made the passage gloomy. In his triptych of short stories dealing with the colonial uprooted, *In A Free State*, the Trinida-dian author V. S. Naipaul has his African narrator express the mood:

The water black, the ship white, the lights blazing. And inside the ship, far below, everybody like prisoners already. The lights dim, everyone in their bunk. In the morning the water is blue, but you can't see the land. You are just going where the ship is going, you will never be a free man again.[77]

Third, the "push-pull" situation that had moved rural populations to urban centers within colonial territories during the interwar era now moved colonial populations to European urban centers. As one Jamaican pithily put the reasons for his move: "I was sort of half and half . . . half of what I was leaving, not making much money, and half that I knew there were good jobs in England."[78]

The end of colonialism was thus marked by the colonization of the colonial countries by the formerly colonized. The attendant social and economic problems have been enormous. In particular a virulent racism, hitherto unknown in most European countries developed, leading to riots in major European cities and to a deep sense of social unrest.

No historical commentary on this migration to Europe can approach the sense of tragedy pervading the story of the vast demographic dislocation caused by the partition of India. Although the end of the British Raj was expeditiously carried out by Lord Mountbatten in a spirit of goodwill, what occurred when Hindus and Moslems formed separate states is unmatched in scope and intensity by any similar event in recorded history. Gandhi's dream of a single state in which Hindu, Sikh, and Moslem would live harmoniously was shattered because of Moslem fears. A minority in India, the Moslems worried about future discrimination, even oppression, under a regime based on a Hindu majority. The leader of the Moslem League, Ali Jinnah, demanded a separate country for his people, a request which was granted to expedite the transfer of power. However, a major dispute arose over the vast and agriculturally rich territory of the Punjab, which the Moslems desired to be part of Pakistan. A special commission, under British leadership, was set up to find a satisfactory solution for the division of the territory. No such solution was found, but the partition took place. As a result, the greatest historical shift of population in the shortest period of time occurred. Moslems and Hindus moved to the area with the regime favorable to them. It is estimated that 7,500,000 people changed location, with as many as 1,000,000 killed in the riots and assassinations that both inspired and accompanied much of the transfer. One author observed that "one convoy contained 800,000 people and was forty-five miles long."[79] Over 2,300,000 people were moved by train alone in the short period of time extending between August 27 and November 6, 1947.[80]

The renting of the imperial political fabric caused some grief and many problems for the Europeans themselves. Colonial administrators, colonial settlers, and men in the colonial military service were all deprived of position and authority as the European national flags were run down. Although some stayed on to serve as advisers and a few others continued in commerce or on the land, most quickly departed from a new world they could not serve to an old world they did not know well. Some 100,000 colonists in Libya, who believed Mussolini's rhetoric about Libya being the "Third Shore" of Italy, returned to one or the other of the two shores of the Italian peninsula. Some 250,000 Dutch settlers left the East Indies for the Netherlands. Most socially disturbing of all was the arrival of 850,000 French from Algeria in the year 1962–63, with 100,000 of these settlers moving to Paris alone. One French analyst noted, with irony, that among the group were 20 men and 80 women who were between 96 and 100 years of age, old enough that their lives were almost conterminous with the history of French colonialism in Algeria.[81]

From such a muddled end of empire one simple conclusion might be reached: imperialism accomplished little and disturbed much. Whether the expansive nature of the modern West would have created the conditions and generated the unrest that have characterized the global scene in this century, even if formal imperialism had not been pursued, is a question interesting in itself and worthy of debate. However, the historical fact is that colonial empire was the agent of change. It never approached the dreams of its most fervent proponents, nor did it reach the depths of human degradation that the infamies of our own age have shown possible.

Modern empire ended as it began, not with ceremony but in confusion.

Aftermath

Years after the French had departed, many of the street signs in Algiers still displayed the incompleteness of change. Old French names enameled in white on a blue background had been partially covered by new Arabic names painted in black. The "revolution of expectations"—a popular term employed during the years of transition—was never fully realized in the former colonial regions. The concern, even the anguish, over this condition has been part of the public debate on decolonization. Europeans have often insisted that they were required to leave too soon, before the good government they desired was ensured by sufficient preparation.[1] Africans and Asians have frequently seen signs of only formal changes, and these changes are of little consequence when compared with their continuing economic dependency.

The jubilation expressed at independence ceremonies did not echo long. All parties involved in the termination of colonial empire soon wondered what actually had been achieved.

The rush of events during world War II swept colonial reform along with it. Considered during the war and implemented shortly thereafter, colonial development was strongly supported by the state. Direct financial and technical assistance in the few remaining years of European domination was provided as it had not been over the previous half century.[2] Colonial planning was no longer a haphazard art performed by an occasional administrator; it was now the well-defined responsibility of teams of technicians schooled in economics as well as in engineering. The intensified concern with development enhanced social and political relationships as well. The idea of partner-

211

ship—"dialogue" was a popular term of the time—was accepted, even encouraged by the colonial administrations.

Not all who heard it found the word "partnership" appealing, however. It was a "notorious word in African politics," wrote an African literary critic who, like others, sensed a continuing subordinate relationship that had been modified only in terminology.[3] Even when European sincerity was not doubted, European purposes were no longer found timely. The division of interests between colonizer and colonized occurred with a rapidity no one had anticipated when World War II ended. What struck the French colonial administrator Robert Delavignette about the independence movements was their "suddenness."[4]

Yet when aware of what was happening, colonial administrators were occasionally baffled by the positions they could assume. They no longer attempted to "hold the ring." Instead, they stood aside and allowed new elites, their forthcoming replacements, to emerge, consolidate power, and gain advantage.

To avoid accusations of racial prejudice and imperialistic deceit we more or less sat back and watched the elite, to whom in practice we were going to hand over the power, build for themselves an unassailable position of privilege.[5]

The transfer of power was generally a lateral move, a shift of responsibility from one elite to another. Structures remained; personnel changed. However, no European colonial administration had desired or expected its institutions to continue in unaltered form in the post-colonial world. Delavignette, for instance, wondered publicly: "With such an administration, unsuited to its needs, how can a poor country achieve economic and social growth and assert full sovereignty on the national scene?"[6]

As European administrators fretted about these immediate and local problems, the intellectual elite in the new nations frequently had a broader view of events. What they saw aroused their complaint that imperialism, not colonialism, was the major Western legacy. The continuation of capitalistic exploitation was accepted as a fact. It is obvious why a Marxist interpretation of history appealed to Third World intellectuals. Not only did it provide a strong repudiation of the recent colonial experience, but it allowed local failures to be attributed to international design—the continuing penetration of world capitalism. According to one recent African analysis, the fifth phase of capitalist activity has now been reached. "Dependency domination" was begun in the 1970s and is considered not the last, but "the latest phase of capitalist domination in Africa," marked by international financial organization and multi-national corporate activity.[7]

No matter from what intellectual perspective it is regarded, the landscape of the post-colonial world resembles a beach after the tide has receded: it is still strewn with much of what the Europeans had earlier floated in. The metaphor seems apt, for most of formal empire—flag-raising empire—was a short-lived phenomenon among the European nation states of the modern age. Excluding the older dependencies such as Java and Australia, European domination was not of long duration. The British were in and out of Kenya within 70 years. The Americans administered the Philippines for 48 years. The Italians could claim Libya as theirs for no more than 30 years. During this short time, few changes penetrated deeply; many of them were only superficial, lightly cast over certain segments of the population, across particular regions. At best a delicate balance existed among what was imposed, what was expected, and what had long been practiced. The coups d'état that have marred recent African history are explained by this elliptical statement. So also are the numbers of unemployed professionals in India, and the larger numbers of underfed in Southeast Asian cities. "Fragile, fragile, this world," wrote V. S. Naipaul in his novel *The Guerrillas*, "requiring endless tolerance, endless forbearance."[8]

The balance sheets of imperialism have not yet been satisfactorily prepared. Even now some critics doubt any such attempt ought to be made; they fear the enterprise may still be in operation. Twenty years ago, the American theologian and philosopher Reinhold Niebuhr wrote that the end of the age of European imperialism was marked by the rise of two anti-imperialist imperialisms, those sponsored by the Soviet Union and the United States.[9] But Niebuhr's ideology was not Third World in thrust. He distinguished between Soviet "universal imperialism," urged on by false economic arguments and real tanks, and an American imperialism the nation sought to deny, but "which we exercise in fact, or ought to exercise, if imperialism means the exercise of the responsibilities of power."[10]

The prevalent definition today is not Niebuhr's, but the one that brings a look of contempt to the face of the speaker. It implies the irresponsible use of power, and it has, in that sense, been used to define direct American involvement in Vietnam and indirect American involvement in Latin America. Moreover, the Soviet Union, Israel, Vietnam, Morocco, and Libya are among the other modern states that have been accused of pursuing imperialistic policies. The word "imperialism" has lost its meaning as it has been charged with emotion by the leaders of contending states, not one of them reluctant to use military power to achieve objectives.

Assuming imperialism to come in many shapes over many centuries of history, one may assert that the distinguishing characteristic of its modern political form is its nationalistic bias. Modern imperialism may thus be defined as overseas nationalism. Expanding nation states created empires; retreating empires created nation states. Niebuhr considered the "creative factors" in modern European imperialism to have been those that ensured the "integral nationhood" of the former colonies.[11] Yet the oneness or wholeness his term implies is not a condition easily found anywhere. If anything, the post-colonial world is characterized by divisiveness. Internal repression and civil war seem to be nearly as common as domestic harmony. "Things fall apart," wrote the Irish poet William B. Yeats at the beginning of the century, "the center cannot hold." So it seems in much of the former colonial world.

Yet nationhood is the formal sign of the passage through and beyond the colonial state of affairs. On the eve of World War II there were 71 sovereign states. Today that number has increased to 161. The responsibility for the proliferation of such nation states has also been attributed to the imperialists. It has been asserted that they "balkanized" much of the colonial world, divided it or allowed it to be split into segments too small to be economically and politically competitive and, hence, of ideal proportions to be dominated from abroad. The problem is not so simply explained, however. The emerging nationalist elites were often unwilling to alter the political shape of things because in so doing they might have deprived themselves of an authority they had desired for years. None of the several experiments with federation succeeded; all collapsed because of internal political dissension.

The formal trappings of the modern state—an airline and diplomatic representation at the United Nations, for instance—were not matched by an effective spirit of nationalism. In the colonial world, nationalism was initially anti-imperialistic. It was also an act of demythification. Ndabaningi Sithole put it well: "African nationalism, in many ways, represented the degree to which the white man's magic spell had worn off."[12]

The new nationalist ideologies that were fostered were, in the words of President Sukharno of Indonesia, "made-up."[13] They were amalgams of indigenous myths and adapted Western ideas. Most of them sought a cultural distinctiveness that would define the new state and place it in contrast with the former colonial power. The special sense of community was extolled. President Sukharno in explaining his five principles, *Pantjasila*, praised *goyong-rojong*, "our ancient Indonesian custom of each and everyone of us joining together in whatever is to be done . . . and together enjoying the results of our common endeavour."[14] President Léopold Sédar Senghor of Senegal wrote that "Negro-African society . . . is a *community-based* society, in which the hierarchy—and therefore power—is founded in spiritual and democratic values . . . in which work is shared out among the sexes and among technico-professional groups, based on religion."[15] In almost every instance of a new nationalist credo, its tenets were opposed to Western individualistic competition—to those qualities of capitalistic development that the English author Samuel Smiles called "self-help" and American authors have called "rugged individualism." The mechanisms of the West—its technology and administrative systems—were retained, but its "soul" was denied.

Unfortunately, modified ideologies did not reflect important modifications in social and economic reality. The post-colonial world was doubly divided: internationally, between the poor countries of Asia, Africa, and Latin America and the rich countries of the West; nationally, between a privileged elite and impoverished masses. Sukharno spoke boldly of "World Revolution," but it has not occurred. On the contrary, some severe critics sense backward motion and discern signs of decay. In his novels, singularly critical of the post-independence world he frequents, V. S. Naipaul describes settings in which new buildings are flawed, gardens go to seed, and people are self-serving or listless. Of Zaire, the former Belgian Congo, he writes:

And then, quickly, the town that had looked whole showed its dereliction. The drives of villas were overgrown, disgorging glaciers of sand and dirt through open gateways. . . . The boulevard was more than bumpy. It was cracked and fissured; the concrete gutters were choked with sand and dirt and weeds.[16]

The progress of time has worked to African and Asian disadvantage. Developments such as the complexity and instability of the international economy, the military aid and advice provoked by the Cold War, and the intensifying responsibilities of the welfare state have, in the last three decades, freighted all vehicles of the modern state. Sovereignty today may be nominal in many instances, but it is a heavy financial burden everywhere. Those writers who bitterly complain about the continuing development of dependency in the post-colonial world fully understand the effects of these conditions, however debatable their appraisal of the causes may be.

Although its impact is still felt and even more intensely debated, European overseas imperialism has ended. It was a global fixture from another age, when, first, sailing ships and, then, four-funneled oceanliners were the fastest form of intercontinental communication, conveying ideas, goods, and armies abroad.

The so-called "salt water fallacy" of imperialism is not a fallacy but a distinguishing characteristic. Obviously, other forms of imperialism exist, but overseas expansion is distinguished from them in structure, if not in motivation. Isolated as well as bound by the sea, the European colonies in Africa and Asia, in the Pacific and the Caribbean, were places of alien rule. The ideals and institutions imposed were purposeless in the context of indigenous culture. The objectives of this rule were also beyond or above local needs and interests. Of equal importance, this rule was not all-pervasive: "The great merit of British rule in Africa," commented a lieutenant governor of Nigeria, "is that there is so little of it."[17]

What this statement describes is the remoteness of colonial government. It was generally dissociated from the interests of the people at home who supported it and the people overseas who sustained it. It is doubtful whether the British and the French were better informed about imperial geography in 1950 than they had been in 1880. It is equally doubtful whether most Africans and Asians knew or cared why the Europeans were present among them. Europeans on a particular colonial site were often perplexed, no matter how long they had observed or participated in local life. Isak Dinesen, more perceptive than most observers, wrote of her experience in Kenya:

When we really did break into the Natives' existence, they behaved like ants, when you poke a stick into their ant-hill; they wiped out the damage with unwearied energy, swiftly and silently—as if obliterating some unseemly action.[18]

Both parties to the colonial act went about their daily business usually unmindful of empire. The monotony and the pettiness, if not the misunderstanding, were only occasionally relieved by spectacular occurrences that bore a resemblance to those seventeenth-century royal pageants by which the state, in the person of its ruler, displayed its authority for all to see. The several trips of the Prince of Wales after World War I are good examples. In his African tour of 1925 he traveled overland with seven touring cars, "his own being a powerful, long-bodied car painted a brilliant scarlet, specially designed to leave an impression on the nations visited."[19] Mussolini's state visit to Libya in 1937 was another such pageant. In Tripoli streets were re-paved, and a large central square hastily laid out where a slum had previously been. Then, a 320-foot-high steel scaffold was constructed so that Musso-lini's evening entry into the city would be brightly illuminated by overhead searchlights. The reception given for him two days later by Marshal Balbo was described as "a sight to make Mr. Cecil B. de Mille [the noted Hollywood film director] green with envy."[20] Had the airship R101 succeeded in making its inaugural trip, it would have been the dramatic setting for a state banquet to be held on the ship at its pylon in Egypt. For that anticipated occasion the main corridor of the dirigible was handsomely outfitted with a 600-foot-long pale blue carpet. Monogrammed crystal was also part of the airship's manifest when it departed on its ill-fated flight.[21]

To the very end the pomp was displayed on special occasions—and on some not so special ones. When Lord Mountbatten, Viceroy of India in 1946, wished to make a brief vacation trip to Simla, he found that the venture was of a magnitude he would not have dared consider. His military secretary, un-willing to hear of hotel reservations, made ready the viceregal lodge in that summer mountain resort. Once arrived at Simla, Mountbatten, disturbed by the flurry of excitement over the trip, inquired how many individuals had come in his entourage. He was supplied with the figure in writing: 333.[22]

Yet like all else, the theatrical aspect of empire was just about played out at that time. Critics have viewed John Osborne's play *The Entertainer* as a statement that the imperial show was over. The play, its author states, des-cribes the end of the music hall as a British art form. The hero of the play is an old trouper named Archie Rice. To a near empty set of seats in a theater located at a beachside resort, Archie wearily sings:

> It's chaps like us—yes you and me,
> Who'll march again to victory.
> Some people say we're finished,
> Some people say we're done
> But if we all stand
> *Spotlight behind gauze reveals a nude in Britannia's*
> *helmet and holding a bulldog and trident.*
> By this dear old land,
> The battle will be won.[23]

As contemporary scholars and polemicists attempt to reassemble the causes, purposes, and effects of modern colonial empire, they never consider it an entertainment, nor are they particularly concerned about its theatrical displays. But the quality of drama remains part of the historical interpretation. Few activities in the modern era have generated more controversy, caused the leveling of more moral judgments, or been the cause of more ideological constructions. Empire was not a simple matter. With this conclusion both the earlier proponents and the more recent critics would agree.

Bibliographical Note

Bibliographical Note

Today, academic research on empire is as far-reaching as the subject itself was when it embraced the globe. The end of empire occurred about the same time that major changes in the methodologies and the organization of disciplines in the social sciences were taking place—developments enhancing and directing the interest in decolonization and its effects. "Modernization" studies then proliferated, with treatment accorded economic development and political mobilization alike. Behavioral and structural analyses led to the re-evaluation of the nature and process of cultural contact and institutional formation.

Comparative studies enlarged the appreciation of the transitional world left behind by a departing colonialism. The concept of "area studies," essentially American, had been introduced during World War II as a means of understanding those regions—almost all colonial—into which American troops were going and about which intelligence was dangerously weak. After that war area studies became something of a rage, as their form of integrated study promised greater knowledge of the Third World. "An area," remarked Benjamin I. Schwartz in his 1980 presidential address to the Association of Asian Studies, "is a cross-disciplinary unit of collective experience within which one can discern complex interactions among economic, social, political, religious and other areas of life." African, Asian, and Middle Eastern institutes were widely established in support of this sort of definition. Some universities even began programs devoted to imperial problems, such as Duke University's Center for Commonwealth and Comparative Studies and the University of Leiden's Centre for the History of European Expansion.

A new generation of scholarly periodicals concerned with comparative or regional studies appeared. Among the first were *Afrique et Asie*, a French publication sponsored by the Center for Advanced Studies on Modern Africa and Asia (CHEAM), which began in 1947; and, in 1951, *Civilisations*, a publication of the Belgian International Institute of Differing Civilizations, an organization that had evolved out of the earlier, productive International Colonial Institute.

The significant clustering of such publications began somewhat later. In 1958 *Comparative Studies in Society and History* was founded, and it was soon followed by a large number of regional publications, among which some of the most prominent are: *Les Cahiers d'Etudes Africaines*, started in 1961; *The Journal of Modern African Studies* begun in 1963; and *Modern Asian Studies* which appeared in 1971.

221

The colonial regions in their period of transition became laboratories of sorts in which case studies of political and social change were conducted. Large foundations, such as the Ford Foundation, supported these activities. University presses fostered the publication of the scholarly results; but no press offered as varied a range of publications on empire as did the Presses universitaires de France. Its *Pays d'Outre-Mer* included monographs on history, geography, art, and literature; a series on the "classics of colonization" was also published.

In such an atmosphere young scholars were easily persuaded to turn their attention from traditional locations of research to investigate the Third World. In British universities nine dissertations on the culture of Sierra Leone were approved between 1953 and 1962. The number increased to 49 for the period between 1962 and 1976. In 1966 alone, 141 dissertations on Southeast Asia were completed in American universities.

The result of all this activity has been a literary output that is most impressive and offers a rich array of materials that concentrate on single colonies and focus on intercontinental problems such as urbanization. Because of the large number of works now readily available, these bibliographical notes will be highly selective. They are designed primarily for the individual who wishes to be initiated into serious study of twentieth-century imperialism—not to be overwhelmed by the immense volume of scholarship about it.

Although few works of grand synthesis have yet appeared, the concern with decolonization has inspired studies that follow the downward sweep of empire. These works quickly displaced one of the most respected general studies, its pages dog-eared long ago: Parker T. Moon, *Imperialism and World Politics* (New York: Macmillan, 1961; first published in 1926). One of the first newer studies was John Strachey, *The End of Empire* (New York: Random House, 1960), written by a renowned member of the British Labour Party, which concentrated on the problems of the British Empire but was also concerned with the general effects of imperialism. In the same year, a more widely used and enthusiastically received book appeared, Rupert Emerson, *From Empire to Nation* (Boston: Beacon Press, 1960), a very successful effort to treat, on a global scale, the devolution of power. Henri Grimal, *Decolonisation, 1919–1963* (Paris: A. Colin, 1965), is also predominantly political in its thrust, but more descriptive than analytical.

The most detailed single volume on the process of decolonization is Rudolf von Albertini, *Decolonization: The Administration and Future of the Colonies, 1919–1960*, trans. Francisca Garvie (New York: Doubleday, 1971; first published 1966). Albertini indicates in his preface that his approach is essentially political and, therefore, the study is not significantly different in format from its predecessors. However, Albertini's later work deviates from this bias. *European Colonial Rule: The Impact of the West on India, Southeast Asia, and Africa*, trans. John G. Williamson (Westport, Conn.: Greenwood Press, 1982; first published 1976), while selective, is an excellent assessment that includes valuable information on labor, communications, and social development. What might serve as a complementary study is A. P. Thornton, *Imperialism in the Twentieth Century* (Minneapolis: University of Minnesota Press, 1977). An erudite, witty, and highly interpretive essay, this book will reward the reader who is familiar with the general lines of modern imperial development. More extended historically, but more topically focused is the recent study of V. G. Kiernan, *From Conquest to Collapse: European Empires from 1815 to 1960* (New York: Pantheon Books, 1982). The theme of "war and society" is stressed and also well-treated in rather short compass. The most sweeping of the recent volumes is David K. Fieldhouse, *The Colonial Empires from the Eighteenth Century* (New York: Dell, 1971; first published 1966), which offers a fine overview.

There are several series that treat many, if not all, of the phases of modern empire. The one in which this book appears, *Europe and the World in the Age of Expansion*, offers two volumes of immediate interest: Henry S. Wilson, Vol. 8, *The Imperial Experience in Sub-Saharan Africa Since 1870* (Minneapolis: University of Minnesota Press, 1977); and W. David McIntyre, Vol.

9, *The Commonwealth of Nations: Origins and Impact, 1869-1971* (Minneapolis: University of Minnesota Press, 1977). The trilogy edited by Prosser Gifford and William Roger Louis on Africa is generally excellent; all the contributors are well-known authorities in the field. Moreover, each volume contains a superb, annotated bibliography. The volumes are: *Britain and Germany in Africa: Imperial Rivalry and Colonial Rule* (New Haven: Yale University Press, 1967); *France and Britain in Africa: Imperial Rivalry and Colonial Rule* (New Haven: Yale University Press, 1971); and *The Transfer of Power in Africa: Decolonization 1940-1960* (New Haven: Yale University Press, 1982). More elaborate is the series edited by L. H. Gann and Peter Duignan, *Colonialism in Africa, 1870-1960* (Cambridge University Press, 1969-1975), a five-volume set that includes reviews of all aspects of the colonial experience and an extensive volume of bibliography.

Individual studies that focus on particular regions are numerous and useful in distinguishing regional problems and particular colonial rivalries that occurred within the larger framework of global expansion. L. H. Gann and Peter Duignan, *Burden of Empire: An Appraisal of Western Colonialism in Africa South of the Sahara* (London: Pall Mall Press, 1968), is a conservative interpretation that highlights the benefits of imperialism. A veritable treasure of detailed information is found in Lord William Hailey, *An African Survey: A Study of Problems Arising in Africa South of the Sahara*, originally published in 1938 but currently available in a revised edition (London: Oxford University Press, 1957). Michael Crowder, *West Africa Under Colonial Rule* (Evanston: Northwestern University Press, 1968) is a first-rate survey. A set of thoughtful essays by a historian long concerned with West Africa is John D. Hargreaves, *The End of Colonial Rule in West Africa: Essays in Contemporary History* (New York: Barnes and Noble, 1979).

Equally good introductions exist for a study of the imperialist encounter in other parts of the world. On the Near East, George Lenczowski, *The Middle East in World Affairs* (4th ed.: Ithaca: Cornell University Press, 1980), is a fine, broad-scaled survey. Elizabeth Monro, *Britain's Moment in the Middle East 1914-1956* (Baltimore: Johns Hopkins Press, 1963), should be considered. Howard N. Schar, *Europe Leaves the Middle East, 1936-1956* (New York, Knopf, 1962), provides a good analysis of World War II and the role the Germans played in the region. The forthcoming work by William Roger Louis, *The British Empire in the Middle East, 1945-1951* (Oxford: Clarendon Press, 1984), will be a welcome addition.

On the other side of the globe, the changing disposition of political power, particularly after the "decline of the diplomacy of imperialism," is most reasonably and closely judged by Akira Iriye, *After Imperialism: The Search for a New Order in the Far East, 1921-1931* (Cambridge, Mass.: Harvard University Press, 1963). A volume that nicely complements it is William Roger Louis, *British Strategy in the Far East, 1919-1939* (Oxford: Clarendon Press, 1971). Two other studies that concentrate on the Pacific Ocean area in World War II and offer balanced appraisals of Japan's role in that activity are: H. P. Willmott, *Empire in the Balance: Japanese and Allied Pacific Strategies to April 1942* (Annapolis: Naval Institute Press, 1982); and Christopher Thorne, *Allies of a Kind: The United States, Britain and the War Against Japan, 1941-1945* (New York: Oxford University Press, 1978).

On the activities of the two major colonial powers, Great Britain and France, the reader will find many individual studies worthy of close attention. Not too long ago, Henri Brunschwig, one of the outstanding scholars of French colonialism, remarked that the French had shown less historical interest in their empire than the British had in theirs. Perhaps this is so, but both subjects have been amply treated. What is striking in the British instance is the number of good, short studies designed for the general reader. Among these one boldly stands out. James Morris, *Farewell the Trumpets: An Imperial Retreat* (Middlesex, England: Penguin Books, 1979; first published 1978), is a beautifully etched narrative about the decline of British colonial power and the idiosyncrasies that accompanied it. Two other short studies command great respect: Bernard

Porter, *The Lion's Share: A Short History of British Imperialism, 1850–1970* (London: Longman, 1974); and Colin Cross, *The Fall of the British Empire, 1918–1968* (London: Palladin, 1968). Two studies that concentrate on the idea and institutions of the British Commonwealth are: Perceval Griffith, *Empire Into Commonwealth* (London: Benn, 1969); and the masterful study of Nicholas Mansergh, *The Commonwealth Experience* (London: Weidenfeld and Nicolson, 1969). Of course, the *Cambridge History of the British Empire*, ed. J. Holland Rose (8 vols; Cambridge: Cambridge University Press, 1929–1940), should be consulted by anyone interested in the various geographical segments of that empire and their particular development. A most lucid study of the British problem of decolonization in its early stages is William Roger Louis, *Imperialism at Bay: The United States and the Decolonization of the British Empire, 1941–1945* (New York: Oxford University Press, 1978).

Concerning the general problems of the French colonial empire, two brief assessments are: Xavier Yacono, *Histoire de la decolonisation française* (Paris: Presses universitaires de France, 1969), a study that begins in the 1930s; and Raymond F. Betts, *Tricouleur: The French Overseas Empire* (London: Gordon and Cremonesi, 1978). On the ideology supporting it all, see the excellent review of Raoul Girardet, *L'Idée coloniale en France, 1871–1962* (Paris: La Table Ronde, 1972). The transformation of colonial empire in Africa immediately after World War II is followed effectively by D. Bruce Marshall, *The French Colonial Myth and Constitution-Making in the Fourth Republic* (New Haven: Yale University Press, 1979). The intellectual debate over the end of the empire, intense and far-ranging, is well reviewed by Paul C. Sorum, *Intellectuals and Decolonization in France* (Chapel Hill: University of North Carolina Press, 1977). The intensity and duration of the struggles in Indochina and Algeria have aroused considerable academic attention and have led to a very large number of scholarly and popular studies on these subjects. Among the older works of lasting value are Paul Mus, *Viet-Nam: sociologie d'une guerre* (Paris: Editions du Seuil, 1952), and Bernard Fall, *Street Without Joy: Indochina at War: 1946–1954* (Harrisburg, Pa.; Stackpole Press, 1961). The background to the collapse of French power in Indochina is carefully reviewed in David G. Marr, *Vietnamese Anticolonialism 1885–1925* (Berkeley: University of California Press, 1971). On Algeria, the following books are good introductions: Alf Andrew Heggoy, *Insurgency and Counterinsurgency in Algeria* (Bloomington: Indiana University Press, 1978); Tony Smith, *The French Stake in Algeria, 1945–1962* (Ithaca, N.Y.: Cornell University Press, 1978); and the highly readable work by Alistair Horne, *A Savage War of Peace, 1954–1962* (New York: Viking Press, 1978). A most critical and personal interpretation is Jean-Jacques Servan-Schreiber, *Lieutenant in Algeria*, trans. Ronald Matthews (New York: Knopf, 1957).

The amount of recent material on the other colonial establishments will be disappointing to the reader. The Italians, who certainly were the most aggressive and ambitious of the imperialists after World War I, have not been subjected to sufficient historical appraisal. In part to fill this need an excellent introduction has been published: Claudio G. Segrè, *The Fourth Shore: The Italian Colonization of Libya* (Chicago: University of Chicago Press, 1974). A complementary volume is John Wright, *Libya* (New York: Praeger, 1969). On Somalia, see Robert Hess, *Italian Colonization of Somalia* (Chicago: University of Chicago Press, 1966). The best overall introduction is the brief volume of Jean-Louis Miège, *L'Impérialisme italien de 1870 à nos jours* (Paris: Société d'Edition d'enseignement supérieur, 1968).

The Germans, who ceased to exercise colonial control after World War I, nevertheless continued to express an interest in colonies and to fulminate about their loss of them. This condition is well-chronicled in Wolfe W. Schmokel, *Dream of Empire: German Colonialism, 1919–1945* (New Haven, Conn.: Yale University Press, 1964). For British attitudes and policies toward Germany's colonies in World War I, see Wm. Roger Louis, *Great Britain and Germany's Lost Colonies, 1914–1919* (Oxford: Clarendon Press, 1967).

On the Belgian Congo, the most convenient introduction is Ruth Slade, *The Belgian Congo* (London: Oxford University Press, 1960); it is, however, exceptionally brief. Roger Anstey, *King Leopold's Legacy: the Congo Under Belgian Rule, 1908–1960* (London: Oxford University Press, 1966) traces the continuation of institutions and policies established under Leopold's regime. For a balanced appraisal of the end of Belgian rule, see René Lemarchand, *Political Awakening in the Belgian Congo* (Berkeley: University of California Press, 1964), a detailed study. A fine work by a Belgian scholar, Michel de Schrevel, *Les Forces politiques de la decolonisation congolaise à la veille de l'indépendance* (Louvain: M. et L. Symons, 1970), analyzes the various political factions contributing to the political movement for independence.

The two older colonial empires that continued until they, too, succumbed to movements for national independence are not yet the subject of good broad introductory studies. The work of John S. Furnivall on the Dutch East Indies, although outdated, still serves: *Netherlands India: A Study of Plural Economy* (New York: Macmillan, 1944); *Colonial Policy and Practice: A Comparative Study of Burma and Netherlands India* (Cambridge: Cambridge University Pess, 1948). The Portuguese in Africa are assessed in two works by James Duffy: *Portuguese Africa* (Cambridge, Mass.: Harvard University Press, 1959): and *Portugal in Africa* (Baltimore: Penguin Books, 1953). More detailed and concentrating on the rise of nationalism is Ronald Chicote, *Portuguese Africa* (Berkeley: University of California Press, 1967).

The theoretical analyses upon which the imperialist activity has been structured are numerous and frequently contentious. The debate over the causes of imperialism has been followed by one of equal importance—and bitterness—over the end of empire. As mentioned in the text of this book, no one has generated more interest in his ideas than André Gunder Frank, who has popularized the concept of the "development of underdevelopment." Among his several works, *Dependent Accumulation and Underdevelopment* (New York: Monthly Review Press, 1979) is the most convenient introduction. His theory, originally focused on Latin America, was amplified in a major study by Walter Rodney, *How Europe Underdeveloped Africa* (Washington: Howard University Press, 1974). Broader studies tracing the nature of capitalistic European exploitation are: Samir Amin, *Imperialism and Unequal Development* (New York: Monthly Review Press, 1979) and Jacques Berque, *Dépossession du Monde* (Paris: Editions du Seuil, 1964). Most recently, the scholarship of Immanuel Wallerstein, a sociologist who has become seriously interested in historical research, has led to a new global scheme of things, what has been called "the world capitalist system," and an idea developed from the work of Fernand Braudel. Wallerstein and his colleagues, for he has in effect established a "school," have produced many works on the subject but the best introduction is the series of essays that Wallerstein has written over the last two decades, which were published as *The Capitalist World Economy: Essays* (Cambridge: Cambridge University Press, 1979). For its historical interest—and its relationship to the earlier volume on imperialism written by Lenin, one ought read Kwame Nkrumah, *Neo-Colonialism: The Last Stage of Imperialism* (New York: International Publishers, 1966).

There are a number of excellent regional economic surveys which ought be read as a complement—or a corrective—to the more theoretical works. Among them, *An Economic History of West Africa* (New York: Columbia University Press, 1973), by Anthony Hopkins, is an excellent overview of the effects of colonialism on the economic life of this part of the world. A classic that has fortunately been reprinted with an excellent introduction by Hopkins is Allan McPhee, *The Economic Revolution in British West Africa* (London: Frank Cass, 1971; first published, 1926). A doctoral dissertation of unusual dimensions and rare insight, this work allows the reader to see how one individual witnessed the changes brought about by British technological engagement. Martin J. Murray, *The Development of Capitalism in Colonial Indochina (1870–1940)* (Berkeley: University of California Press, 1980), is an excellent and detailed analysis of the intensifying capitalist hold on Indochina written from a Marxist perspective. A comprehensive study of industrial development in India is Rajat K. Ray, *Industrialization in India: Growth and Conflict in the Private Corporate Sector, 1914–1947* (Delhi: Oxford University Press, 1979). Another work, which complements this study well, is Amiya Kumar Bagchi, *Private Investment in India, 1900–1939* (Cambridge: Cambridge University Press, 1972). On economic policy in the British empire, a very valuable introduction is Ian Drummond, *British Economic Policy and the Empire 1919–1939* (London: George Allen and Unwin, 1972). Grander in scale is William Keith Hancock, *Problems of Economic Policy, 1918–1939* (London: Oxford University Press, 1940). Finally, mention ought be made of the majesterial UNESCO volume, *Social Implications of Industrialization and Urbanization in Africa South of the Sahara* (Paris: UNESCO, 1956).

Certainly one of the more interesting sets of material on twentieth-century empire is the recently gathered oral history. Testimonies from individuals who were part of the empire scene since the interwar period are available in well-edited studies that provide fascinating reading because of their local color and poignancy. One of the first of these, and perhaps the best in its organization and style, is Charles Allen, ed., *Plain Tales from the Raj: Images of British Rule in the Twentieth Century* (London: Futura Books, 1979; first published 1975). Originally a series of tape recordings broadcast on the British Broadcasting Corporation radio service, the work is an assessment of interviews with English who lived in India, primarily in the interwar period. The success of this endeavor caused Allen to turn toward Africa, and a second volume which he edited appeared: *Tales from the Dark Continent* (New York: St. Martin's Press, 1979). Of a similar sort, but focused on the administrators of India, is Roland Hunt and John Harrison, *The District Officer in India, 1930–1947* (London, Scolar Press, 1980). This volume is also well organized, and its informants are a remarkably reflective group. Jean Daniel Scherb, *Le Soleil ne chauffe que les vivants* (Paris: Robert Laffont, 1964), is a probing narrative about the difficulties endured by the *pieds noirs* who returned to France from Algeria and whom Scherb, himself born in Algeria, purposely met and interviewed while he toured France. The sense of sadness that permeates this volume is quickly forgotten when one turns to *Les enfants d'Algérie: témoinages et desseins d'enfants réfugiés en Tunisie, en Libye et au Maroc* (Paris: François Maspero, 1962), a series of interviews with youngsters ranging in age from 4 to 15, who fled Algeria during the war. The accompanying sketches, some in color, drawn by the youngsters as an expression of their sentiments, heighten the pathos of the accounts.

Individual memoirs from colonial officials are abundant and quite good. One spritely account of the new experience of colonial service is John Smith, *Colonial Cadet in Nigeria* (Durham, N.C.: Duke University Press, 1962). Penderel Moon, *Strangers in India* (New York: Reynal and Hitchcock, 1945), presents a personal interpretation of the Indian Civil Service through a series of fictional characters whose dialogue clearly expresses Moon's sentiments and experiences. Senior officials have also summed up their experiences. Sir Arthur Burns, *Colonial Civil Servant* (London: George Allen and Unwin, 1949); and Robert Delavignette, *Freedom and Authority in West Africa* (London: Frank Cass, 1968) merit special attention. Indeed, so does the volume which consists of the Reith Lectures given on BBC radio by Margery Perham, *The Colonial Reckoning* (New York: Knopf, 1962).

Academic studies of the colonial administrator in training, in the bush, and on the governor's staff have proliferated now that administrative history has become a major scholarly concern. Philip Mason, *The Men Who Ruled India*, is a monumental study. Volume 2: *The Guardians* (New York: St. Martin's Press, 1954), covers the period with which this volume is concerned. William B. Cohen, *Rulers of Empire: The French Colonial Service in Africa* (Stanford: Hoover Institute Press, 1971), creates an excellent social profile of the men who served France and, additionally, contains a fine assessment of their training. A very recent and thoughtful volume concerned with the development of West African elites is Henri Brunschwig, *Noirs et blancs en Afrique noire française, ou comment le colonisé devient colonisateur (1870–1914)* (Paris: Flammarion, 1983). A frequently cited work and a pacesetter at the time is Robert Heussler, *Yesterday's Rulers: The Making of the British Colonial Service* (Syracuse, N.Y.: Syracuse University Press, 1966). Richard Symonds, *The British and Their Successors: A Study in the Development of Government Services in New States* (Evanston, Ill.: Northwestern University Press, 1966), contains a country-by-country survey that is most useful. The historical introduction provided in A. L. Adu, *The Civil Service in Commonwealth Africa: Development and Transition* (London: George Allen and Unwin, 1969), is worth reading. Heather Sutherland, *The Making of a Bureaucratic Elite: The Colonial Transformation of the Javanese Piyayi* (Singapore: Heinemann Education Books [Asia], 1979), is a fine assessment of the changing role of a traditional ruling elite in a disturbing colonial situation.

The critical literature on the ideology and practice of protest in the colonial world is impressive in amount and quality of analysis. An excellent example is Robert July, *The Origins of Modern African Thought: Its Development in West Africa in the Nineteenth and Twentieth Centuries* (New York: Praeger, 1967). More specifically concerned with the meaning of *négritude* are Thomas Melone, *De la négritude dans la littérature négro-africaine* (Paris: Présence africaine, 1962), and the critical, Marxist-directed interpretation of René Dépestre, *Bonjour et adieu à la négritude* (Paris: Robert Laffont, 1980). Far broader in scope and very provocative in its approach—a denial of the Marxist outlook—is the long introduction to a valuable set of documents edited by Elie Kedourie, *Nationalism in Asia and Africa* (New York: World Publishing Company, 1970). Walter Z. Laqueur, *Communism and Nationalism in the Middle East* (New York: Praeger, 1956), offers a country-by-country description of these forces. William J. Duicker, *The Rise of Nationalism in Vietnam, 1900–1941* (Ithaca, N.Y.: Cornell University Press, 1976); and George M. Kahin, *Nationalism and Revolution in Indonesia* (Ithaca, N.Y.: Cornell University Press, 1952), should also be consulted.

Among works by leaders of these different movements, a few should be mentioned because of their influence, insight, and/or the quality of protest. Jawaharlal Nehru's autobiography, *Toward Freedom* (New York: John Day, 1942), is a remarkable account by this thoughtful man of his growing involvement in the movement led by Gandhi. The poet-philosopher who was also the first president of Senegal, Léopold Sédar Senghor, has fully enunciated the idea of *négritude*, of which he was the principal spokesman, in *Liberté I: Négritude et humanisme* (Paris: Editions du Seuil, 1964). Patrice Lumumba, *Congo, My Country* (New York: Praeger, 1966), provides a set of interesting statements made at the time of colonial transition by the individual who would be so important in the turbulent first years of Zaire's existence. For an appreciation of Gandhi's thought, his early *The Story of My Experiments With Truth* has been published as his *Autobiography*, trans. by Mahadev Desai, (Washington: Public Affairs Press, 1948). A handbook on guerrilla warfare left behind by the schoolteacher-strategist Vo Nguyen Giap is *People's War, People's Army* (New York: Bantam Books, 1968).

On the side of institutional development, urban studies flourish. Although most are concerned with social growth and change immediately after the colonial era, or are directed to the study of a particular city—such as Janet Abu-Lugard's fascinating *Cairo: 1001 Years of the City Victorious* (Princeton: Princeton University Press, 1971)—several general studies ought to be mentioned in an introductory bibliography such as this. Gerald Breeze, *Urbanization in Newly Developing Countries* (Englewood Cliffs: Prentice-Hall, 1966), is a very brief, highly analytical introduction to the subject. D. J. Dwyer, ed., *The City in the Third World* (London: Macmillan, 1979), is a series of individual essays; as is Horace Miner, ed., *The City in Modern Africa* (New York, Praeger, 1967). Anthony D. King, *Colonial Urban Development: Culture, Social Power and Development* (London: Routledge and Kegan Paul, 1976) is an original sociological interpretation attempting to describe the unique qualities of the hyphenated city. The book, centered on India, has far broader implications. Similarly thoughtful and theoretical in approach is T. G. McGee, *The Urbanization Process in the Third World: Exploration in Search of a Theory* (London: G. Bell and Sons, 1971). Particular mention must be made of the splendid volume—so described because of the excellence of its contents and the lavishness of its format—by Robert Grant Irving, *Indian Summer: Lutyens, Baker and Imperial Delhi* (New Haven, Conn.: Yale University Press, 1981).

Finally, a few words ought to be said about the fictional literature on modern empire. While few great colonial novels exist—with perhaps E. M. Forster, *A Passage to India* (New York: Harcourt Brace, 1965) and André Malraux, *The Royal Way*, trans. by Gilbert Stuart, (London: Methuen, 1935) at the top of the list—the novelist as social critic has played an important part in evaluating the colonial situation, particularly the problems of transition from the colonial to the national era. General literary histories that will serve well as introductions to this aspect of colonial literature are: Meenkshi Mukherjee, *Twice Born Fiction: Themes and Techniques of the Indian Novel in English* (New Delhi: Heinemann, 1971); William Walsh, *A Manifold Voice: Studies in Commonwealth Literature* (London: Chatto and Windus, 1970); and G. D. Killam, *Africa in English Fiction, 1874–1939* (Ibadan: Ibadan University Press, 1968). Janheinz Jahn, *Neo-African Literature: A History of Black Writing*, trans. Oliver Coburn and Ursula Lehrrburger, (New York: Grove Press, 1968), is a valuable compendium of modern African, Caribbean, and American literature of this genre.

The aftermath of imperialism has provided a rich harvest of studies, among which some of the most interesting and provocative are those concerned with the modernization process. A minor classic in its own right is Daniel Lerner, *The Passing of Traditional Society: Modernizing the Middle East* (Glencoe, Ill.: The Free Press, 1958). Therein the author describes the characteristics distinguishing the old from the new—the pitchfork from the television aerial. Worthy of a place in any bibliography on the subject is the remarkable "case study" by Clifford Geertz, *Peddlars and Princes: Social Development and Economic Change in Two Indonesian Towns* (Chicago: University of Chicago Press, 1965), from which the author extrapolates concepts that have informed the broader subject, as this volume has already demonstrated (see Chapter 4, p. 17). The issue of technology transfer once held the attention of social scientists. An exceptional work on the subject is Denis Goulet, *On the Ethics of Development Planning: General Principles, Special Applications to Value Conflicts in Technology* (Los Angeles: University of California Press, 1975). As a prefatory historical note to this development, perhaps the work by Daniel R. Headrick, *Tools of Empire: Technology and European Imperialism in the Nineteenth Century* (New York: Oxford University Press, 1981), should be mentioned, even though its period of inquiry ends before the subject of this volume begins.

The politics of change have received ample attention and have often led to multi-authored works in which particular regions of the former colonial world are analyzed according to institutional and functional change. One such work, still of value today, was edited by Gabriel A. Almond and James C. Coleman, *The Politics of Developing Areas* (Princeton, Princeton University Press, 1960). A far more theoretical study, one that returns the primacy of politics to the process, is David Apter, *The Politics of Modernization* (Chicago: University of Chicago Press, 1965). A standard work, most useful to an understanding of the politics in Africa shortly after independence is Thomas L. Hodgkin, *African Political Parties* (Harmondsworth: Penguin, 1961). Finally, for a clear overview, see Brian Crozier, *The Morning After: A Study of Independence* (New York: Oxford University Press, 1963).

Notes

Notes

INTRODUCTION. THE SETTING

1. Carlo M. Cippola, in editor's introduction to *The Economic Decline of Empire* (London: Methuen, 1970), p. 12.

2. Air Commodore C. F. A. Portal, "Air Force Co-Operation Policing the Empire," *Journal of the Royal United Service Institute,* 82: 351–55 (1937).

3. A. A. Walker, "Air Power and the Empire," *The Nineteenth Century,* 92:359 (1922).

4. Harold R. Hardless, *The Indian Gentleman's Guide to English Etiquette, Conversation and Correspondence* (2nd ed.; Chumar: Sanctuary Press, 1920), pp. 15 and 51.

5. Kimar Goshal, *People in Colonies* (New York: Sheridan House, 1948), p. 163.

6. Two particularly laudatory biographies of Lyautey are: André Maurois, *Lyautey* (Paris: Plon, 1931); and Georges Hardy, *Portrait de Lyautey* (Paris: Bloud et Gay, 1949). The most recent and very critical assessment of the resident-general is found in Douglas Porch, *The Conquest of Morocco* (New York: Knopf, 1982), a well-written interpretation.

7. The most readily available biographical statement on Balbo is Georges Bourgin, "I. Balbo" in Charles-André Julien, ed., *Les Techniciens de la colonisation (XIXe-XXe siècles),* (Paris: Presses universitaires de France, 1947).

8. George Orwell, "Shooting an Elephant," in *Shooting an Elephant and Other Essays* (New York: Harcourt Brace, 1950), p. 8.

9. Robert Delavignette, *Freedom and Authority in West Africa* (London: Cass, 1968), p. 12.

10. Raymond Aron, in preface to Pierre Bourdieu, *The Algerians,* trans. Alan C. M. Ross (Boston: Beacon Press, 1962), p. vi.

11. Frantz Fanon, *A Dying Colonialism,* trans. Haakon Chevalier (New York: Grove Press, 1965), pp. 51 and 65. The entire chapter, "Algeria Unveiled," is a provocative interpretation of the social role of clothing.

12. n.a., *The Colonial Problem* (London, Oxford University Press, 1937), p. 2.

13. Delavignette, *Afrique occidentale française* (Paris: Société d'Editions géographiques, 1931), p. 68.

14. Philip Mason, in introduction to Charles Allen, *Plain Tales from the Raj* (London: Futura Publications, 1976), p. 16.

15. Philip Napier, *Raj in Sunset* (Ilfracombe: Arthur H. Stockwell, 1966), p. 30.

16. Guy Mounerau, "Une Enquête en A.O.F.," *L'Ouest africain français*, September 28, 1927.

17. Delavignette, *Afrique occidentale française*, p. 68.

18. Herbert Baker, *Cecil Rhodes by His Architect* (London: Oxford University Press, 1934), p. 53.

19. William McKinley, November 21, 1899, to a committee of the Methodist Episcopal Church, quoted in Garel A. Grunder and William E. Livezey, *The Philippines and the United Staes* (Norman: University of Oklahoma Press, 1951), p. 36.

20. Mary Hastings Bradley, *On the Gorilla Trail* (New York: D. Appleton, 1922), p. 31.

CHAPTER 1. EMPIRES AT WAR

1. *The Times,* February 2, 1921.

2. Sir Julian Corbett, *Naval Operations* (London: Longmans, 1938), pp. 130–31; and Lord Fisher, quoted in D. M. Schurman, "Historians and Britain's Imperial Strategic Stance in 1914," John Flint and Glyndwr Williams, eds., *Perspectives of Empire* (London: Longmans, 1973), p. 179.

3. Minutes of the War Committe, March 19, 1915, reprinted in C. J. Lowe and M. L. Dockrill, *The Mirage of Power*, Vol. III: *The Documents* (London: Routledge and Kegan Paul, 1972), p. 527.

4. L. S. Amery, *My Political Life*, Vol. II: *War and Peace, 1914–1929* (London: Hutchinson, 1953), p. 102.

5. The figures on British colonial manpower are from C. E. H. Carrington, "The Empire at War," *Cambridge History of the British Empire*, Vol. III: *The Empire Commonwealth, 1870–1939* (Cambridge: Cambridge University Press, 1959), pp. 641–42. Those on the French come from Albert Sarraut, *La Mise en valeur des colonies françcaises* (Paris: Payot, 1923), pp. 40–44.

6. Reprinted in W. K. Hancock and Jean van der Poel, *Selections from the Smuts Papers*, Vol. III: June 1910–November 1918 (Cambridge: Cambridge University Press, 1966), p. 508.

7. Joseph Chailley, "Le Maroc dans la guerre," *Revue de Paris*, October 15, 1916, p. 785; Abel Ferry, quoted in André Kaspi, "French War Aims in Africa, 1914–1919," in Prosser Gifford and Wm. Roger Louis, eds., *French and Great Britain in Africa* (New Haven, Conn.: Yale University Press, 1971), p. 312. Paul von Lettow-Vorbeck, *East African Campaigns* (New York: Robert Speller, 1957), p. 1. War Cabinet statement cited in Paul Guinn, *British Strategy and Politics, 1914 to 1918* (Oxford: Oxford University Press, 1965), p. 126.

8. Articles in the *Dépêche coloniale*, July 1, 1913; quoted in Christopher Andrew and A. S. Kanya-Forstner, *The Climax of French Imperial Expansion, 1914–1924* (Stanford, Calif.: Stanford University Press, 1981), p. 18.

9. "The Round Table," *The Round Table*, 1:1 (1910).

10. "Memorandum of 1917: The General Strategic and Military Situation," reprinted in Hancock and van der Poel, *Selections*, p. 482.

11. Serge Sazonov, *Fateful Years, 1909–1916* (New York: Kraus Press, 1971; first published, 1928), p. 242.

12. The De Bunsen Committee, quoted in V. H. Rothwell, *British War Aims and Diplomacy, 1914–1918* (Oxford: Clarendon Press, 1977), p. 26.

13. Quoted in Robert Hess, "Italy and Africa: Colonial Ambitions in the First World War," *Journal of African History*, 4:108 (1963).

14. The general argument presented here is the basic thesis of the provocative and penetrating study by Andrew and Kanya-Forstner previously cited.

15. Commandant Davin, "L'Angleterre dans la Golfe persique," *Revue des deux mondes*, July 15, 1916, p. 448.

16. Eastern Committee Minutes, quoted in Wm. Roger Louis, *Great Britain and Germany's Lost Colonies* (Oxford: Clarendon Press, 1964), p. 120. Also see H. G. Wells, "A Forecast of the World's Affairs," n.a., *These Eventful Years*, Vol. II (London: Encyclopedia Britannica, 1924), pp. 12-14.

17. Amery, *My Political Life*, p. 161.

18. Quoted in Guinn, *British Strategy*, p. 193.

19. All of the above information in this paragraph comes from Fritz Fischer, *Germany's Aims in the First World War* (New York: W. W. Norton, 1967), notably pp. 101-103; 586-91.

20. Quoted in Hancock and van der Poel, *Selections*, p. 482.

21. See Andrews and Kanya-Forstner, *Climax*, pp. 144-45 as the source for the information in this paragraph.

22. See Wm. Roger Louis, *Ruanda-Urundi, 1884-1919*, Part III (Oxford: Clarendon Press, 1963).

23. Hess, "Italy and Africa," p. 108. This paragraph is a recapitulation of Hess' analysis, pp. 108-11.

24. An excellent summary is Peter Lowe, *Great Britain and Japan, 1911-1915* (London: Macmillan, 1939), chapter 6.

25. Quoted in Arthur J. Marder, *From the Dreadnought to Scapa Flow* (London: Oxford University Press, 1961), p. 235.

26. Letter dated March 22, 1915, in David Garnett, ed., *The Letters of T. E. Lawrence* (New York: Doubleday, 1939), p. 196.

27. Lowe and Dockrill, *The Mirage of Power*, Vol. II: *British Foreign Policy, 1914-1922* (London: Routledge and Kegan Paul, 1972), p. 209.

28. David Lloyd George, *War Memoirs*, Vol. II: *1915-1916* (Boston: Little, Brown, 1937), p. 238.

29. A. J. Barker, *The Bastard War: The Mesopotamian Campaign of 1914-1918* (New York: Dial Press, 1967), p. 29.

30. Quoted in Alan Moorehead, *Gallipoli* (London: Hamish, Hamilton, 1956), p. 109.

31. The incident is beautifully described in James Morris, *Farewell The Trumpets: An Imperial Retreat* (Harmondsworth: Penguin, 1980), pp. 176-77.

32. Among the most perceptive is Jeremy Meyer, *The Wounded Spirit: A Study of the Seven Pillars of Wisdom* (London: Martin Brian and O'Keefe, 1973), notably chapter 7.

33. Letter dated July 15, 1918, reprinted in Garnett, ed., *Letters*, p. 244.

34. Letter from government of India to Mallat Committee, dated September 29, 1916, quoted in Rothwell, *British War Aims*, p. 88.

35. Jan Karl Tannenbaum, *France and the Arab Middle East, 1914-1920* (Philadelphia: American Philosophical Society, 1978), p. 6.

36. The story of the negotiations is well told. On the French side, see Andrews and Kanya-Forstner, *Climax*, notably pp. 87-97, 99-102; and Tannenbaum, *France and the Arab Middle East*, pp. 9-15. A favorable interpretation of the treaty is found in Elie Kedourie, *England and the Middle East* (Hassocks: Harvester Press, 1978), chapter 2.

37. *Ibid.*, p. 132.

38. See Tannenbaum, *France and the Arab Middle East*, pp. 24-25.

39. Quoted in Andrew and Kanya-Forstner, *Climax*, p. 177.

40. House of Commons Speech, March 17, 1914, reprinted in Randolph S. Churchill, ed., *Winston S. Churchill*, Vol. II: *Young Statesman, 1901-1914* (London: Heineman, 1967), p. 683. An even more interesting comment is that of Edward Grey, who asked this question at the War

Committee Meeting of March 19, 1915: "If we acquire fresh territory shall we make ourselves weaker or stronger?" Quoted in Lowe and Dockrill, *Mirage*, Vol. III, p. 524.

41. Meeting of April 23, 1917, quoted in Louis, *Great Britain and Germany's Lost Colonies*, p. 84.

42. Gabrielle M. Vassal, "D'Indo-chine en France, aôut–décembre 1914," *Revue de Paris*, June 1, 1917, p. 570.

43. See Alan Schamm, *Lyautey in Morocco* (Berkeley: University of California Press, 1970), pp. 24–25.

44. One of his most frequently cited comments is: "A construction site spares a batallion." Quoted in J. Marrast, "Maroc," in n.a., *L'Oeuvre d'Henri Prost* (Paris: Academie d'Architecture, 1960), p. 56.

45. See Jean-Louis Miège, *L'Impérialisme italian de 1870 à nos jours* (Paris: Société d'Édition d'enseignement supérieur, 1968), pp. 108–9.

46. Philip Mason, *A Matter of Honor: An Account of the Indian Army, Its Officers and Its Men* (London: Joanthan Cape, 1974), p. 426.

47. T. R. H. Davenport, "The South African Rebellion," *English Historical Review*, 78:93 (1963).

48. Quoted in Carlton Younger, *Ireland's Civil War* (London: Frederick Muller, 1978), p. 23.

49. Quoted in Michael Crowder, *West Africa Under Colonial Rule* (Evanston: Northwestern University Press, 1968), p. 255.

50. Hughes quoted in the *Sydney Daily Telegraph*, March 11, 1916; article reprinted in F. K. Crowley, *Modern Australia in Documents*, Vol. I: *1901–1939* (Melbourne: Wren, 1973), p. 267.

51. n.a., *Canada in the Great War*, Vol. II: *Days of Preparation* (Toronto: United Publishers, n.d.), p. 87.

52. P. M. Gibson, "The Conscription Issue in South Australia, 1916–1917," *University Studies in History, 1963–64*, ed., J. I. W. Brash (Nedlands, 1964), p. 80.

53. Alan J. Ward, "Lloyd George and the Irish Conscription Crisis," *The Historical Journal*, 17:110 (1974). The details of the conscription and its effects are very well described in this article.

54. Charles Mangin, *La Force noire* (Paris: Hachette, 1910), p. 343.

55. For details on this conscription issue, see Marc Michel, "La Genèse du recrutement de 1918 en Afrique noire française," *Revue française d'histoire d'outre-mer*, 58: 433–50 (1977); and G. Wesley Johnson, *The Emergence of Black Politics in Senegal* (Stanford, Calif.: Stanford University Press, 1971), pp. 183–95.

56. Quoted in Michel, "La Genèse," p. 444.

57. On Diagne see Johnson, *Emergence*, Chapter 9.

58. Quoted in Crowder, *West Africa*, p. 265.

59. Lord Beaverbrook, *Canada in Flanders*, Vol. II (London: Hodder and Stoughton, 1917), p. 244.

60. House of Commons Speech, May 17, 1918, quoted in Amery, *My Political Life*, p. 108.

61. Quoted in R. Craig Brown and Robert Rothwell, "The 'Canadian Resolution'," in Michael Cross and Robert Rothwell, eds., *Policy by Other Means* (Toronto: Charles Irwin, 1972), p. 165. The article provides a good summary of the origins of the resolution.

62. Quoted in John Blum, *Woodrow Wilson and the Politics of Morality* (Boston: Little, Brown, 1956), p. 159.

63. Lloyd George, *Memoirs of the Peace Conference*, Vol. I (New Haven, Conn.: Yale University Press, , 1939), p. 4.

64. Andrews and Kanya-Forstner, *Climax*, p. 146.

65. A notable effort to fill this gap is the special issue, entitled "World War I and Africa," of the *Journal of African History*, 19(1) (1978). See also the majesterial study by Marc Michel, *L'Appel à l'Afrique. Contributions et réactions à l'effort de guerre en A.O.F. (1914-1919)*. (Paris: Publications de la Sorbonne, 1982).

66. Amiya Kumar Baggchi, *Private Investment in India 1900-1939* (Cambridge: Cambridge University Press, 1972), p. 192.

67. Richard Rathbone, "World War I and Africa: Introduction," *Journal of African History* 19(1):7 (1978).

68. Michel, *L'Appel*, pp. 100-112.

69. Kenneth Good, "Settler Colonialism: Economic Development and Class Formation," *Journal of Modern African Studies*, 14(4):590 (1976).

70. See the comments of Martin J. Murray, *The Development of Capitalism in Colonial Indochina (1870-1940)* (Berkeley: University of California Press, 1980), pp. 118-19.

71. Michel, *L'Appel*, pp. 189-192.

72. On this scheme, see *supra*, p. 97.

73. Nehru, *Toward Freedom* (New York: John Day, 1942), p. 78.

74. Sir Herbert Russell, *With the Prince in the East: A Record of the Royal Visit to India and Japan* (2nd ed.; London, 1922), p. 23.

CHAPTER 2. COLONIAL RULE AND ADMINISTRATION

1. Information found in a letter of T. W. Pollock, Honorable Treasurer of the Over-Seas Club and Patriotic League, Tientsin, China, printed in *Overseas*, 4(40):90 (1919).

2. Parker T. Moon, *Imperialism and World Politics* (New York: Macmillan, 1926), p. 566.

3. Georges Hardy, *La Politique coloniale et le partage de la terre aux 19e et 20e siècles* (Paris: Albin Michel, 1937), p. 465.

4. See, for instance, A. D. A. Kat de Angelino, *Colonial Policy*, Vol. I, trans. G. J. Renier (Chicago: University of Chicago Press, 1931), pp. 471-86; Albert Sarraut, *La Mise en valeur des colonies françaises* (Paris: Payot, 1923), pp. 103 and 120; Georges Hardy, *Nos grands problèmes coloniaux* (Paris: Armand Colin, 1929), pp. 208-9.

5. *Congressional Record* (55th Congress, 3rd Session), quoted in Grayson L. Kirk, *Philippine Independence: Motives, Problems, and Prospects* (New York: Farrar and Rinehart, 1936), p. 21.

6. See Henry Winkler, *The League of Nations Movement in Great Britain, 1914-1919* (Metuchen, N.J.: Scarecrow, 1967), pp. 201-6.

7. Rudolf von Albertini, *Decolonization: The Administration and Future of Colonies*, trans. Francisca Garvie (New York: Doubleday, 1971), p. 80.

8. On this subject see Claudio Segrè, *Fourth Shore: The Italian Colonization of Libya* (Chicago: University of Chicago Press, 1974), notably chapter 5; and Jean-Louis Miège, *L'Impérialisme italien de 1870 à nos jours* (Paris: Société d'Édition d'enseignement supérieur, 1968), pp. 248-50.

9. Herbert Bailey, "The Colonisation of Libya," *Fortnightly Review*, 151:200 (February 1934).

10. Segrè, *Fourth Shore*, p. 106.

11. See Miège, *L'Impérialisme italien*, pp. 135-36.

12. Segrè, *Fourth Shore*, pp. 104-5.

13. The concept is that of Melville Herskovits, *The Human Factor in Changing Africa* (New York: Vintage, 1967), pp. 56-58.

14. Lucien Lévy-Bruhl, in preface to *La Mentalité primitive* (11th ed.; Paris: Presses Universitaires de France, 1960), p. i.

15. Robert Briffault, *The Making of Humanity* (London: George Allen and Unwin, 1919), p. 73.

16. On this matter see Jean Cazeneuve, *Lucien Lévy-Bruhl et son oeuvre* (Paris: Presses Universitaires de France), p. 20.

17. Lévy-Bruhl, "preface", p. 1.

18. Malinowski made the following remark on the use of language by "primitive" man: "The meaning of the thing is made up of experience in its active uses and not of its contemplation." Bronislaw Malinowski, *Magic, Science, and Religion* (Glencoe, Ill.: Free Press, 1948), p. 257.

19. Lucy Mair, *Primitive Government* (Harmondsworth: Penguin, 1964), p. 8.

20. Frederick D. Lugard, *The Dual Mandate in Tropical Africa* (3rd ed.; Edinburgh: William Blackwell, 1926), p. 68.

21. Jomo Kenyatta, *Facing Mt. Kenya* (New York: Vintage, n.d.), p. 121.

22. *Indians in Kenya*, Cmd. 1922 (London, 1923), p. 9.

23. Lugard, *Dual Mandate*, p. 7.

24. V. I. Lenin, *Imperialism, the Highest Stage of Capitalism* (New York: International Publishers, 1939), p. 82.

25. Lugard, *Dual Mandate*, p. 618.

26. *Ibid.*, p. 58.

27. Quoted in Winkler, *League of Nations*, pp. 204-5.

28. See the assessment of Heinrich Schnee, *German Colonization Past and Future* (New York: Knopf, 1926), pp. 63-66; and the difficulties of making comparisons in John D. Fage, "British and German Colonial Rule: A Synthesis and Summary," in Prosser Gifford and Wm. Roger Louis, eds., *Britain and Germany in Africa: Imperial Rivalry and Colonial Rule* (New Haven, Conn.: Yale University Press, 1967), pp. 691-706. An interwar comment found in the British Colonial Office states that the "dreadful example of the Cameroons" was cited in a Ministry of Information memorandum of 1917, because "no fewer than 29 punitive expeditions during the years 1891-1903" were undertaken. The commentator then notes that 38 or 40 such punitive expeditions were undertaken by the British between 1900 and 1906 in Northern Nigeria. See CO 323/1398/6656 (Part 1), 1936, *Public Records Office; Great Britain; henceforth: PRO.*

29. Jean Stengers, "British and German Imperial Rivalry: A Conclusion," in Gifford and Louis, *Britain and Germany in Africa*, p. 345.

30. Schnee, *German Colonization*, p. 66.

31. PRO: CO 323/1398/6656/ (Part 1), 1936.

32. Saurraut, *La mise en valeur*, p. 91.

33. Quoted in Garel A. Grunder and William E. Livezey, *The Philippines and the United States*, (Norman: University of Oklahoma Press), p. 37.

34. Earl of Cromer, *Ancient and Modern Imperialism* (London: John Murray, 1910), p. 118.

35. An interesting dissenting view, one that suggested the use of existing indigenous institutions in the structuring of modern democracy, was that of Mukerjee, *Democracies of the East* (1923), briefly analyzed in Kat de Angelino, *Colonial Policy*, pp. 433-34.

36. Charles Lucas, *United Empire* (March 1919), quoted in Lugard, *Dual Mandate*, p. 608.

37. Kat de Angelino, *Colonial Policy*, p. 493.

38. William H. Taft, "Civil Government in the Philippines," in *The Philippines* (New York: Outlook, 1902), pp. 105-6.

39. Hardy, *Nos grands problèmes coloniaux*, p. 208.

40. Quoted in Albertini, *Decolonization*, p. 312.

41. *Ibid.*, p. 116.

42. Quoted in Partha Sarathi Gupta, *Imperialism and the British Labour Movement, 1914–1964* (New York: Holmes and Meir, 1975), p. 325. G. D. H. Cole, author and active member of the Labour Party, remarked in 1949: "Except in Burma and the Philippines and in Siam . . . complete independence, even in name, seems for the present to be beyond the grasp of the peoples of southeast Asia," G. D. H. Cole, *World in Transition: A Guide to the Shifting Political and Economic Forces of Our Time* (New York: Oxford University Press, 1949), p. 530.

43. See the revisionist interpretation of John Darwin, "Imperialism in Decline: Tendencies in British Imperial Policy Between the Wars," *The Historical Journal*, 23:647–79 (1980).

44. Margery F. Perham, *The Colonial Reckoning: The End of Imperial Rule in Africa in the Light of the British Experience* (New York: Knopf, 1962), p. 141.

45. Quoted in William B. Cohen, "The Colonial as Child: British and French Colonial Rule," *Journal of African Studies*, 3:427–31 (1970).

46. Quoted in David Gardinier, "The British in the Cameroons, 1919–1939," in Gifford and Louis, *Britain and Germany in Africa*, p. 513.

47. Robert Lansing, *The Peace Negotiation: A Personal Narrative* (Boston: Houghton Mifflin, 1921), p. 157.

48. Quoted in Louis, "The United States and the African Peace Settlement of 1919: The Pilgrimage of George Louis Beer," *Journal of African History*, 4:421–22 (1963).

49. Quoted in R. N. Chowdhuri, *International Mandates and Trusteeship Systems: A Comparative Study* (The Hague: Martinus Nijhoff, 1955), p. 4.

50. See Louis, *Germany's Lost Colonies*, pp. 119–21.

51. Quoted in David Lloyd George, *Memoirs of the Peace Conference*, Vol. I (New Haven, Conn.: Yale University Press, 1939), p. 35.

52. Quoted in *ibid.*, p. 353.

53. Quoted in *ibid.*, p. 360.

54. *Ibid.*, p. 367.

55. *Ibid.*, p. 68.

56. Gardinier, "The British in the Cameroons," p. 528.

57. Quoted in Duncan Hall, *Mandates, Dependencies and Trusteeship* (Washington, D.C.: Carnegie Endowment, 1948), p. 205.

58. Lord Hailey, *An African Survey: A Study of Problems Arising in Africa South of the Sahara* (Revised ed.; London: Oxford University Press, 1957), p. 242.

59. Robert Delavignette, *Service africain* (8th ed; Paris: Gallimard, 1946), p. 121.

60. *Instructions to Political and Other Officers on Subjects Chiefly Political and Administrative*, 1906, p. 191; quoted in Margery Perham, *Lugard, The Years of Authority, 1898–1945* (London: Collins, 1960), p. 144.

61. Margery Perham, "A Restatement of Indirect Rule," *Africa*, 7:331 (1934).

62. Harry J. Benda, "Decolonization in Indonesia: The Problem of Continuity and Change," *American Historical Review*, 70:1065 (1955).

63. Donald K. Emmerson, *Indonesia's Elite: Political Culture and Cultural Politics* (Ithaca, N.Y.: Cornell University Press, 1976), p. 40.

64. Jules Harmand, *Domination et colonisation* (Paris: Flammarion, 1910), p. 163.

65. Joost von Vollenhoven, "Circulaire au sujet des chefs indigènes," in *Une âme de chef* (Paris: Plom-Nourrit, 1920), p. 207.

66. On this subject see in particular, Robert Tignor, "Colonial Chiefs in Chiefless Societies," *The Journal of Modern African Studies*, 9:339–59 (1971); and John Tosh, "Colonial Chiefs in a Stateless Society: A Case Study from Northern Uganda," *Journal of African History*, 14:473–90 (1973).

67. "Programme d'action économique, politique et sociale," 1933, p. 185; quoted in Jean Suret-Canale, *French Colonialism in Tropical Africa, 1900–1945*, (New York: Pica Press, 1971), p. 323. Italics in author's original.

68. Delavignette, *Service africain*, p. 29.

69. Mair, *Primitive Governments*, p. 253.

70. Quoted in Hailey, *An African Survey*, p. 428.

71. "Conference du jeune barreau de Bruxelles," quoted in Pierre Ryckmans, *Dominer pour servir* (Brussels: Universelle, 1948; first published, 1931), p. 180.

72. Lugard, *The Dual Mandate*, pp. 69-70.

73. Ida G. Greaves, *Modern Production Among Backward Peoples* (London: George Allen and Unwin, 1935). See, in particular, chapter 2.

74. John S. Furnivall, *Netherlands India* (New York: Macmillan, 1944), p. 354.

75. See *The Colonial Problem* (London: Oxford University Press, 1937), p. 182, footnote 1.

76. Quoted in William B. Cohen, ed., *Robert Delavignette on the French Empire* (Chicago: University of Chicago Press, 1977), p. 56.

77. See Martin J. Murray, *The Development of Capitalism in Colonial Indochina (1870–1940* (Berkeley: University of California Press, 1980), p. 83.

78. *The Colonial Problem*, p. 178.

79. Interview with William B. Cohen, February 2, 1965, in William B. Cohen, *Rulers of Empire: The French Colonial Service in Africa* (Stanford: Calif.: Hoover Institution Press, 1971), p. 61.

80. F. S. V. Donnison, quoted in Roland Hunt and John Harrison, *The District Officer in India, 1930–1947* (London: Scolar Press, 1980), p. 45.

81. Penderel Moon, *Strangers in India* (New York: Reynal and Hitchcock, 1945), p. 165.

82. C. M. Lloyd-Jones quoted in Hunt and Harrison, *The District Officer*, p. 135.

83. On the squire analogy, see Prosser Gifford, "Indirect Rule: Touchstone or Tombstone for Colonial Policy?" in Gifford and Louis, *Britain and Germany in Africa*, pp. 358–60; on the constable analogy, see C. H. Masterman quoted in Hunt and Harrison, *The District Officer*, p. 95.

84. J. D. Shulka, quoted in *ibid.*, p. 78.

85. Benda, "Decolonization in Indonesia," p. 1065.

86. Mair, *Primitive Government*, p. 272.

87. Philip Woodruff, *The Men Who Ruled India*. Vol. II, *The Guardians* (London: 1954), p. 244; quoted in T. H. Beaglehole, "From Rulers to Servants: The I.C.S. and the British Demission of Power in India," *Modern Asian Studies*, 2(2):237 (1977).

88. Perham, *The Colonial Reckoning*, p. 143.

89. See John H. Kautsky, "An Essay on the Politics of Development," in Kautsky, ed., *Political Change in Underdeveloped Countries: Nationalism and Communism* (New York: John Wiley, 1966), pp. 32–33.

90. John Smith, *Colonial Cadet in Nigeria* (Durham, N.C.: Duke University Press, 1968), p. 22.

CHAPTER 3. IMPERIAL DESIGNS: TECHNOLOGY AND ECONOMIC DEVELOPMENT

1. *Life*, January 10, 1937, p. 50.

2. Commander Sir Denniston Burney, address to Royal Empire Society printed in *United Empire*, 21(3):137 (1930).

3. The term "buckle" was Winston Churchill's, used in 1919; cited in John Higham, *Brit-*

ain's *Imperial Air Routes, 1918 to 1929* (Hamden, Conn.: Shoestring Press, 1960), p. 11. "Links" appeared in M. de P. Webb, "Links in the Imperial Chain," *Asiatic Review*, 29:693 (1933).

4. Laurens Van der Post, *Venture to the Interior* (Harmondsworth: Penguin, 1963), p. 8.

5. Bronislaw Malinowski, *The Dynamics of Culture Change: An Inquiry into Race Relations in Africa* (New Haven, Conn.: Yale University Press, 1965) p. 15.

6. Isak Dinesen, *Out of Africa* (New York: Modern Library, 1952), p. 292.

7. Frank Perlin, "Proto-Industrialization and Pre-Colonial South Asia," *Past and Present*, No. 98:33 (February 1983).

8. M. Johnson, "Proto-Industrialization in West Africa," in *Eighth International Congress of Economic History, Budapest, 1982: Communications Presented to Section A2: La Proto-industrialisation, theorie et réalité* (Lille: Université des arts, lettres et sciences humaines, 1982.)

9. H. F. Wilson, "Imperial Aviation," *United Empire*, 11(4):152 (1920).

10. Memorandum of J. E. W. Flood, dated August 8, 1930, in PRO:CO 323 1080/70329 (1930).

11. Sir William P. Andrew, *Indian Railways as Connected with the Power and Stability of the British Empire in the East* (London, W. H. Allen, 1846), p. 9.

12. John Strachey, *The End of Empire* (New York: Random House, 1964), p. 58.

13. Allan McPhee, *The Economic Revolution in British West Africa* (London: Frank Cass, 1971; first published, 1926), pp. 113–14.

14. See J. N. Schni, *Indian Railways: One Hundred Years, 1853 to 1953* (New Delhi: Government of India, 1953), pp. 35–6.

15. See M. Devallon, "Notes sur le Transsaharen," in *Congrès d'outillage economique et des communications: Rapport* (Paris, 1931), p. 297.

16. See Marcel Migeo, *Saint-Exupéry* (Paris: Flammarion 1958), p. 79.

17. Higham, *Britain's Imperial Air Routes*, pp. 110–11.

18. The story is fully described—and dramatically—in James Leasor, *The Millionth Chance: The Story of the R-101* (New York: Reynal, 1957).

19. Antoine de Saint-Exupéry, *Wind, Sand and Stars* in *An Airman's Odyssey*, trans. Lewis Galantiere (New York: Reynal and Hitchcock, 1942), p. 116.

20. *Illustration*, June 20, 1936, p. 257.

21. On the nautical appearance of British Imperial Airways, see James Morris, *Farewell The Trumpets: An Imperial Retreat* (Harmondsworth: Penguin, 1980), pp. 358–60.

22. Van den Post, *Venture to the Interior*, p. 37.

23. Andre Citröen quoted in n.a., "Motoring Across the Sahara," *Literary Digest*, 76:69 (1923).

24. See Georges Marie Hardt, "Through the Deserts and Jungles of Africa by Motor," *National Geographic Magazine*, 49:650–720 (1926).

25. Yves-J. Saint Martin, "Les Premières automobiles sur les bords du Niger," *Revue française d'historie d'outre-mer*, 60:602 (1973).

26. General Jean Charbonneau, *Gallieni à Madagascar* (Paris: Bibliothèque de l'Union française, 1950), p. 145.

27. See the letter from V. Hippolite to the minister of colonies, dated Saigon, August 20, 1910, in Archives nationales: Section outre-mer: Indochine: 15.315.

28. Joseph Friedland, "Opening Up the Orient," *Living Age* 338:184 (April 1, 1930).

29. Arnold Toynbee, "The Best Way to See Japan," *Contemporary Review* 138:163 (1930).

30. On the Nairn's equipment see "A Modern Desert Coach," *Scientific American* 150:98

(February 1934); and "Streamlined Bus Replaces Camels in Desert," *Popular Mechanics* 61:40 (March 1934).

31. Virginia Thompson, *French Indochina* (New York: Macmillan, 1937), p. 212.

32. R. E. Fulton, Jr., "Roads of Asia," *Asia* 34 (April 1934), p. 206.

33. Alice Guibon-Poulleau, "La Grande route littorale Tripoli-Alexandre," *Illustration*, March 20, 1937, p. 296.

34. See the description provided by E. D. O'Brien, "With the Duce in Libya," *English Review*, 54:553 (May 1937).

35. Carey, *Mister Johnson* (New York: Harper, 1948), p. 43.

36. McPhee, *The Economic Revolution*, p. 110.

37. Frederick D. Lugard, *The Dual Mandate in Tropical Africa* (3rd ed; Edinburgh: William Blackwell, 1926) p. 476; and Albert Sarraut, *La Mise en valeur des colonies françaises* (Paris: Payot, 1923), p. 389.

38. McPhee, *The Economic Revolution*, pp. 117–18.

39. Lord Hailey, *An African Survey* (London: Oxford University Press, 1957), p. 1574; and Paul E. Pheffer, "Political and Economic Strategies for French Colonial Railroads in West Africa, 1885–1914," *Proceedings of the Second Annual Meeting of the French Colonial Historical Society* (Athens, Georgia, 1977), particularly pp. 65–66.

40. n.a. "A Gigantic Trans-Desert Road," *Great Britain and the East*, June 1, 1939, p. 607.

41. See Geoffrey Hindley, *A History of Roads* (London: Peter Davies, 1971), p. 98; and Richard Pankhurst, "Road Building During the Italian Fascist Occupation of Ethiopia (1936–1940)," *Africa Quarterly (India)*, 15:3 (January 1976), p. 37.

42. On this subject see the detailed assessment in Pankhurst, *Road Building*, pp. 21–63, on which the above description is largely based.

43. *Ibid*, p. 26.

44. W. B. Courtney, "Dark and Bloody Roads," *Collier's*, March 21, 1939, p. 29.

45. Walter H. Malloy, "The Burma Road," *Foreign Affairs* 17:625–627 (April 1939).

46. See the assessment of McPhee, *The Economic Revolution*, pp. 114 and 126.

47. See McPhee's favorable comment, *The Economic Revolution*, p. 126; and the unfavorable one of André Huybrechts, *Transports et structures de dévelopment au Congo: Etude du progrès économique de 1900 à 1970* (Paris: Mouton, 1970), pp. 74–75.

48. As good a summary statement as any on the role and effects of transportation systems in colonial empire is "Transportation and Imperatives of Colonial Rule," the last chapter in Semil Kumar Munsi, *Geography of Transportation in Eastern India Under the British Raj* (Calcutta: K. R. Bagchi, 1980). A fine, preliminary interpretation of the history and effects of road-building on one colony is A. M. Hay, "The Development of Road Transport in Nigeria, 1900–1940," *Journal of Transport History*, New Series 1(12):95–107 (1971).

49. Anthony G. Hopkins, *An Economic History of West Africa* (New York: Columbia University Press, 1973), p. 196.

50. On the lack of any immediate effect of Chamberlain's proposal, see John M. Carland, "Public Expenditure and Development in a Crown Colony: The Colonial Office, Sir William Egerton, and Southern Nigeria, 1900–1912," *Albion*, 12:368–386 (1981).

51. L. S. Amery, *My Political Life,* Vol. II: *War and Peace, 1914–1929* (London: Hutchinson 1953), p. 340.

52. Sarraut, *La Mise en valeur des colonies françaises*, pp. 18–19.

53. Documents on Franck's plan are apparently no longer extant. See Barbu Niculescu, *Colonial Planning: a Comparative Study* (London: Allen and Unwin, 1958), p. 73. The best brief account of the plan is found in Sarraut, *La Mise en valeur*, pp. 352–53.

54. R. E. Wraith, *Guggisberg* (London: Oxford University Press, 1969), p. 124.

55. Cited in *ibid.*, p. 116.

56. A brief survey of these institutions is found in Hailey, *An African Survey*, pp. 1601-1609; and L. H. Gann, "Economic Development in Germany's African Empire, 1884-1914," in Peter Duignan and L. H. Gann, *Colonialism in Africa, 1870-1960*; Vol. IV: *Economics of Imperialism*, pp. 241-42.

57. Quoted in *Nature*, January 12, 1929, p. 39. On Dutch scientific institutions, see John S. Furnivall, *Netherlands India* (New York: Macmillan, 1937), pp. 304-7.

58. The most interesting statement on this proposed committee, from which information here cited comes, is that of its most ardent proponent, H. Wilson-Fox, "The Development of the Empire's Resources," *Nineteenth Century*, 82:835-858 (1917).

59. Amery, *My Political Life*, p. 350.

60. Sarraut, *La Mise en valeur*, p. 346.

61. Amery, *My Political Life*, p. 345.

62. See Cathérine Coquéry-Vidrovitch, "L'Afrique française et la crise de 1930: crise structurelle et genèse du sous-développement," *Revue Française d'historie d'outre-mer*, 63:405 (1976).

63. On the conference and its failure, see Lucien Hiquily, *La Politique impériale et la conférence coloniale de 1935* (Lyon: Basc, 1937), notably pp. 240-41; Georges Ngango, *Les Investissements d'origine extérieure en Afrique francophone: statut et incidence sur le développément* (Paris: Présence africaine, 1973), pp. 84-86.

64. Melvin M Knight, *Morocco As a French Economic Venture* (New York: D. Appleton-Century, 1937), p. 201.

65. "Rationalizing the Empire," *The Spectator*, September 27, 1930, p. 400.

66. Martin J. Murray, *The Development of Capitalism in Colonial Indochina (1870-1940)* (Berkeley: University of California Press, 1980), p. 459.

67. For Great Britain, see Ian M. Drummond, *British Economic Policy and the Empire, 1919-1939* (London: George Allen and Unwin, 1972), p. 18; for France, see Jacques Marseille, "L'Investissement française dans l'Empire colonial: l'enquête du gouvernement de Vichy (1943)," *Revue historique*, 252:2 (1974), p. 421.

68. See the interpretation of René Gallissot, "Rapports coloniaux, rapports sociaux et impérialisme," *Revue française d'histoire d'outre-mer*. 52:644-95, (1976).

69. "Empire Trade," *The London Times*, August 8, 1929.

70. Glenn D. Babcock, *History of the United States Rubber Comany* (Bloomington: Indiana University Graduate School of Business, 1966), p. 179.

71. Neville Chamberlain, "The Empire and Industry," *The Empire Review*, 50(342):93 (1929).

72. See "British Industry and the Future," *The Round Table*, 15:702-7 (1924-1925); and "Towards Industrial Renaissance," *ibid.*, 19:262-65 (1928-1929).

73. *Ibid.*, p. 264.

74. V. V. Giri, *Labour Problems in Indian Industry* (London: Asia Publishing House, 1959), pp. 158-160.

75. Coquéry-Vidrovich, "L'Afrique française," p. 406.

76. Speech to the Académie des sciences coloniales, May 18, 1923, cited in Thomas E. Ennis, *French Policy and Development in Indochina* (Chicago, 1936), pp. 132-33.

77. Hans Zache, one of the editors of *Kolonial gesellschaft*, cited in Charles-Robert Agéron, "L'Idée d'Eurafrique et le débat colonial franco-allemand de l'entre-deux-guerres," *Revue d'histoire moderne et contemporaine*, 22:452 (1975).

78. A. D. A. Kat de Angelino, *Colonial Policy, II: The Dutch East Indies*, trans. G. J. Renier (Chicago: University of Chicago Press, 1931), p. 427.

79. "Report and Correspondence Relating to the Expediency of Maintaining the Royal Indian

Engineering College," cited in Amiya Kumar Bagchi, *Private Investment in India, 1900–1939* (Cambridge: Cambridge University Press, 1972), p. 152.

80. Commission report cited in Margaret Read, *The Indian Peasant Uprooted* (London: Longmans, Green, 1931), p. 83.

81. See Bagchi, *Private Investment in India*, pp. 300–303.

82. Rajat K. Ray, *Industrialization in India: Growth and Conflict in the Private Corporate Sector, 1914–47* (Delhi: Oxford University Press, 1979), p. 62.

83. K. F. Creutzberg in *Neerlands Indie*, cited in Kat de Angelino, *Colonial Policy, II*, p. 230.

84. See, particularly, the statement reprinted in David G. Scanlon, ed., *Traditions of African Education* (New York: Columbia University Teachers College, 1964), p. 53.

85. Cited in *Education in India in 1932–33* (Delhi: Government of India, 1935), p. 18.

86. See the popular work of Robert Delavignette, *Paysans noirs* (Paris: Stock, 1931).

87. See Henri Brunschwig, *Noris et blancs en Afrique noire française, ou comment le colonisé devient colonisateur (1870–1914)* (Paris: Flammarion, 1983), chapter 6.

88. E. M. Forster, *A Passage to India* (New York: Harcourt, Brace, 1924), p. 42.

89. J. C. Schook quoted in Kat de Angelino, *Colonial Policy, II*, p. 238.

90. On this matter, see J. S. Furnivall, *Colonial Policy and Practice: A Comparative Study of Burma and Netherlands India* (Cambridge: Cambridge University Press, 1948), pp. 380–81.

91. See Ray, *Industrialization in India*, p. 91.

92. Quoted in Hailey, *An Africay Survey*, p. 1231.

93. This subject is well treated in Kenneth James King, *Pan-Africanism and Education* (Oxford: Oxford University Press, 1971), notably pp. 43–127. The information here presented is derived principally from this source.

94. Brévié's statement is quoted in *The Colonial Problem: A Report by a Study Group of Members of the Royal Institute of International Affairs* (London: Oxford University Press, 1937), p. 209.

95. Murray, *Development of Capitalism in Indochina*, p. 241. Also see Thompson, *French Indochina*, p. 153.

96. Kat de Angelino, *Colonial Policy, II*, p. 504.

97. *Ibid.*, pp. 507–8.

98. Harley F. MacNair, *The Chinese Abroad* (2nd ed.; Shanghai: Ch'eng Wen Publishing Company, 1971; first published, 1933) p. 209.

99. The term was one used by the Lebanese in West Africa. See R. Bayley Winder, "The Lebanese in West Africa," in L. A. Fallers, ed., *Immigrants and Associations* (The Hague: Mouton, 1966), p. 105.

100. Kat de Angelino, *Colonial Policy, II*, pp. 274–76.

101. Session of July 23, 1923, Chamber of Commerce, Dakar. *Chambre de Commerce, Proces-Verbaux, 1921–23*, Archives de la Chambre de Commerce, Archives nationales; République de Sénégal.

102. H. E. Scott, head of the Church of Scotland Mission in East Africa, quoted in King, *Pan-Africanism*, p. 105.

103. See Charles Robequain, *The Economic Development of French Indochina* (London: Oxford, 1944), p. 40; William E. Willmott, *The Chinese in Cambodia* (Vancouver: University of British Columbia Press, 1967), p. 57.

104. Winder, *The Lebanese in West Africa*, p. 108.

105. Furnivall, *Netherlands India*, notably chapter 13.

106. The concept is that of Immanuel Wallerstein, most accessible in *The Capitalist World Economy* (Cambridge: Cambridge University Press, 1979).

107. This idea and slogan, now widespread, were developed by André Gunder Frank. See his essay, "The Development of Underdevelopment," in *Latin America: Underdevelopment or Revolution* (New York: Monthly Review Press, 1969).

108. Frank, *Dependent Accumulation and Underdevelopment* (New York: Monthly Review Press, 1979), pp. 113-21.

109. *Ibid.*, p. 115.

110. *Ibid.*, p. 130.

111. These figures come from Walter Rodney, *How Europe Underdeveloped Africa* (Washington, D.C.: Howard University Press, 1974), p. 151.

112. See Samir Amin, *Le Monde des affaires sénéglaises* Paris: Editions du Minuit, 1969), pp. 20-26.

113. Bitter comment on this class is found in Frantz Fanon, *The Wretched of the Earth*, trans. Constance Farrington (New York: Grove Press, 1966), notably, pp. 139-45.

114. Paul Bairoch, "The Main Trends in Economic Disparities Since the Industrial Revolution," in P. Bairoch and M. Lévy-Leboyer, eds. *Disparities in Economic Development Since the Industrial Revolution* (New York: St. Martin's Press, 1981), p. 4.

115. Paul Bairoch, "Le Bilan éconnomique du colonialisme: mythes et réalités," in L. Blussé, H. L. Wesseling, G.D. Winius, eds., *History and Underdevelopment* (Leiden: Leiden University Press, 1980), p. 37.

116. *Ibid.*

117. *Ibid.*, pp. 34-35.

118. Quoted in "Mr. Ormsby-Gore and Tropical Development,"*Nature*, January 12, 1928, p. 37.

119. "L'Esprit africain," reprinted in William B. Cohen, ed., *Robert Delavignette on the French Empire: Selected Writings* (Chicago: University of Chicago Press, 1977), p. 65.

120. H. A .N. Bluett, British Commercial Agent in Java, quoted in John H. Harris, *Slavery or "Trust?"* (New York: Negro Universities Press, 1968; first published, 1926), p. 85.

CHAPTER 4. COLONIAL CITIES

1. This incident is briefly recounted in J. Marrast, "Maroc," in n.a., *L'Oeuvre d'Henri Prost* (Paris: Académie d'Architecture, 1960), p. 83.

2. Huxley quoted in Charles Allen, ed., *Plain Tales From the Raj* (London: Futura, 1979), p. 54.

3. Geoffrey Gorer, *Africa Dances* (New York: Knopf, 1935), pp. 24-25.

4. D'Anfreville de Salle, "Dakar et la colonisation française," *La Revue*, 37:501 (1912).

5. The best, brief, but highly laudatory account available on this historically ignored subject is Vero Roberti, "L'Archittetura Libica e i nouvi centri agricoli," *Emporium*: 88:309-18 (December 1938).

6. Jean Austin, "The Tri-Polis of Ancient Fame and Wondrous Modern Beauty," *Country Life*, 75:36-40 (April 1939).

7. Letter of March 21, 1912, reprinted in Christopher Hussey, *The Life of Sir Edwin Lutyens* (London: Country Life, 1953), p. 247.

8. On the Dutch in the East Indies, see J. S. Furnivall, *Netherlands India* (New York: Macmillan, 1937), p. 348; on the French in West Africa, see Robert Delavignette, *Afrique occidentale française* (Paris: Société d'Editions, 1931), pp. 177-78. The percentage from the figures contained therein has been determined by Raymond F. Betts.

9. Isak Dinesen, *Out of Africa*, (New York: Modern Library, 1952), p. 11.

10. For a brief review of the subject, see Melville J. Herskovits, *The Human Factor in Changing Africa* (New York: Vintage, 1967), pp. 287–88.

11. Gerald Breeze, *Urbanization in Newly Developing Countries* (Englewood Cliffs, N.J.: Prentice-Hall, 1966), p. 47.

12. Bert F. Hoselitz, "Urbanization and Economics Development," in Roy Turner, ed., *India's Urban Future* (Berkeley: University of California Press, 1962), p. 157.

13. Mary P. Holmsteiner and Marie Elena Lopez, "Manila: The Face of Poverty," in n.a., *Asia Urbanizing: Population Growth and Concentration* (Tokyo: Simul Press, 1976), p. 70.

14. Joseph J. Spengler, "Africa and the Theory of Optimum City Size," in Horace Miner, ed., *The City in Modern Africa* (New York: Praeger, 1967), p. 59.

15. From Kingsley Davis and Hilda Hertz, "Patterns of World Urbanization," table reprinted in Breeze, *Urbanization*, p. 22.

16. Janet L. Abu-Lughod, "Varieties of Urban Experience: Contrast, Coexistence and Coalesence in Cairo," in Ira M. Lapidus, ed., *Middle Eastern Cities* (Berkeley: University of California Press, 1969), p. 164.

17. Most of the material and the general interpretation found in these two paragraphs come from the close study of Lim Heng Kow, *The Evolution of the Urban System in Malaya* (Kuala Lumpur: Penerbit Universities Press, 1978).

18. *Ibid.*, pp. 67–71.

19. *Ibid.*, p. 71

20. *Ibid.*, p. 64

21. *Ibid.*, pp. 89 and 111.

22. Geddes, *Town Planning in Colombo: A Preliminary Report* (Colombo: Government of Ceylon Printer, 1921), p. 21.

23. Prakash Tandon, *Beyond Punjab, 1937–1960* (Berkeley: University of California Press, 1971), p. 21.

24. Canard, *Rapport*, dated May 1, 1877, Archives de la République du Sénégal, 13G 308.

25. See Swee-Hock, *Singapore Population in Transition* (Philadelphia: University of Pennsylvania Press, 1970), p. 25.

26. H. P. White, "The Morphological Development of West African Seaports," in B. S. Hoyle and D. Hilling, eds., *Seaports and Development in Tropical Africa* (London: Macmillan, 1970), p. 18.

27. For an overview of transportation's effects on urban form and location, see the "Sequence to Transportation Development," presented in Edward J. Taaffe, Richard L. Morrill, and Peter J. Gould, "Transportation Expansion in Underdeveloped Countries: A Comparative Analysis," *The Geographical Review*, October 1963, p. 503.

28. Paul Nizan, *Aden, Arabie*, trans. by Joan Pinkham (New York: Monthly Review Press, 1968), p. 96.

29. Akin L. Mabogunju, *Urbanization in Nigeria* (New York: Africana Publishing Co., 1968), p. 250.

30. James Bird, *Seaport Gateways of Australia* (London: Oxford University Press, 1968), p. 77.

31. Marcel Monnier, *France noire*, (Paris: Plon et Nourrit, 1894), p. 23.

32. "Résumé retrospectif," in *Annuaire Statistique de L' A.O.F.* (Paris: Agence Economique de l'A.O.F., 1939), p. 127.

33. L. H. Hoyez, "Rapport général sur le plan directeur," dated Paris, June 27, 1938, Archives de la République du Sénégal 4P 408/32.

34. Mamdou Diop, "L'Avenir de Dakar et l'évolution de la politique africaine," in *Dakar à cent ans, France d' outre-mer*, 330:16 (1957).

35. For the cultural effect of such emigration on the community of origin, see Ta Chen, *Emigrant Communities in South China* (New York: Institute of Pacific Relations, 1940).

36. Gerald H. Blake, "Urbanization in North Africa: Its Nature and Consequences," in D. J. Dwyer, ed., *The City in the Third World* (London: Macmillan, 1979), p. 69.

37. Jacques Dresch, "Villes d'Afrique occidentale," *Cahiers d'outre-mer*, 11:204-5, (1950).

38. Dinesen, *Out of Africa*, p. 11.

39. Georges Balandier, *La Sociologie des Brazzavilles noires* (Paris: A. Colin, 1955), pp. 43-44.

40. Chinua Achebe, *No Longer At Ease* (Greenwich, Conn.: Fawcett, 1969), p. 20.

41. The term is that of W. F. Wertheim, *East-West Parallels—Sociological Approaches to Modern Asia* (Chicago: Quadrangle, 1964), pp. 164-81, and is mentioned in effective analysis as part of "urban involution" in T. G. McGee, *The Urban Process in the Third World* (London: G. Bell and Sons, 1971), pp. 64-94.

42. Clifford Geertz, *Peddlers and Princes: Social and Economic Modernization in Two Indonesian Towns* (Chicago: University of Chicago Press, 1971), chapter 3.

43. This is a variation of Geertz's metaphor which is that "of a long line of men passing bricks . . . to build . . . a large wall." *Ibid.* p. 31.

44. Tandon, *Beyond Punjab*, pp. 17-18.

45. Swee-Hock, *Singapore Population*, p. 128.

46. Quoted in P. K. Nambiar, "Slums of Madras City," in A. R. Desai and S. Devadas, eds., *Slums and Urbanization* (Bombay: Popular Prakashan, 1970), p. 176.

47. n.a., "Housing Problem in Singapore: Background," in *ibid.*, p. 130.

48. Marcel Léger, "Considérations sur l'habitation des noirs à Dakar," *Compte Rendu, Académie des sciences coloniales*, VIII, 1926-1927, p. 219.

49. Robert S. Harrison, "Migrants in the City of Tripoli, Libya," *The Geographical Review*, July 1967, p. 415.

50. Kow, *Evolution*, p. 49.

51. Mabogunji, *Urbanization in Nigeria*, p. 117.

52. Kow, *Evolution*, p. 49.

53. *Ibid.*, p. 90.

54. "Note de Service" from the résident-supérieur of Tonkin to the Governor-General, dated October 8, 1901. Archives Nationales, section outre-mer: Indochine, Folder 6329.

55. Mabougunji, *Urbanization in Nigeria*, p. 193.

56. Letter No. 10, Minister of War to *Directeur des Affaires de l'Algérie*, dated January 18, 1849, Archives nationales, section outre-mer: Alger, 4M23, Folder 9.

57. T. Alwyn Lloyd, "The Town Planning Exhibition" in *Town Planning and Housing*, supplement to the *Architectural Review*, 1:249 (1910).

58. The development of the plague and the statistical information here given are from the article "Plague" in the eleventh ed. of the *Encyclopedia Britannica*, Vol. 21, pp. 699-700.

59. The information that follows on this subject is derived from Maynard Swanson, "The Sanitation Syndrome: Bubonic Plague and Native Policy in the Cape Colony, 1900-1909," *Journal of African History*, 18: 387-410 (1977); and Raymond F. Betts, "The Establishment of the Medina in Dakar, Senegal, 1914," *Africa*, 41:143-59 (1971).

60. See, for instance, Henry Vernon Lanchester, "Town Planning in Southern India," *Papers and Discussions, Town Planning Institute*, 3:100 (1916-17).

61. Furnivall, *Netherlands India*, p. 363.

62. The term is that of Swanson, "The Sanitation Syndrome." See note 59 above.

63. On this subject, see Anthony D. King, *Colonial Urban Development* (London: Routledge and Kegan Paul, 1976), pp. 108-15.

64. René Schoentjes, "Considérations générales sur l'urbanisme au Congo belge," in Jean Royer, *L'Urbanisme aux colonies et dans les pays tropicaux*, Vol. I (Charité-sur-Loire: Delaynce 1932). Also see the memorandum of J. E. W. Flood, dated August 22, 1930, in PRO: CO 323/1080 70329 (1930), wherein Flood complained of a "blank space of 440 yards" placed between each quarter.

65. See his statement on this twin concern in his preface to Jean Royer, *L'Urbanisme aux colonies*, p. 7.

66. For an excellent summary of his views, see his speech to the *Université des Annales*, December 10, 1926, reprinted in Hubert Lyautey, *Paroles d'action* (Paris: Armand Colon, 1927), pp. 444-57.

67. J. Marrast, "Maroc," *L'Oeuvre d'Henri Prost*, p. 53.

68. For earlier criticisms and Lyautey's defense against them, see Ladreit de Lacharrière, "L'Urbanisme colonial français et ses réalisations au Maroc," *Afrique française*, 42 (32):161-63 (1932). The chief urbanist in Morocco after 1945, Michel Ecochard, offered this criticism: "It was easy to hide behind a respect for local customs and the character of local populations so as to allow these people to become crowded behind medieval walls." Ecochard, "L'Urbanisme dans les pays en voie de développement," *Conférence au Centre de formation des experts de la coopération technique internationale*, 5th Session: November 1955-February, 1956. (Mimeographed: Commissariat du plan, Dakar, 1962), p. 1.

69. Marrast, "Maroc," *L'Oeuvre d'Henri Prost*, p. 54.

70. Henry Vaughn Lanchester, *The Art of Town Planning* (London: Chapman and Hall, 1925), p. 201.

71. Lanchester, "Town Planning in Southern India," *Papers*, pp. 92-93.

72. George Orwell, *Burmese Days* (New York: Harcourt-Brace 1950), p. 17.

73. Quoted in Allen, *Plain Tales from the Raj*, p. 117.

74. *Ibid.*

75. *Ibid.*, p. 119.

76. Described in Herbert Baker, *Architecture and Personalities* (London: Country Life, 1944), p. 36.

77. Philip Boardman, *Patrick Geddes* (Chapel Hill: University of North Carolina Press, 1944), p. 327.

78. Quoted in *ibid.*, p. 318.

79. Geddes, "Town Planning in Kapurthala," in Jacqueline Tyrewhitt, ed., *Patrick Geddes in India* (London: Lund Humphries, 1947), pp. 24-27.

80. See "Town Planning in Lucknow: A Second Report to the Municipal Council, 1917," reprinted in *ibid.*, p. 57; and Boardman, *Patrick Geddes*, p. 327.

81. Professor Abercrombie's discussion of H. V. Lanchester, "Town Planning in Southern India," *Papers*, p. 117.

82. Letter to Lord Passfield, dated July 14, 1930 in PRO: CO 323/1080 70329 (1930).

83. Letter dated September 18, 1930, *ibid.*

84. E. du Vivier de Streel, introduction, in Royer, *L'Urbanisme aux colonies*, p. 9.

85. Guillaume de Tarde, *Lyautey: Le Chef en action* (Paris: Gallimard 1949), p. 132.

86. Letter to King O'Malley, Minister for Home Affairs, dated December 1, 1913, and printed in *Parliamentary Papers, Commonwealth of Australia*; No. 346: Federal City. (Melbourne: Government of the Commonwealth of Australia, 1916), p. 7.

87. George S. C. Swinton, "New Delhi," *Empire Review* 53:441 (1931). The subject of New Delhi's construction has attracted a considerable amount of historical commentary. How-

ever, the most outstanding work—both the most recent and the most elegant in format—is Robert Grant Irving, *Indian Summer: Lutyens, Baker, and Imperial Delhi* (New Haven: Yale University Press, 1981)

88. Robert Byron, "New Delhi," *Architectural Review*, 49:1 (1931).

89. Herbert Baker, "The New Delhi," *Journal of the Royal Society of Arts*, July 2, 1926, p. 776.

90. Sten Nilsson, *The New Capitals of India, Pakistan and Bangladesh* (Lund: Studentlitter atur, 1973), p. 54.

91. Letter to his wife, quoted in Hussey, *Life of Sir Edwin Lutyens*, p. 280.

92. *Ibid.*, p. 298.

93. Quoted in Robert Lutyens, *Sir Edwin Lutyens: An Appreciation in Perspective* (London: Country Life, 1942), p. 49.

94. See Herbert Baker's critical comment on Lutyens's "Olympian attitude" as he grew older, in *Architecture and Personalities*, pp. 207-8.

95. Quoted in Mark Bence-Jones, *Palace of the Raj.* (London: George Unwin and Allen, 1973), p. 203.

96. n.a., "Rabat capitale," in *Rabat capitale*, special issue of *Notre Maroc*, 5-7:13-14 (1953).

97. Lyautey, speech to the *Université des Annales*, December 10, 1926, Lyautey, *Paroles d'action*, p. 445.

98. See, for instance, the comments of Albert Laprace, "Une Ville crée spécialement pur les indigènes à Casablanca," in Royer, *L'Urbanization aux colonies*, pp. 96-97; and Jules Borely, *Le Maroc au pinceau* (Paris: Denoel, 1950), pp. 9-10.

99. Henri Prost, "Le Développement de l'urbanisme dans le protectorat du Maroc de 1914 à 1923," in Royer, *L'Urbanisme aux colonies*, p. 66.

100. See Fernand Benoit, "L'Evolution des villes et le decor architectural au Maroc," *La Renaissance*, 4 (8): 24 (1931); and D'Arcos, "Le Maroc à la recherche d'une formule d'archi-tecuture," *L'Art et Les Artistes*, 24:204 (1930).

101. *Ibid.*, p. 207.

102. Marrast, "Maroc," *L'Oeuvre d'Henri Prost*, p. 103. Lyautey said much the same thing of Prost: "Thanks to him urbanism has moved in entirely new directions in our country." Statement written in 1932 on the occasion of Prost's election to the Académie des Beaux-Arts, reprinted in *L'Oeuvre d'Henri Prost*, p. 119.

103. The paragraphs that follow on Le Corbusier, with some slight modification, come from Betts, "The Architecture of French Empire: A Neglected History," appear in n.a., *Études Africaines offertes à Henri Brunschwig* (Paris: Editions de l'Ecole des Hautes Etudes en Sciences Sociales, 1982), pp. 307-15.

104. Le Corbusier, *Towards A New Architecture* (New York: Payson and Clarke, 1927) p. 223.

105. Quoted in a letter to M. Brunel, mayor of Algiers, dated December 1933, and reprinted in Willy Boesinger, ed., *Corbusier: oeuvre complète, 1929-1934* (7th ed.; Zurich: Éditions d' Architecture, 1964), p. 174.

106. Siegfried Giedion, *Space, Time and Architecture: The Growth of a New Tradition* (5th ed.; Cambridge, Mass.: Harvard University Press, 1971), p. 159.

107. On Nemours, see Le Corbusier, "Nemours," *L'Architecture d'aujourd'hui*, 16 (3):29 (1945); and S. Van Moos, *Le Corbusier: l'Architect et son mythe* (Paris: Horizons de France, 1971), pp. 162-63.

108. Dugold Macfayden, *Sir Ebenezeer Howard and the Town Planning Movement* (Manchester: University of Manchester Press, 1933), p. 134.

109. Howard, *Tomorrow: A Peaceful Path to Real Reform* (London: Swann Sownenschevi, 1898), p. 7.

110. *Ibid.*, p. 114.

111. See Colonel E. Weithas, "L'Urbanisme en Afrique tropicale," in Royer, *L'Urbanisme aux colonies*, p. 112.

112. Geddes, *Town Planning in Colombo*, p. 6.

113. Helen Rosenau, *The Ideal City: Its Architectural Evolution* (London: Routledge and Kegan Paul, 1959), p. 139.

114. Gide, préface to Georges Benoit-Lévy, *La Cité-jardin*, Vol. I (Paris: Editions des Citiés-Jardins de France, 1911), p. 19.

115. Baker, *Cecil Rhodes and His Architects* (London: Oxford University Press, 1943), pp. 46–47 and 59.

116. *Ibid.*, p. 60.

117. *Ibid.*, p. 67.

118. J. M. Linton Bogle, *Town Planning in India* (London: Oxford University Press, 1929), p. 72.

119. Lt. Col. R. H. Rowe, "Memorandum on Town and Regional Planning," August 13, 1930, p. 2. PRO: CO 232 1080/70329 (1930).

120. Geddes, "Town Planning Towards City Development. A Report to the Durber of Indore, 1918," reprinted in Tyrewhitt, *Patrick Geddes in India*, p. 28.

121. Lanchester, *Town Planning in Madras* (London: Constable, 1918), p. 110.

122. See his letter to his wife, no date given, quoted in Hussey, *Life of Sir Edwin Lutyens*, p. 285; and see Nilsson, *The New Capitals*, p. 41.

123. Swinton, "New Delhi," pp. 443–44.

124. Allen Greenberg, "Lutyens' Architecture Restudied," *Perspecta*, 12:142 (1969).

125. G. Flieringa, "L'Habitation aux Indes neerlandaises," *Urbanisme*, 4(32): 204–205 (1935).

126. See Prosper Ricard, *Le Maroc* (Paris: Hachette, 1930), p. 223; and Jacques Caille, "Rabat touristique," in *Rabat Capitale*, p. 48.

127. Anthony King, *Colonial Urban Development*, p. 238.

128. Consider only this comment: "The so-called green zones which separate the European quarters from the African are barricades. But in order to deceive us, they are planted with trees and flowers in the form of gardens." Patrice Lumumba, *Le Congo: terre d'avenir est-il menacé?* (Brussels: Office de Publicité, 1961), p. 181.

129. Quoted in Henri Prost, "Rapport General," in Royer, *L'Urbanisme aux Colonies*, p. 22.

130. Swinton, "New Delhi," p. 442.

131. Such criticism is found in D. Hywel Davies, "Lusaka, Zambia: Some Town Planning Problems in an African Capital City at Independence," *Zambia Urban Studies*, 1:7 (1969); and John Collins, "Lusaka: The Myth of the Garden City," *Zambia Urban Studies*, 2:1–32 (1969).

132. See "Note au sujet de la réorganisation de l'OHE," dated March 30, 1932, Archives de la République du Sénégal: 4P 423 (32).

133. *Procès-verbal de la 4ème Réunion du Conseil d'Administration de l'OHE de l'AOF*, March 16, 1927, Archives de la République du Sénégal: 4P 416 (32).

134. Henry Vernon Lanchester, preface to Tyrewhitt, *Patrick Geddes in India*, p. 19.

135. An effort to get something of a "diagnostic survey" undertaken for New Delhi was already tried in 1912 by Henry Vernon Lanchester who had been appointed adviser to the planning committee. See Nilsson, *The New Capitals*, pp. 44–45.

136. Patrick Geddes, *Cities in Evolution* (London: Williams and Norgate, 1915), pp. 240-241.

CHAPTER 5. VOICES OF PROTEST

1. *New York Times*, August 3, 1920; and cited in E. David Cronin, *Black Moses: The Story of Marcus Garvey and the Universal Negro Improvement Association* (Madison: University of Wisconsin Press, 1969), p. 64. The following narrative on Garvey is largely based on Cronin's lively account.

2. Marcus Garvey, *Philosophy and Opinions of Marcus Garvey* (New York: Universal Publishing House, 1923), p. 10.

3. UNIA Manifesto quoted in Cronin, *Black Moses*, p. 17.

4. *Negro World*, September 11, 1920; quoted in *ibid.*, p. 60.

5. Lord Reading to Lloyd George, May 4, 1922, reprinted in B. N. Pandey, ed., *The Indian Nationalist Movement, 1885-1947: Select Documents* (New York: St. Martin's Press, 1979), p. 109.

6. As one of the anticolonialists in André Malraux's novel *The Conquerors* remarks: "Now I know what the British Empire is. Stubborn, unrelenting force. Running things. Making decisions." André Malraux, *The Conquerors*, Trans. Stephen Becker (New York: Holt, Rinehart and Winston, 1976), p. 173.

7. Mohandas Gandhi, "Hindu Swaraj," in *The Collected Works of Mahatma Gandhi*, Volume X: *November 1909-March 1911* (Delhi: Government of India, 1963), p. 58.

8. Aimé Césaire, *Discours sur le colonialisme* (Paris: Présence africaine, 1955), p. 63.

9. The dating and the citation are from Leo Marx, *The Machine in the Garden: Technology and the Pastoral Ideal in America* (New York: Oxford University Press, 1977), pp. 11 and 13.

10. André Malraux, *The Temptation of the West*, Trans. Robert Hollander (New York: Vintage, 1961), pp. 20-21.

11. Quoted in Krishna Kripalani, *Rabindranath Tagore: A Biography* (London: Oxford University Press, 1962), p. 277.

12. Quoted in William Walsh, *Commonwealth Literature* (London: Oxford University Press, 1973), p. 7.

13. Claude McKay, *Banana Bottom* (Chatham, N.J.: Chatham Bookseller, 1970), p. 226.

14. Black African criticism of Western civilization has been analyzed carefully by Mercer Cook in Cook and Stephen E. Henderson, *The Militant Black Writer* (Madison: University of Wisconsin Press, 1969), p. 23-27.

15. Gandhi, *Collected Works*, p. 24.

16. *Ibid.*, pp. 26-28; 32-36.

17. *Ibid.*, p. 37.

18. Rabindranath Tagore, *Nationalism* (New York: Macmillan, 1917), p. 19.

19. *Ibid.*, p. 28.

20. *Ibid.*, pp. 35-36.

21. *Ibid.*, pp. 16-17. It should be noted that Tagore appreciated much of British culture. He wrote: "I have a deep love and a great respect for the British race as human beings. It has produced great-hearted men, thinkers of great thoughts, doers of great deeds." *Ibid.*, p. 28.

22. Quoted in Cosmo Pieterse, "Conflict in the Germ: William Plomer and Benedict Vilakazi," in Cosmo Pieterse and Donald Monro, eds., *Protest and Conflict in African Literature* (London: Heinemann, 1968), p. 24.

23. André Bréton, "Un Grand poet noir," preface to *Cahier du retour au pays natal* (Paris: Bordes, 1947), p. 22.

24. Aimé Césaire, *Return to My Native Land* (Paris: Présence africaine, 1968), p. 13.

25. Gerald Moore, "The Politics of Négritude," in Pieterse and Munro, *Protest and Conflict*, pp. 32-33.

26. David Nicholls, *From Dessalines to Duvalier: Race, Colour and National Independence in Haiti* (Cambridge: Cambridge University Press, 1979), p. 150.

27. Quoted in Jean Price-Mars, *De Sainte-Dominique à Haiti: Essai sur la culture, les arts et la littérature* (Paris: Présence africaine, 1959), p. 51.

28. Jean Price-Mars, *Ainsi parla l'oncle: Essais d'Ethnographie* (Compiègne: Imprimérie de Compiègne, 1928), p. 78. An excellent recent analysis of Price-Mars' influence is found in René Dépestre, *Bonjour et adieu à la négritude* (Paris: Robert Laffont, 1980), chapter 2.

29. *Ibid.*, p. 121. For another interesting interpretation of the dance in African life, see Louis-Thomas Achille, "L'Art et le noir," *Revue du Monde Noir*, No. 2 (December 1932), pp. 28-31.

30. Alain Locke, "The New Negro," in Alain Locke, ed., *The New Negro: An Interpretation* (New York: Johnson Reprint Co., 1968), p. 7.

31. Langston Hughes, *The Big Sea* (New York: Alfred Knopf, 1940), p. 162.

32. Léopold Senghor, introduction to "Trois poètes négro-américains," *Poésie 45*, No. 23 (February-March 1945), p. 32.

33. *Ibid.*

34. On this subject and the development of the literary reviews, see Lillian Kesteloot, *Les Écrivains noirs de langue française* (Brussels: Université libre de Bruxelles, 1963), notably pp. 25-28, 46-47; 52.

35. Guy Zuccarelli, "Une Etape de l'évolution haitienne," *Revue du Monde Noir*, No. 5 (March 1932), p. 30.

36. Countee Cullen, "Heritage," in Countee Cullen, *On These I Stand* (New York: Harper and Row, 1953), p. 24.

37. Jawaharlal Nehru, *An Autobiography* (London: The Bodley Head, 1953), p. 37.

38. Jawaharlal Nehru, *Toward Freedom* (New York: John Day, 1943), p. 278.

39. Quoted, in this instance, in Hisham Sharabi, *Arab Intellectuals and the West: The Formative Years, 1874-1914* (Baltimore: The Johns Hopkins University Press, 1970), p. 44. For a very critical interpretation of Western scholarship on the Near East, see Edward Said, *Orientalism* (New York: Pantheon, 1978).

40. Sun Yat-Sen, *San Min Chu I* (Tapei: China Cultural Service, 1953), p. 26.

41. n.a., "The Durbar from the Crowd," *Blackwell's Magazine*, February 1912, p. 289.

42. The London Times, reprinted as "Pacifying Effect of the Durbar," *Literary Digest*, January 6, 1912, p. 9.

43. Ndabaningi Sithole, *African Nationalism* (2nd ed.; London: Oxford University Press, 1970), p. 57.

44. Ziya Gokalp, *Turkish Nationalism and Western Civilization*, quoted in Elie Kedourie, ed., *Nationalism in Asia and Africa* (New York: World Publishing Co., 1970), p. 190.

45. Rosalynde Ainslie, *The Press in Africa: Communications Past and Present* (New York: Walker and Co., 1967), p. 21.

46. Charles C. Clayton, "Hong Kong," in John A. Lent, ed., *The Asian Newspaper: Reluctant Revolution* (Ames: Iowa State University Press, 1971), pp. 56-57.

47. Quoted in Walter G. Langlois, *André Malraux: The Indochina Adventure* (New York: Praeger, 1966), p. 55.

48. Margarita Barnes, *The Indian Press: A History of the Growth of Public Opinion in India* (London: George Allen and Unwin, 1940), p. 335.

49. Langlois, *André Malraux*, p. 58.

50. Roland E. Wolseley, "India: History and Development," in Lent, *The Asian Newspaper*, p. 272.

51. Quoted in Ainslie, *The Press in Africa*, p. 34.

52. Quoted in Henry S. Wilson, ed., *Origins of West African Nationalism* (London: Macmillan, 1969), p. 267.

53. Gokalp, *Turkish Nationalism*, p. 191.

54. Karl Marx and Friedrich Engels, *The Communist Manifesto* (New York: International Publishers, 1948), p. 12.

55. V. I. Lenin, *Imperialism: The Highest State of Capitalism* (New York: International Publishers, 1939), p. 82.

56. See Robert C. North and Xenia J. Eudin, *M. N. Roy's Mission to China: The Communist Kuomintang Split of 1927* (Berkeley: University of California Press, 1963), pp. 1 and 12.

57. *Ibid.*, pp. 4, 10, and 128.

58. *Ibid.*, p. 12.

59. Xenia J. Eudin and Robert C. North, *Soviet Russia and the East, 1920-1927. A Documentary Survey* (Stanford, Calif.: Stanford University Press, 1957), p. 66.

60. *Ibid.*, p. 65.

61. *Ibid.*, p. 265. Also see Nehru's comments on the conference in *Toward Freedom*, pp. 123-25

62. Arthur Holitscher, "A Race Congress at Berlin," from the *Berliner Tageblatt*, reprinted in *Living Age*, April 15, 1927, p. 669.

63. Quoted in Eudin and North, *Soviet Russia and the East*, p. 15.

64. In an indirect response to Lord Irwin's claim that "the disquieting spread of the methods of Communism has for some time been causing my Government anxieties," Nehru said that he did not doubt the problems caused by Communism but that "this cry of Communism is meant to cover a multitude of sins of the Government." Jawaharlal Nehru to Walter Citrine, June 22, 1929, quoted in Pandey, *The Indian Nationalist Movement*, p. 97.

65. Walter Z. Laqueur, *Communism and Nationalism in the Middle East* (New York: Praeger, 1951), p. 34.

66. Robert Legvold, *Soviet Policy in West Africa* (Cambridge: Harvard University Press, 1970), p. 9.

67. André Malraux, *The Conquerors*, p. 98.

68. Joseph Stalin, "Do not Forget the East," reprinted in Eudin and North, *Soviet Russia and the East*, p. 156.

69. Quoted in *ibid.*, p. 79.

70. Quoted in *ibid.*, p. 146

71. Mao Tse-tung, "Report of an Investigation into the Peasant Movement in Hunan," reprinted in Stuart R. Schram, *The Political Thought of Mao Tse-tung* (New York: Praeger, 1963), p. 252.

72. The term forms part of the title of Regis Debray, *Revolution in the Revolution? Armed Struggle and Political Struggle in Latin America.*, trans. Bobbye Otis (New York: Monthly Review Press, 1967).

73. Speech delivered on May 15, 1917, and reproduced in Keith Hancock and Jean Van der Poel, *Selections From the Smuts Papers*; Vol. III: *June 1910-November 1918* (Cambridge: Cambridge University Press, 1966), pp. 510-11.

74. Quoted in Percival Spears, *India: A Modern History* (Ann Arbor: University of Michigan Press, 1961), p. 347.

75. Nehru, *Toward Freedom*, p. 50.

76. Letter dated August 1, 1920 and reproduced in Pandey, *The Indian Nationalist Movement*, p. 53.

77. Frantz Fanon, *The Wretched of the Earth* (New York: Grove Press, 1968), p. 94.

78. See, for instance, Harry J. Benda and Ruth T. McVey, eds,. *The Communist Uprisings of 1926–1927 in Indonesia: Key Documents* (Ithaca, N.Y.: Cornell University, Department of Far Eastern Studies, 1960), pp. xxi–xxii.

79. David D. Marr, *Vietnamese Anticolonialism, 1885–1925* (Berkeley: University of California Press, 1971), p. 190.

80. The following assessment comes directly from the carefully wrought analysis of Edmond Rabbath, "L'Insurrection syrienne de 1925–1927," *Revue historique*, 267 (2):405–47 (1982).

81. n.a., "Europe, The League and Abyssinia," *The Roundtable* 25:667 (1934–35).

82. George Padmore, *Pan-Africanism or Communism* (Garden City, N.Y.: Doubleday, 1971), pp. 123–24.

83. *Ibid.*, pp. 116–17.

84. *Ibid.*, p. 124.

85. On this reaction see the fine monograph of S. K. B. Asante, *Pan-African Protest: West Africa and the Italo-Ethiopian Crisis 1934–1941* (London: Longmans, 1977).

86. *Ibid.*, pp. 58–60.

87. Vittorio Mussolini, *Due donne nella Tempesta*, quoted in Ivone Kirkpatrick, *Mussolini: A Study in Power* (New York: Hawthorn Books, 1964), p. 189.

88. Winston Churchill to President Roosevelt, April 12, 1943, reprinted in Pandey, *The Indian Nationalist Movement*, p. 181.

CHAPTER 6. THE END OF EMPIRE

1. King George VI had originally intended to undertake the trip himself, but he was too ill to do so. He died shortly after Princess Elizabeth arrived in Kenya, and she immediately returned to England and thus cancelled the remainder of the tour.

2. *Life*, February 18, 1952, p. 32.

3. Georges Catroux, *Dans la bataille de la Meditérrranée* (Paris: Rene Juillard, 1949), p. 431; and speech delivered by Harold Macmillan in Cape Town, February 3, 1960, and frequently cited in studies of the British Commonwealth. See, for instance, Colin Cross, *The Fall of the British Empire* (London: Palladin, 1970), p. 351.

4. K. M. Panikkar, *Asia and Western Dominance* (New York: Collier, 1969), p. 234.

5. Quoted in Percival Spear, *India: A Modern History* (Ann Arbor: University of Michigan Press, 1961), p. 352.

6. Nehru, *Toward Freedom* (New York: John Day, 1943), p. 422.

7. Quoted in P. S. Payne, *The Life and Death of Mahatma Gandhi* (New York: Dutton, 1964), p. 404.

8. Speech at Lord Mayor's Day Luncheon, November 10, 1942, reprinted in *Winston S. Churchill: His Complete Speeches, 1897–1963*; Vol. VI: *1935–1942*; ed. Robert R. James (New York: Chelsea House, 1974), p. 6695.

9. On this subject, see Wolfe W. Schmokel, *Dream of Empire: German Colonialism 1919–1945* (New Haven, Conn.: Yale University Press, 1964), chapter 2.

10. See Alan Moorehead, *The Desert War: The North African Campaign, 1940–1943* (London: Hamish Hamilton, 1965), p. 194. Moorehead compares desert warfare with naval warfare.

11. *Ibid.*, p. 45.

12. Erwin Rommel, *Krieg Ohne Hass* (Heidenheim: Verlag Heidenheimer Zeitung, 1950), pp. 391-92.

13. Winston S. Churchill, *The Second World War*, Vol. IV: *The Hinge of Fate* (Boston: Houghton Mifflin, 1950), p. 92.

14. Mamoru Shigemitsu, *Japan and Her Destiny: My Struggle for Peace*, trans. Oswald White (New York: E. P. Dutton, 1958), p. 208.

15. Quoted in W. David McIntyre, *The Rise and Fall of the Singapore Naval Base, 1919-1942* (New York: Archon Books, 1979), p. 22.

16. The previous assessment is largely derived from McIntyre's study.

17. H. P. Willmott, *Empires in the Balance: Japanese and Allied Pacific Strategies to April 1942* (Annapolis: Naval Institute Press, 1982), p. 63. On the general strategy of the war, see Christopher Thorne, *Allies of a Kind: The United States, Britain and the War Against Japan, 1941-1945* (New York: Oxford University Press, 1978).

18. The symbolism of this act is well described in Paul Mus, *Le Destin de l'Union française. De l'Indochine à l'Afrique* (Paris: Editions du Seuil, 1954), pp. 52-55.

19. John Wright, *Libya* (New York: Praeger, 1969), pp. 198-201.

20. Louis, *Imperialism at Bay: The United States and the Decolonization of the British Empire, 1941-1945* (Oxford: Oxford University Press, 1978), p. 29.

21. On Eboué, see Brain Weinstein, *Eboué* (New York: Oxford University Press, 1972).

22. Translated and quoted in D. Bruce Marshall, *The French Colonial Myth and Constitution Making in the Fourth Republic* (New Haven, Conn.: Yale University Press, 1973), p. 107.

23. The assessment in the next few paragraphs draws heavily on the detailed study of Louis, *Imperialism at Bay*.

24. *Ibid.*, p. 139.

25. Quoted in *ibid.*, p. 537.

26. Guy Malengrau, "Recent Developments in the Belgian Congo," in C. Groves Haines, ed., *Africa Today* (Baltimore: Johns Hopkins Press, 1954), p. 340.

27. Quoted in R. D. Pearce, "Morale in the Colonial Service in Nigeria during the Second World War," *Journal of Imperial and Commonwealth History* 11(2):177 (1982).

28. Maurice Collis, *Last and First in Burma (1941-1948)* (London: Faber and Faber, 1966), p. 182.

29. See George M. Kahin, *Nationalism and Revolution in Indonesia* (Ithaca, N.Y.: Cornell University Press, 1952), pp. 132-33.

30. Bernard Fall, *The Two Vietnams: A Political and Military Analysis* (2nd ed; London: Pall Mall Press, 1967), p. 48.

31. Pearce, "Morale in Colonial Service."

32. Malengrau, "Recent Developments in the Belgian Congo," p. 340.

33. T. H. Beaglehole, "From Rulers to Servants: The ICS and the British Demission of Power in India," *Modern Asian Studies* 2:240-42; (1977).

34. *Ibid.*, notably pp. 237-38, 252-55.

35. Hunt and Harrison, *The District Officer in India*.

36. See the statement in *Tales from the Dark Continent*, pp. 133-34.

37. As an example of this attitude, see the statement of Philip Mason in Allen, ed., *Plain Tales from the Raj*, p. 244.

38. Quoted in Cohen, *Rulers of Empire*, p. 175.

39. Achebe, *No Longer At Ease*, p. 103.

40. Charles Meek quoted in Allen, ed., *Tales from the Dark Continent*.

41. Fanon, *The Wretched of the Earth*, p. 30.

42. Perham, *The Colonial Reckoning*, p. 70.

43. Dwight D. Eisenhower, *Waging Peace, 1956–1961* (New York: Doubleday, 1961), p. 486.

44. Chou en Lai, speech given on April 19, 1955, reproduced in *Vital Speeches*, 21:1275 (Oct. 1954–Oct. 1955).

45. Dean Acheson, *Power and Diplomacy* (Cambridge, Mass.: Harvard University Press, 1959), pp. 6–7.

46. See Wm. Roger Louis and Ronald Robinson, "The U.S. and the End of British Empire in Tropical Africa," in Prosser Gifford and Wm. Roger Louis, ed., *The Transfer of Power in Africa: Decolonization, 1940–1960* (New Haven, Conn.: Yale Universit. Press, 1982), pp. 53–55.

47. A variation of this argument is found in *ibid.*, pp. 51 and 52.

48. Kwame Nkrumah, *Neo-Colonialism, The Last Stage of Imperialism* (New York: International Publishers, 1970), p. xi.

49. This argument is persuasively made, with respect to the British Empire by B. R. Tomlinson, "The contraction of England: National Decline and the Loss of Empire," *Journal of Imperial and Commonwealth History* 11(1):58–72 (1982).

50. E. A. Midgley, quoted in Hunt and Harrison, *District Officer in India*, p. 224.

51. See the remarkable study by Gyorgy Doczi, *The Power of Limits: Proportional Harmonies in Nature, Art and Architecture* (Boulder, Colo.: Shambhala, 1981).

52. Smith, *Colonial Cadet in Nigeria*, p. 15.

53. On this subject, but with particular reference to West Africa, see John D. Hargreaves, *The End of Colonial Rule in West Africa: Essays in Contemporary History* (New York: Barnes and Noble, 1979), chapter 4.

54. Quoted in John D. Hargreaves, *France and West Africa: An Anthology of Historical Documents* (London: Macmillan, 1969), p. 265.

55. Speech reproduced in Colum Legum, ed., *Zambia, Independence and Beyond: The Speeches of Kenneth Kaunda* (London: Nelson, 1966), p. 83.

56. Quoted in *The London Times*, October 3, 1960, p. 8.

57. Lord Mountbatten, *Reflections on the Transfer of Power and Jawaharlal Nehru* (Cambridge: Cambridge University Press, 1968), p. 6.

58. Bernard Fall, *Street Without Joy: Insurgency in Indochina, 1946–1963* (3rd ed.; Harrisburg, Pa.: Stackpole, 1963), p. 27.

59. See Kahin, *Nationalism and Revolution in Indonesia*, p. 101.

60. Jean Lacouture, *Le Vietnam entre deux paix* (Paris: Editions du Seuil, 1965), p. 26.

61. Kahin, *Nationalism and Revolution in Indonesia*, p. 396.

62. Lacouture, *Le Vietnam entre deux paix*, p. 27.

63. See George Herring, *America's Longest War: The United States and Vietnam, 1950–1970* (New York: Wiley, 1979).

64. Figures taken from Alf Andrew Heggoy, *Insurgency and Counterinsurgency in Algeria* (Bloomington: Indiana University Press, 1972), p. 79.

65. Jean-Jacques Servan-Schreiber, *Lieutenant in Algeria*, trans. Ronald Matthews (New York: Knopf, 1957), p. 192.

66. On the intellectual opposition to the Algerian War, see Paul C. Sorum, *Intellectuals and Decolonization in France* (Chapel Hill: University of North Carolina Press, 1977), chapters 5 and 6.

67. S. A. de Smith, "Westminster's Export Model: The Legal Framework of Responsible Government," *Journal of Commonwealth Political Studies*, 1(1):2 (1961).

68. See the interesting comments of Hubert Deschamps, "Et Maintenant Lord Lugard?" *Africa* 33(4):293–305 (1963).

69. Comment of Frank Lloyd, quoted in Allen, ed., *Tales from the Dark Continent*, p. 144.

70. Deschamps, speech translated by Mary Paquette and reprinted in Robert O. Collins, ed., *Problems in the History of Colonial Africa, 1860–1960* (Englewood Cliffs, N.J.: Prentice-Hall, 1970), p. 211.

71. *Ibid.*

72. James L. Watson, "The Chinese: Hong Kong Villagers in the British Catering Trade," in James L. Watson, ed., *Between Two Cultures: Migrants and Minorities in Britain* (Oxford: Basil Blackwell, 1979), pp. 182–83.

73. H. L. Wesseling, "Post-Imperial Holland," *Journal of Contemporary History* 15:137 (1980).

74. Quoted in Jean-Daniel Scherb, *Le Soleil ne chauffe que les vivants* (Paris: Robert Laffont, 1964), pp. 53-54.

75. Zahia Bent Abdallah quoted in n.a., *Les Enfants d'Algérie: témoinages et desseins d'enfants réfugiés en Tunisie, en Libye et au Maroc* (Paris: Francois Maspero, 1962), p. 109.

76. Pierre George, *Les Migrations internationales* (Paris: Presses Universitaires de France, 1976), pp. 82–83.

77. V. S. Naipaul, *In a Free State*, (London: Penguin, 1982), p. 79.

78. Quoted in Nancy Foner, "The Jamaicans, Culture and Social Change among Migrants in Britain," in Watson, ed., *Between Two Cultures*, p. 123.

79. Stephen L. Keller, *Uprooting and Social Change: The Role of Refugees in Development* (Delhi: Manohar Book Service, 1975), p. 37.

80. Joseph B. Schechtman, *The Refugee in the World: Displacement and Integration* (New York: A. S. Barnes, 1963), p. 102.

81. Scherb, *Le Soleil ne chauffe que les vivants*, p. 234.

AFTERMATH

1. See J. M. Lee, *Colonial Development and Good Government: A Study of the Ideas Expressed by the British Official Classes in Planning Decolonization, 1939-1964* (Oxford: Clarendon Press, 1967). notably pp. 17–25.

2. *Ibid.*, p. 29.

3. Ezekiel Mphahlele, *The African Image* (New York: Praeger, 1962), p. 75.

4. Cohen, ed., *Robert Delavignette on the French Empire*, p. 133.

5. Smith, *Colonial Cadet in Nigeria*, p. 85.

6. Cohen, ed., *Robert Delavignette on the French Empire*, p. 130.

7. Amechi Okalo, "Dependency in Africa: Stages of African Political Economy," *Alternatives*, 19:237 (1983).

8. V. S. Naipaul, *The Guerrillas* (New York: Vintage Books, 1980; first published, 1975), p. 119.

9. Rheinhold Niebuhr, *The Structure of Nations and Empires: A Study of the Recurring Patterns and Problems of the Political Order in Relation to the Unique Problems of the Nuclear Age* (New York: Charles Scribner's Sons, 1959), p. 9.

10. *Ibid.*, p. 15.

11. *Ibid.*, p. 13.

12. Ndabaningi Sithole, *African Nationalism* (2nd ed; London: Oxford University Press, 1968), p. 163.

13. President Sukarno, *New Nationhoods and New Forums* (Djarkata: Department of Information, Republic of Indonesia, 1963), p. 6.

14. *Ibid.*, p. 16.

15. Leopold Sedar Senghor, "African-Style Socialism," in William H. Friedland and Carl G. Rosberg, Jr., ed., *African Socialism: A General Survey of African Socialism with Detailed Studies of Ghana, Guinea, Mali, Senegal and Tanganyika* (Palo Alto, Calif.: Stanford University Press, 1964), p. 265.

16. V. S. Naipaul, *In a Free State*, p. 166.

17. Quoted in Joyce Cary, *The Case for African Freedom and Other Writings on Africa* (Austin, University of Texas Press, 1962), p. 17.

18. Isak Dinesen, *Out of Africa*, pp. 18–19.

19. Hal O'Flaherty, London correspondent, *Chicago Daily News*, quoted in "England's Prince Goes to Africa," *The Literary Digest*, April 18, 1925, p. 40.

20. E. D. O'Brien, "With the Duce in Libya," *English Review*, 54:551 and 554 (May 1937).

21. James Leasor, *The Millionth Chance: The Story of the R. 101*, pp. 43–44.

22. Lord Mountbatten, *Reflections of the Transfer of Power* (Cambridge: Cambridge University Press, 1968), p. 26.

23. John Osborne, *The Entertainer* (London: Faber and Faber, 1957), pp. 60–61.

Index

Index

Raymond Betts earned his doctorate in history at Columbia University in 1958; he also holds degrees from the universities of Grenoble and Paris. Betts has taught at Bryn Mawr and Grinnell colleges and, since 1971, at the University of Kentucky. A specialist in French colonial history, Betts is the author of *Assimilation and Association in French Colonial Thought, 1890–1914, Europe Overseas: Phases of Imperialism, The False Dawn: European Imperialism in the Nineteenth Century* (Minnesota, 1975), and *Tricouleur: The French Overseas Empire.*